MARXIST
GOVERNMENT
in INDIA

Marxist Regimes Series

Series editor: Bogdan Szajkowski,
Department of Sociology,
University College, Cardiff

Afghanistan Bhabani Sen Gupta
Angola Keith Somerville
Bulgaria Robert J. McIntyre
China Marc Blecher
Ethiopia Peter Schwab
German Democratic Republic Mike Dennis
Ghana Donald I. Ray
Grenada Tony Thorndike
Guinea-Bissau Rosemary E. Galli and Jocelyn Jones
Guyana Colin Baber and Henry B. Jeffrey
Hungary Hans-Georg Heinrich
Kampuchea Michael Vickery
Laos Martin Stuart-Fox
Madagascar Maureen Covell
Marxist Local Governments in Western Europe and Japan ed. Bogdan Szajkowski
Marxist State Governments in India T. J. Nossiter
Mongolia Alan J. K. Sanders
Nicaragua David Close
P.D.R. Yemen Tareq and Jacqueline Ismael
Romania Michael Shafir
Soviet Union Ronald J. Hill
Surinam Henk E. Chin and Hans Buddingh'
Vietnam Melanie Beresford
Yugoslavia Bruce McFarlane

Further Titles

Albania
Benin and The Congo
Cape Verde, São Tomé and Príncipe
Cuba
Czechoslovakia
Democratic People's Republic of Korea
Mozambique
Poland
Zimbabwe
Adaptations of Communism
Comparative Analysis
Cumulative Index

MARXIST STATE GOVERNMENTS in INDIA

Politics, Economics and Society

T. J. Nossiter

 Pinter Publishers
London and New York

© T. J. Nossiter 1988

All rights reserved. No part of this publication may be reproduced, stored in a retrieval system, or transmitted by any means without the prior written permission of the copyright holder. Please direct all enquiries to the publishers.

First published in Great Britain in 1988 by
Pinter Publishers Limited
25 Floral Street, London WC2E 9DS

British Library Cataloguing in Publication Data
A CIP catalogue record for this book is available from the British Library.
ISBN 0-86187-456-0
ISBN (Pbk) 0-86187-457-9

Library of Congress Cataloging-in-Publication Data
Nossiter, T. J. (Thomas Johnson)
   Marxist state governments in India.
   (Marxist regimes series)
   Bibliography: p.
   Includes index.
   1. Communism—India—History. 2. Communist parties—India—History. 3. India—Politics and government—1947- . 4. State governments—India. 5. Kerala (India)—Politics and government. 6. West Bengal (India)—Politics and government. I. Title. II. Series.
HX394.N67   1987   320.5'32'0954   84-62673

Typeset by Joshua Associates Limited, Oxford
Printed in Great Britain by SRP Ltd, Exeter

Editor's Preface

The overriding aim of this series on Marxist Regimes is to provide an in-depth analysis and appraisal of a whole range of Marxist experimentation on the various levels at which Marxist parties exercise political control. Understandably, therefore, such a wide-ranging evaluation should also include discussion of the performance of the Marxist-led State governments in India. This study provides the reader with the most comprehensive and up-to-date analysis published thus far of the Marxist parties in power in Kerala, West Bengal and Tripura.

In 1957 Kerala became the first—and until 1977 the only—Indian state to elect a communist government.[1] The CPI took the biggest share of the vote with 38 per cent of the poll and although it was one seat short of an overall majority in the Assembly, the party formed the government with the support of independents. The experiment was short-lived. The ministry was dismissed and the Assembly dissolved by Presidential decree in 1959 but the ensuing elections in 1960 showed that popular support for the CPI had grown, not diminished, even though this was not translated into seats because of the nature of the electoral system. Subsequently, and despite a damaging split in the Indian communist movement in 1964, there have been communist-led governments in Kerala more often than not. Between 1967 and 1981 there were only eighteen months when the Chief Minister of the State was not a communist. Following the 1987 elections, a CPI(M)-led ministry is again in office.

West Bengal, with 55 million people (the same as Britain), is the fifth biggest state in India and a major province. Here, after two brief United Front experiments in which the communists participated in 1967 and 1969, CPI(M)-led Left Front ministries have been in power since 1977. The CPI(M) enjoys an absolute majority in the Legislative Assembly.

In the north-eastern hill state of Tripura, with a population of only two million, the CPI(M) were in power from 1977 until narrowly defeated in the 1988 elections. It is worth remembering that neither now nor in the past have the communists come close to power in any of the Hindi-speaking heartland

---

[1] Kerala was only the second example of a communist party returned to power in competitive elections. In the Republic of San Marino in 1945 the elections to the Grand National Council brought to office a coalition of the San Marino Communist Party and the San Marino Socialist Party.

states of India. Significant communist presence is mainly confined to regional redoubts and on a national level the communist party share of the national vote amounts to about 8 per cent (see Table P.1).

Table P.1 Communist performance in Indian general elections, 1952–84

	1984	1980	1977	1971	1967	1962	1957	1952
Seats won								
CPI	6	11	7	23	23	29	27	16
CPI(M)	22	36	22	25	19	—	—	—
Percentage vote								
CPI	2.7	2.6	2.8	4.7	5.1	9.9	8.9	3.3
CPI(M)	5.8	6.1	4.3	5.1	4.4	—	—	—

Source: T. J. Nossiter, 'Communism in Rajiv Gandhi's India', *Third World Quarterly*, vol. 7, 1985, p. 924.

The political units dealt with in this study are not, of course, sovereign entities; but neither are they (just) regional governments, much less municipal administrations. In the Indian Constitution and everyday usage they are called *states* and the complex and often vexed relations between the Indian government in Delhi and the provincial governments in the state capitals are referred to as centre–state relations. The constitution declares that India is a union of federated states and centrally administered territories. Curiously the existence of states as such is guaranteed but not that of a particular state. The central parliament can create new states, abolish existing states and alter state boundaries by simple majority vote, although the actual number of states, at present twenty-five, has grown—not diminished—over time. Each state is an individual political system as well as part of a larger polity and significantly in some states popular turn-out at elections is higher for the provincial assemblies than for the central parliament.

Politically, India is as much an exception to the normal categories of government and political science as it is socially and culturally unique. States are frequently classified as federal or unitary but, strictly speaking, India is both and neither. It is a quasi-federal hybrid. Relations between the centre and the states have varied from time to time and place to place, and there has been no consensus about the nature of the system.

As a country with 15 per cent of the world's population and some 250 different languages and an alarming contrast in wealth and resources between different groups of the population, anything but quasi-federal arrangements is unthinkable. The chances of any subgroup in the nation imposing its hegemony on the rest seem remote. The largest linguistic community, the Hindi speakers, compose less than a third of the population and are themselves divided by culture and history. In the Soviet Union, by contrast, the Russians form more than half of the population. Conversely, there is no possibility of any state breaking away. From Nehru's swift response to the Nizam of Hyderabad's attempt to set up an independent state in 1947 to the massive deployment of troops in Punjab in 1984, the Indian Government has demonstrated its ability as well as determination to crush separatism. However it is worth remembering that successive administrations in Delhi have been less effective in putting down class-based insurrections (e.g. West Bengal, 1948; Telengana, 1951; Naxalitism, in the late 1960s). Indian communists often remark that the Soviet Union—with whom India has a Defence Treaty—is more supportive of the central government than the fraternal movement.

The autonomy of the Indian states is, of course, relative not absolute. The legislative and executive powers of the state governments are limited but they derive from the Constitution as such, not delegation of authority by the central government alone; and they are not derisory powers. In Kerala and West Bengal productive relations have been profoundly altered by means of land reform, which is largely a state subject. Similarly the character of policing is predominantly a matter for the state executive, so that provincial governments, if they wish, can contribute to the democratization of the state apparatus.

For the Indian communists the ballot box is a weapon in the popular struggle but it is only part of the armoury. Parliamentary assemblies are propaganda platforms for exposing the real nature of class government, and ministerial office is to be used to build the party through patronage on the one hand and on the other to show that no real change in social relations is possible through the bourgeois democratic process. Nevertheless, the Marxist experiences of Kerala, West Bengal and Tripura have facilitated the opening of a rich new seam of communist praxis.

This book examines communist praxis by analysing two key issues. First, has India, the second most populous country in the world, developed what could be called an Indian form of communism? And second, how far have the Marxist-led state governments of Kerala, West Bengal and Tripura been successful in creating genuine communist policies despite their limited autonomy? In addition the book examines the future prospects of communism in India.

Bogdan Szajkowski
University College, Cardiff

Contents

Editor's Preface *by Bogdan Szajkowski*	v
List of Illustrations and Tables	x
Acknowledgements	xi
Glossary	xiii
List of Abbreviations	xv
1 India: An Overview	1
2 Communism in India	14
3 History and Political Traditions of Kerala	38
4 Social Structure of Kerala	55
5 The First Communist Government, 1957–9	64
6 From United to Disunited Front	82
7 National Democracy: CPI and Congress, 1969–79	95
8 Left and Democratic Fronts	103
9 West Bengal: History and Political Traditions	109
10 Modern History of West Bengal	122
11 The Hegemony of the CPI(M)	137
12 Communism in a Micro State: Tripura and the Nationalities Question *by Harihar Bhattacharyya and T. J. Nossiter*	144
13 Conclusion	170
Bibliography	199
Index	209

List of Illustrations and Tables

Maps

Map 1 Kerala	xii
Map 2 West Bengal	110
Map 3 Tripura	145

Tables

P.1 Communist performance in Indian general elections, 1952–84	vi
2.1 Communist percentage support in State Assembly elections, 1967	22
2.2 CPI membership, 1934–59	31
2.3 CPI and CPI(M) membership, 1967–85	32
10.1 Number of seats and percentage of votes won by Congress, CPI(M) and CPI in Assembly elections, West Bengal, 1967–72	136
12.1 Electoral College, Territorial Council and Legislative Assembly election results, Tripura, 1952–88	147
12.2 Lok Sabha elections, Tripura, 1952–84	148
12.3 Tripura: Tribal Area Autonomous District Council results, 1982 and 1985	152
12.4 Tripura: municipal election results, 1978 and 1983	168

Acknowledgements

I am most grateful to the many members of the communist movement in India who have spared their time to talk with me. It would be invidious and lengthy to name them all but I would particularly wish to mention the kindness of the Chief Ministers of West Bengal (Mr Jyoti Basu) and Kerala (Mr E. K. Nayanar) and the former Chief Minister of Tripura (Mr Nripen Chakrabarty). I owe the latter an apology. After he had so whetted my enthusiasm to visit his state, the anonymous bureaucrat in Delhi whose task it was to decide whether or not I could have a permit for entry into Tripura declined to answer my letter. Several civil servants in West Bengal and Kerala were most helpful in answering queries and directing me to sources; but, proper though they were, I do not suppose they would thank me for mentioning them. The maps are based upon the Survey of India, Government of India copyright 1981, by kind permission of the Survey of India. I have benefited greatly from discussions with journalists, who are often of very high calibre in India, and from academics great and small. My own and colleagues' doctoral students have taught me a lot, Dr Guharpal Singh about the 'failed' case of communism in Punjab, and Mr Harihar Bhattacharyya on the complexities of neglected Tripura. Among personal friends the late Dr Sambhu Ghosh, Minister for Higher Education in West Bengal, was generous in many ways, and Dr Prasanto Ray has, without knowing it, encouraged me when I needed it. The publishers have been very tolerant and the editor, Heather Bliss, should be decorated for her patience as well as her professionalism. I feel far less well disposed to those responsible for the pressures on universities which make it extraordinarily difficult to conduct research any more. I acknowledge with real gratitude the financial assistance of the University of London's Central Research Fund and the British Council in making visits to India possible. Carolyn Cowey and Marion Osborne have been marvellous with typing throughout; and Zarina Khan has assisted in the last rites. Dr D. Chakrabarty made contacts in West Bengal; Mr Rameshwar Rao was unfailingly generous. From my family I can only crave forgiveness: 'it won't always be like this'.

T. J. Nossiter
London School of Economics

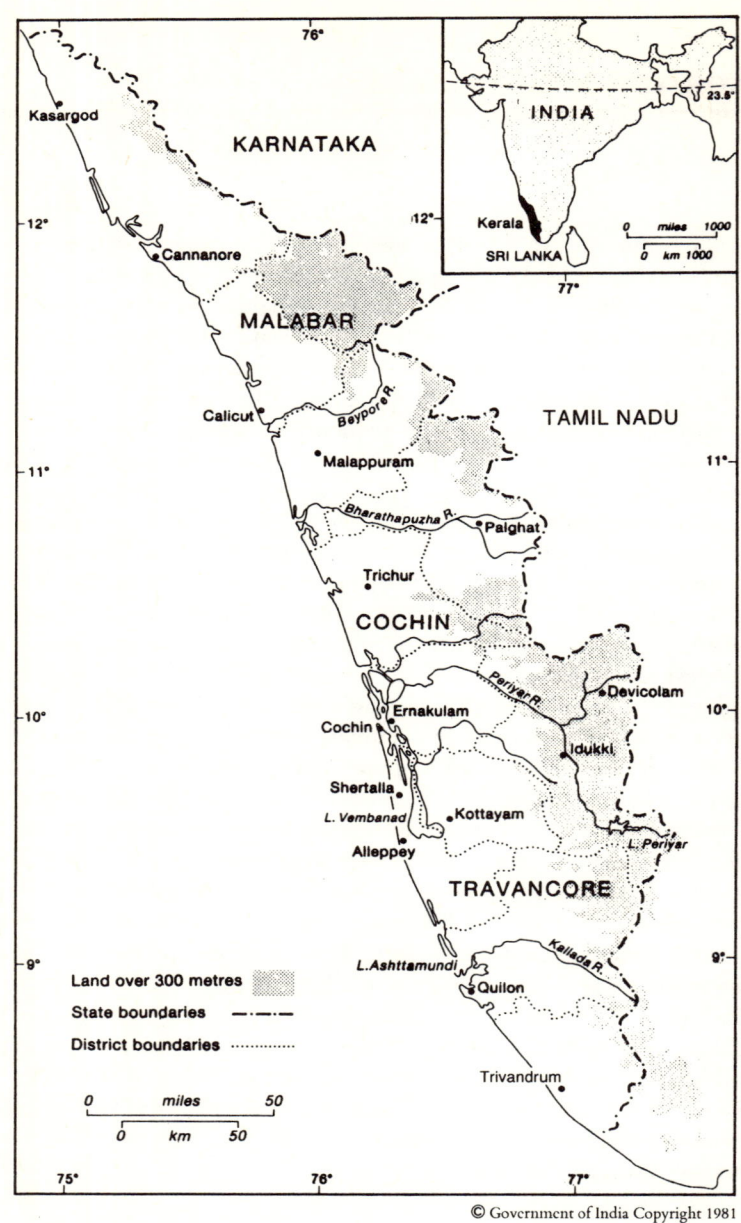

Map 1: Kerala
Source: First published in T. J. Nossiter, *Communism in Kerala*, London, Hurst, 1982.

Glossary

ashraf	honourable
bandh	agitation
bhadralok	Bengali urban ruling elite
abhijata	aristocrats
grihastha	middle-class, bourgeoisie
burra	brown
Bustee	urban slum
dewan	chief minister
gherao	encirclement
jawan	soldier
jenmi	landlord
jhumia	those who practice *jum*
jum	slash-and-burn agricultural method
kanomdar	rent-collector
kayal	low-lying land reclaimed from Vembanad Lake in Kerala; paddy land in this region
kisan sabha	peasant association
lathi	police cane
mahisya	cultivator caste
madhyabitta sreni	middle-class, petty bourgeois
panchayat	lowest unit of local government in rural areas, composed of a small number of villages
panchayati raj	rural local government
pukka	proper, true, best quality
puramboke	land reserved for public purposes
raja	king or chief
ryot	cultivator
ryotwari	land revenue system under which assessments are made on individual holdings
sanyasi	holy man
sudra	service
satyagraha	a fast
taluk	a local administrative unit; revenue subdivision of a district

yogam association
zamindar landlord
zilla parishad a local authority at district level in Independent India

List of Abbreviations

AIAWU	All-India Agricultural Workers' Union
AIDWA	All-India Democratic Women's Association
AISF	All-India Student Federation
AITUC	All-India Trade Union Congress
BJP	Bharatiya Janata Party
BPC	Bengal Provincial Congress
CFD	Congress for Democracy
CITU	Congress of Indian Trade Unions (CPI(M) trade-union federation)
CPC	Communist Party of China
CPGB	Communist Party of Great Britain
CPI	Communist Party of India
CPI(M)	Communist Party of India—Marxist
CPI(ML)	Communist Party of Indian—Marxist-Leninist
CPSU	Communist Party of the Soviet Union
CSP	Congress Socialist Party
FB	Forward Bloc
GMP	Gana Mukti Parishad
IAS	Indian Administrative Service
INC	Indian National Congress
INTUC	Indian National Trade Union Congress (Congress trade union federation)
JPC	Joint Political Congress
KC	Kerala Congress
KMPP	Kisan (or Karshaka) Mazdoor Praja Party
KPCC	Kerala Pradesh Congress Committee
KSP	Kerala Socialist Party
KTP	Karshaka Thozhilali Party
LDF	Left and Democratic Front
MLA	Member of the Legislative Assembly
MP	Member of Parliament
NSS	Nair Service Society
PEPSU	Patiala and East Punjab States Union
PSP	Praja Socialist Party
PUSF	People's United Socialist Front

RSP	Revolutionary Socialist Party
RSS	Rashtriya Swayamsevak Sangh (a Hindu organization)
SFI	Students' Federation of India
SNDP	Sree Narayana Dharma Paripalana Yogam
SSP	Samyuktha Socialist Party
TGP	Tripura Ganamukti Parishad
THPP	Tripura Hill People's Party
TLA	Travancore Labour Association
TNV	Tripura National Volunteers
TSC	Travancore State Congress
TUJS	Tripura Upujati Juba Samity
UDF	United Democratic Front
UF	United Front
ULF	United Left Front
USOI	United Socialist Organization of India
UTUC	United Trade Union Congress
WPP	Worker and Peasant Party
YC	Youth Congress

1 India: An Overview

The Republic of India is the major part of the Indian sub-continent and the principal successor state to British India—which included present-day Pakistan and Bangladesh. It is the world's second most populous state and in area the seventh largest country. The estimated (1985) population of 750 million is growing at the rate of 1 million per month and it is virtually certain that within fifty years there will be more Indians than Chinese. Over twice the population of Europe is squeezed into an area two-thirds its size. Generalizations about India are fraught with difficulty. Its twenty-five states and six Union territories range from the Himalayan Jammu and Kashmir to the near-equatorial Kerala. Despite positive discrimination, the disparities between rich and poor states have changed little since Independence. The dominant religion may be Hinduism but India is the second largest Muslim nation in the world; and the contrasts in life styles are often measurable in centuries, and in the case of a few of the tribal peoples, millennia. No greater challenge to communist revolutionaries exists anywhere; and the answer to the often put question of 'Why has there been no revolution in India?' may be that 'India' exists as an imperial accident.

The dominant features of the Indian landscape are the Himalayan barrier to the north, the inverted triangle to the south known as the Deccan, and the crescent-shaped Indo-Gangetic Plain in between. This vast alluvial plain is the India the tourist sees: Delhi, Agra's Taj Mahal and Benares. At its western end lay the remarkable urban civilization of the Indus Valley (4000–2000 BC); and it was this which attracted raiding Aryan tribes from the north-west. Around 1500 BC they began to colonize and gradually imposed their distinctive social order on the indigenous Dravidian and Austric peoples over most of the subcontinent. By the second century BC, Hinduism, and the caste system developed by the Aryans, had emerged in their recognizable essentials. Although Buddhism and Jainism had some impact, Hinduism proved the more resilient creed. Today it is the religion of 83 per cent of Indians. Muslims form 11 per cent, Christians 3 per cent, Sikhs 2 per cent and Buddhists less than 1 per cent of the population. From AD 1206 Muslim invaders, again from the north-west, steadily established their hold in northern India and by the late seventeenth century the Mughal Empire extended over virtually all of India south of the Himalayas. Conversion, especially among those at the bottom of the Hindu caste ranking, had taken place on a considerable scale but the dynasty was rapidly weakened with the abandonment of religious toleration, coupled with quarrels over the imperial succession and the growing intrusion of European traders, backed by superior military and naval technology.

In the late eighteenth century, after defeats by the British, the Mughals rapidly declined. The last emperor, effectively a pensioner of the British, was formally deposed in 1858. Of the European powers—Portuguese, Dutch, French and English—it was the British East India Company that established its supremacy. By the mid-nineteenth century the company, however, had lost its commercial monopoly and acted as the administrative agent of the British Government. Finally, after the so-called Indian Mutiny of 1857, power was transferred to the Crown, and the Company liquidated. At the wickedly fawning suggestion of the Tory Prime Minister, Benjamin Disraeli, Queen Victoria assumed the title of Empress of India in 1877; and, though she never visited her 'Jewel in the Crown', ordinary Indians wept in Calcutta, then the capital, on hearing of her death in 1901.

Under the British Raj two-thirds of the country was ruled directly through the Viceroy, the India Office and the Imperial Civil Service, in a famous phrase, the steel frame of India, backed by the British-officered Indian Army. The other third—some five hundred princely states—was ruled indirectly through Agents or Residents whose task was to make sure the native rulers did nothing inimical to British interests. The British did not colonize India, in contrast to parts of Africa, although some families—in commerce, in tea-planting, as well as in the military and the civil service—worked in India through several generations. The word 'posh', originating in the preference of 'commuting' Britishers for a ship's cabin away from the sun—'Port Outward, Starboard Home'—sums up the relationship. The total British presence in India at any one time would not have exceeded 100,000; and the Indian Army in the interwar years was about one-seventh of the armed forces of the subcontinent today.

Under the British a nation was forged from peoples of different race, language, religion and tradition. By the late 1930s, however, it had become clear that when independence came there would be two successor nations, a Muslim 'Pakistan' and a secular, though predominantly Hindu, India. Even today language and culture within India constitute a major barrier to the creation of a unified society.

Karl Marx, in a series of letters in 1853 as correspondent of the *New York Daily Tribune* (Marx, 1936, pp. 55-6), concluded with a somewhat Eurocentric but not altogether specious assessment of the 'Future Results of British Rule in India':

Indian society has no history at all, at least no known history. What we call its history is but the history of the successive intruders who founded their empires on the passive basis of that unresisting and unchanging society. The question, therefore, is not whether the English had a right to conquer India, but whether we are to prefer India conquered by the Turk, by the Persian, by the Russian, to India conquered by the Briton.

It was a rhetorical question. Marx saw Britain, the leading capitalist country of his day, as engaged on a double historic mission: to destroy the old Asiatic society and to lay the material foundation of Western society in Asia. 'Asiatic society' proved much more virile than his enthnocentricism foresaw; and while India is today the tenth largest industrial nation in the world, the village and its values still prevail over metropolitan and capitalist ones.

The greatest difference in life style in India is between urban and rural dwellers. Though backward to Western eyes, Indian towns do offer amenities generally unknown in the countryside; the town dweller acquires 'modern' values, albeit mediated through Indian familial structures; and, outside the many slums, he or she enjoys a far higher standard of living than the villager. Four-fifths of the population live in 600,000 villages, although the distinction between town and village is not always clear cut. (Technically, in India a town is defined as a settlement of 5,000 of more people where at least 75 per cent of the adult male work-force is engaged in non-agricultural pursuits.) The rate of urbanization is less than that of many developing countries and the amount of rural to urban migration is surprisingly small when compared to Africa or Latin America. The migrants are also disproportionately drawn from the wealthier sections (and higher castes) of rural society. The poor lack the capital to sustain themselves while they seek work in the towns, which as a result of discrimination is often hard to find. Despite the scale of India there are only ten cities of over one million inhabitants, led by the former imperial cities of Calcutta, Bombay, Delhi and Madras. Calcutta, the largest, is already an ageing city and it is unlikely that Indian cities will develop into megalopolises. The implications of the limits to, and the nature of urbanization in India for a communist movement are considerable. In the cities communism has taken root only in Calcutta and Bombay but the communist base in the mills of Bombay has been eroded with the decline of the textile industry as well as internecine communist disputes. Neither the relatively small scale of factories nor the dispersal of the population into housing colonies far from the city centre are conducive to the mobilization of the working classes.

In the urban areas, caste and communal solidarities remain central to marriage and important in personal relationships but their role in life generally has diminished. Both individualism and class-based stratification have become significant. In contrast, in the countryside, despite noteworthy exceptions, the pattern of life is still dominated by caste and poverty. The poorest of the poor are the scheduled castes (14 per cent of the population) and the scheduled tribes (7 per cent) for whom the constitution provides special protection and governments special provision. Nevertheless, the outcastes remain more nearly 'untouchables' than the 'sons of god' (harijans) as they were renamed by Gandhi. Given the acute pressure of population on land, high caste status by no means guarantees a subsistence standard of living, but for the lower castes—and especially the untouchables—poverty is virtually their birth-right, and discrimination and exploitation an everyday experience. Under-employment, malnutrition, disease, poor housing, illiteracy, high infant mortality (134:1,000) and low life expectancy are the lot of many in most rural areas and the majority in some.

Officially, 40 per cent of the population are below the poverty line. Most rural families are either landless or cultivate a 'dwarf holding', too small to provide for the barest subsistence. With no financial security, they are forced to borrow money from the village moneylender at usurious rates at times of family crisis; and debt rather than property is the legacy of one generation to the next. Children, especially boys, are the surest insurance in old age. When the estimated percentage of children surviving to 10 years of age is only 75, birth-control campaigns, short of the appalling sterilization campaign of 1975-7, will have minimal effect. Forty-two per cent of the population are under 15 years of age and 51 per cent below 19. In contrast only 3.5 per cent are 65 years old or more. Male life expectancy (53) exceeds female (52) and only in Kerala do females outnumber males in the population. Many writers—including Marx—have supposed that Hinduism itself induces fatalism but there is no warrant for this aspersion. Where government has systematically sought to restructure village society through health care, ration shops and basic education, low-caste Hindus have proved as responsive to opportunities as have Christian converts from the degraded castes and they have also broken out of the vicious spiral of caste-related poverty. Kerala, as we shall see, is a remarkable example.

The states and Union Territories of India vary as widely in their demographic and economic characteristics as the social groups within them. The state of Uttar Pradesh with over 100 million inhabitants would, if independent, be one of the biggest countries in the world. At the other end of the scale there are five states with populations of little more than 2 millions. Density ranges from 50 per square kilometre in the extreme north-east to over 500 in Kerala and West Bengal. Urbanization varies between 8 and

31 per cent; and the working percentage of the population from below 30 to above 50 per cent. Electricity is connected to more than 90 per cent of villages in four states and less than 30 per cent in five others. Literacy varies from 25 per cent to 70 per cent and hospital beds per 100,000 population from 40 to 200. Gladstone once described the Naples of his time as the 'negation of God erected into a system of Government' (Gladstone, 1851, p. 9 n). It is a description which equally aptly could be used of the state of Bihar which scores least on virtually every indicator of social provision, including GDP (US$51 per capita), and where atrocities on untouchables are little remarked.

Government and Politics

Although, prompted by major agitations in the wake of the First World War and in the early 1930s, the British gradually introduced a measure of Indian participation in government which culminated in the 1935 Government of India Act, progress was too slow to avert a freedom struggle and, paradoxically, too fast to precipitate a revolution. Terrorism—chiefly associated with Bengal and Punjab—and guerrilla warfare—the wartime Indian National Army—played a small part in the fight for independence which was strikingly non-violent in character. More importantly, the relative peacefulness of the Transfer of Power entailed no fundamental transformation in social relations: Raj remained Raj, albeit run by *burra* sahibs.

The granting of independence on 15 August 1947 owed something to the coming to power of a majority Labour government in Britain but probably rather more to the collapse of the British will and ability to maintain their empire, in the face of a naval mutiny and the uncertain loyalty of the Indian army. The freedom movement had been led by the Indian National Congress and the communist role was a very minor one, further reduced after 1941, when, following the German invasion of the Soviet Union, the communists were ordered by the Comintern to support the Allied War effort. The CPI thus boycotted India's greatest mass protest, the Quit India agitation of 1942.

Congress had, beyond achieving independence, no clear ideology: Gandhism, the utopian ideology of village democracy, traditional cottage industry and the non-violent winning of hearts and minds to social justice, virtually died with the Mahatma, who was assassinated in January 1948 by a Hindu extremist. Indigenous capitalists, who had provided much of the funding for the Congress campaign, shrewdly preferred to operate behind the scenes; and the character of the new India was set by Pandit Jawaharlal

Nehru, who was Prime Minister till his death in 1964. With only brief interruptions (Shastri, 1964-5; Morarji Desai, 1977-9 and Y. B. Chavan, 1979), the Nehru family have held the office of prime minister since independence although the policies of Indira Gandhi, Nehru's daughter, and Rajiv Gandhi, his grandson, have differed greatly from those of Nehru himself.

Under Nehru India became a secular competitive democracy, a planned mixed economy, dedicated to socialist goals, and, in foreign affairs, leader of the non-aligned movement. The Constitution, quite the longest in the world, was largely modelled on the Raj's 1935 Government of India Act. To this were added Directive Principles of a socialist character and, in incipient conflict, such fundamental rights as the right to property. Following the British pattern there was parliamentary government through prime minister and cabinet, a head of state (the President) who was dignified not executive; and elections conducted on the same simple plurality system as Westminster. Parliamentary sovereignty was however constrained by a constitution amendable by two-thirds majority of national and state assemblies, and a supreme court to enforce it. The parliament consists of two houses, the lower, or Lok Sabha, and the upper, or Rajya Sabha, with the Lok Sabha the more important.

The states reproduce in miniature the national constitutional system. In place of the President is the Governor, who, however, unlike his national counterpart, is no mere figurehead. He or she is appointed by the central government and is, normally, the eyes and ears of Delhi. His discretionary powers, exercised in close consultation with the ruling party nationally, include the initiation of the formation of a ministry and the right to decide that no democratic ministry is possible. On more than one occasion this power has been used to frustrate the creation of left-wing ministries. He also has the right to dismiss the state government and the assembly if he determines there is a political crisis and to govern personally through one or more Advisers. This so-called Presidential Rule had up to 1984 been used with growing regularity and doubtful propriety. Some states have upper houses but again it is the lower house which counts. Under the Constitution, legislative powers are divided into three groups, the Union, State and Concurrent Lists of which the longest, and most important, is, of course, the Union's. Of the sixty-six items on the State List, thirty deal with ordinary police functions and twenty-two with taxation, leaving fourteen items of 'development', of which the important ones are education, health and industry, agriculture and agrarian relations. They are hedged about with qualifications; and, in certain cases, the centre may override state powers. The Concurrent List throws in 'economic and social planning' and trade.

Practically no legislation proposed by a state government can avoid the hurdles of 'consultation' with three or four central ministries. The Governor may 'reserve' bills passed by the provincial assembly for 'Presidential' consideration, which was the fate of the first Kerala communist government's land reform bill. The majority party or parties form a state cabinet (council of ministers) under a Chief Minister. Such ministries are, however, notoriously unstable: state-level party systems have fragmented even more than the national one; party discipline is at a discount; powerful vote bankers are close at hand. Quite simply, too many state legislators can be bought. Since the accession to office of the CPI(M)-led United Front government in 1977, West Bengal has been immune from such problems but the defection of non-left coalition partners in the 1980-1 Kerala Left Democratic Front brought down that government.

The actual administration of the state is in the hands of a bureaucracy known as the All-India Services; and the Chief Secretary, the most senior administrative officer in the state, though chosen by the Chief Minister, can be a victim of divided loyalties. Below state level are the district, block, *taluk* and *panchayat*, in descending order, and in the urban areas a variety of authorities of generally limited powers. Despite repeated calls from across the political spectrum, local democracy has generally been stillborn though there are one or two states with a meaningful *panchayati raj* (village government). The key functionaries are local officers and state-level politicians.

Power lies with the authority to write the cheques. In this respect the states are disadvantaged by the distribution of taxation. The central government enjoys the most important and growing sources of revenue. The states depend on three limited sources: their own constitutionally sanctioned powers of taxation; a share of centrally raised taxes decided on the basis of quinquennial Finance Commission reports; and Plan allocations. The main state taxes are land revenue—a legacy of the Raj—agricultural income tax, local excise and estate duties and vehicle and sales taxes. Since there is no more land to bring under the plough any increase in land revenue would mean an enhancement of the rates and the ordinary cultivator cannot afford it. Agricultural income tax could raise a great deal but big farmers are too powerful a lobby to offend. Thus the chief source of state taxation has become sales tax on items of mass consumption: regressive, unpopular and, given the low standard of living, finite.

The Finance Commission, a quasi-judicial body, has the invidious task of deciding how centrally collected resources shall be divided between the central government and the states, and between one state and another. The transfer is unconditional: the monies may be spent as the state government wishes. The Planning Commission is concerned with 'plan' as opposed to revenue expenditure, something of an unreal distinction. It disposes of funds in two ways: Central Investment, which goes to projects of all-India significance; and Central Assistance, which supports projects of local importance. The arguments that ensue when resources are so scarce and need so great are inevitably bitter.

In sum, the states have many responsibilities and, as the seat of government nearest both the voter and the vested interests, demand upon them is inordinate. Yet their capacity to raise revenue is both legally and politically highly constrained. They rely on the centre in one way or another; and since (at least until Rajiv Gandhi's Government actually declined overdraft facilities to Uttar Pradesh in 1985) the Reserve Bank of India has always bailed out those state governments unable to honour their cheques, there has been little incentive to good housekeeping nor indeed to financial probity.

Such a summary of the legislative, executive and financial aspects of centre-state relations may leave the impression that they are more lop-sided than is actually the case and exaggerate the degree to which the states propose and the centre disposes. Relations are bound to vary with a whole array of political factors: how strong, united, and popular the central government is; how much clout particular states and their governments carry; whether there are powerful regional interests to be conciliated; and, in the case of Kerala and West Bengal, as well as other states, whether the same party or parties govern in Delhi and the state capital. Personal connections cannot be discounted: the route to Delhi for either politicians or bureaucrats is through the state government. This does not always mean that central ministers or officials will oblige their old friends. The Finance Minister who declined to extend an overdraft to Uttar Pradesh in the case mentioned above formerly had been the Chief Minister of that state. In the last resort, the sheer amount of knowledge required and the length of the chain of command ensure that determined state authorities can win battles if not the war. The victory of the centre in anything short of a set-piece confrontation is by no means a foregone conclusion, even with a troublesome communist administration. Left-front governments genuinely believe that they have been discriminated against in the allocation of resources but their very agitation to publicize the fact make the centre more cautious since elections are never far away.

The Economy

Under Nehru's direction the Indian economy rapidly became a joint enterprise of public and private sectors. His admiration for the achievements of Soviet planning led to the establishment of the Planning Commission, five year plans and the immediate target of building a heavy industrial base for the country. The private sector, already well-established before Independence, had done comparatively well, in part because such big business houses as the Tatas and Birlas have wielded political as well as economic influence. Agriculture on the other hand was underfunded and its progress has owed more to the Green Revolution and capitalist farming of the 1960s and 1970s than to government support. The public sector has been notoriously inefficient, and rather than guide and stimulate growth, it has tended to stifle it. After the mid-1960s when wars with Pakistan and China, disastrous monsoon failures and political uncertainty necessitated a 'Plan Holiday' for three years, the growth rate of real value added in manufacturing decreased significantly but, even before this, Indian industrialization never matched the rates of expansion of a variety of newly industrializing countries. Improvement in the foreign exchange position in the mid-1970s and a rise in the rate of domestic savings, which had been presumed to be important bottlenecks, did little to improve matters. Nor did the drastic assumption of quasi-dictatorial powers by Mrs Gandhi during the state of emergency of 1975-7.

The causes of India's slow pace of industrialization do not lie in any serious deficiency in natural or human resources. Both are extensive. Coal is plentiful and India is among the world's leading producers of iron ore. Oil is so far produced from Assam in the north-west and the Bombay High Offshore field and now provides for two-thirds of consumption. The level of skills in engineering and science is high enough for India to build its own rockets and the pool of skilled labour is enormous. The real explanation lies in the country's economic policies and the political forces that have affected their formulation and implementation. The immediate economic causes lie in the inefficiencies induced by the high degree of insulation from the marketplace, lack of demand for industrial products, and inadequate investment in the public sector. Key industries have been confined to the public sector with no incentive to show a profit, propped up by subsidies, and often for political reasons, hopelessly overmanned. In the drive for self-sufficiency the import of goods has been severely restricted, foreign investment heavily curtailed and an elaborate system of licensing and regulation developed, which is not only slow but not infrequently corrupt. The tax structure and the financial system have featherbedded private industry. It is difficult for all but the smallest capitalist to go bankrupt. The ailing company becomes a patient of the department for 'sick' industries. The protected high-cost structure and the outdated technologies and design of India's products limit its export market for manufactured goods; and the slow progress of agriculture has not created enough demand for mass consumption items at home. The better-off urban classes and the rich farmers have gone to inordinate lengths to secure 'white goods', electronic equipment and cars on the black market. In 1985 one enterprising individual actually smuggled a Mercedes in 'kit' form through customs. The net effects were that the poor could not afford consumer durables, the rich could not find them (legally), and the economy experienced the massive distortions of a thriving black economy.

The political causes of economic stagnation are more controversial (Joshi & Little, 1987 pp. 371-8). The CPI(M) attributes India's economic problems to the fact that India is mainly linked with the capitalist world and its market and so experiences the capitalist crisis like other Third World countries. Western imperialism—witness the large IMF loan of 1983—increasingly interferes in the Indian economy in collaboration with local capitalist interests. Undoubtedly world economic factors, including oil price increases, have had their repercussions on the Indian economy. It is also true that approaching 90 per cent of India's trade is with the non-communist world, led by the United States. However the links with the capitalist world economy are too slender to bear the weight this analysis places upon them: India's share of world trade is less than 1 per cent.

An even more implausible explanation is encapsulated in Gunnar Myrdal's (1968, p. 124) notion of the 'soft state' where:

National governments require extraordinarily little of their citizens. There are few obligations to do things in the interest of the community or to avoid actions opposed to that interest. Even those obligations that do exist are enforced inadequately if at all. This low level of social discipline is one of the most fundamental differences between the South Asian countries today and Western countries at the beginning of their industrialisation.

The argument that 'all Indians are feckless and lazy' is on a par with 'all Germans were bad'. It has no sociological warrant.

A much more interesting argument is Bardhan's 'proprietory class' analysis, which starts from the generally agreed view that the private industrialists, the big farmers (and large landowners) have heavily influenced politics both nationally and at state levels and adds the professional politicians and bureaucrats themselves, who have a vested interest in the growth of the state *per se* (Bardhan, 1984). The state apparatus in this context is not just the more far-sighted servants of capital, arbitrating between different fractions of capital, and even allowing particular capitalists to go to the wall, the better to preserve capitalism as a system; the managers of state capital have their own economic base and use their control of investment, subsidies, licences and so on, to strengthen it. Politics is indeed big business, supported by its own special currency, 'black money', the grubby notes of the parallel economy, which the tax-man never sees.

Awareness of the importance of broad social forces should not preclude a recognition of the role of prime ministerial decision (and in Mrs Gandhi's case, indecision) in a political system which, like the British, can produce not only cabinet government but prime ministerial government. During the 1950s Nehru was at the peak of his powers but during his last years India experienced a loss of direction and a crisis of confidence on military, economic and political fronts. After a brief interval under the premiership of Lal Bahadur Shashtri (died January 1966), Mrs Gandhi succeeded her father. Congress chiefs found it easier to nominate Nehru's daughter as leader than to agree on one of their own number, especially as they all underestimated her determination to have her way. Her first election (1967) proved a disaster. For the first time Congress suffered a setback at the polls. In about half the state assemblies it lost control; and its majority in the Lok Sabha was slashed. By 1969 Mrs Gandhi had declared war on the party barons over the selection of a new President of India and in consequence Congress split into a Ruling (or Indira) and an Organization Congress. Her supremacy was confirmed in the 1971 elections when Mrs Gandhi's slogan of 'Remove Poverty' proved more potent than the opposition slogan of 'Remove Indira'. The defeat of Pakistan in the Bangladesh War was the zenith of her career. By 1975 the lustre had gone. Beset by economic and political difficulties—harvest failures, the oil price increase and the Jayprakash Narayan Movement against corruption—but devoid of any real policy, Mrs Gandhi reacted to a guilty verdict on a minor charge of electoral malpractice in the Allahabad High Court by declaring a state of national emergency.

The following two years, aptly characterized by Morris-Jones as a period of 'constitutional authoritarianism', tarnished India's image and stained Indira Gandhi's reputation (Morris-Jones, 1977). Opposition politicians were incarcerated and freedom of opinion suppressed while her younger son, Sanjay Gandhi, grew in power. The forcible campaign of sterilization and brutal slum-clearance schemes were his immediate responsibility; and Congress (Indira) became in all but name Congress (Sanjay). Against her son's advice Mrs Gandhi called elections in 1977. For once the opposition united as the Janata (People's) party and Mrs Gandhi was defeated although not by as great a margin as might have been expected. Bitter differences within Congress over the character of the Emergency and the role of Sanjay during it led to a second split in Congress in 1978. Sadly for Indian democracy the Morarji Desai Government proved divided and ineffectual and after a brief effort to sustain an alternative government under Y. B. Chavan in 1979, elections were again held in 1980. Although in terms of the vote Mrs Gandhi's Congress at 42.7 per cent did not reach the 1971 level of 43.7 per cent, the combined effect of the simple plurality electoral system and the opposition disarray was to give her a sweeping victory of over two-thirds of the seats.

Sanjay, who had been his mother's campaign manager, now re-emerged into the limelight and quickly became recognized—not without apprehension—as the heir apparent. However within a few months he was killed in a flying accident; and after great pressure had been brought to bear on his elder brother, Rajiv, this Indian Airlines pilot with no experience of, or inclination towards politics, was persuaded to take Sanjay's place beside Mrs Gandhi. With his mother's assassination on 31 October 1984 at the hands of Sikh extremists, Rajiv became Prime Minister of India after the briefest of apprenticeships. In the December 1984 general elections he became, so to speak, premier in his own right with an unexpectedly large majority. If it is too early to do more than speculate how his growth-oriented, 'high-tech' leadership will develop, Mrs Gandhi's era comes into clearer perspective. Though a statesman on the world stage and the greatest crowd-puller of her time in India, greatness eluded Indira Gandhi. Despite her imperious nature and her authoritarian streak, she proved strangely indecisive. The incipient socialism of the 1971 election campaign was not matched by deeds. She conquered her rivals but in the process all but destroyed the Congress Party. Her advisers were too often sycophants and sometimes crooks. In her later years she increasingly failed to show the political agility which marked her early years and as a result the fabric of national unity was torn by separatism in Punjab, Assam and elsewhere. Despite her failings, however, no official opposition or 'government in waiting' emerged, save half-heartedly in 1977. The electoral system of 'first past the post', constituency-based polling militates against the development of a new national party. Economic difficulties exacerbated regional competition and so nourished state level parties. With the exception of the communist parties, all the parties with any claim to be national in character were Congress fragments; and since Mrs Gandhi clasped socialism to her bosom while holding hands with private capital, she hindered any polarization of the Indian party system into a left-right dichotomy. One does not need to accept the dynastic theory of Indian politics to believe that Indian history would have been very different without her premierships. Nor indeed the rule of her older son, Rajiv Gandhi, who succeeded her in 1984 with his Business School approaches to managing India. In both cases concentration of power in the prime minister's office has been accompanied by the neglect of party organization to the detriment not just of the Congress party but the political integration of India. In contrast the communist movement, to which we now turn, has learnt from bitter experience the importance of a party organization which is at once democratic and centralist but not personalist.

2 Communism in India

The Communist Party of India (CPI) is usually dated from 26 December 1926. It remained effectively an illegal organization until 1942 when the British accepted its support for the Allied war effort. Its origins antedate 1926 and lie in the linkages between the Comintern and educated nationalist *émigrés*, many of whom came from Punjab and Bengal. India was for the Comintern the weakest link in the armour of the greatest imperial power. By the second congress of the Third International (July–August 1920) an Indian communist centre had been set up under M. N. Roy and later in the year a training school for Indian revolutionaries was established, again under Roy, at Tashkent. Its activities were transferred to the Eastern University in Moscow in 1921. From 1922 contact was being made with radical and proto-communist groups in Bombay, Madras, Calcutta and Lahore. The Raj was, however, alert and the 1923 Kanpur Conspiracy Case temporarily interrupted efforts to implant communism in India. In the lull in Congress activity following Gandhi's abrupt (and unpopular) withdrawal of the Non-cooperation Movement, militant class-based Worker and Peasant parties began to mushroom, climaxing in major strikes and the establishment of a national WPP. Again the Raj struck, arresting virtually all the leadership of the CPI, which largely controlled the WPPs, and prosecuting them (1929) in the Meerut Conspiracy Case. The trial dragged on for over three years and gave the communists invaluable publicity as well as—perversely on the part of their gaolers—giving the prisoners considerable liberty to further their studies in Marxism. However two developments placed the CPI in opposition to the mainstream of Indian political life: the Comintern in 1929 instructed the CPI to break with the Congress; and Gandhi launched a new and powerful phase of mass mobilization, the Civil Disobedience Movement. Not until 1935, when the rising tide of fascism as a threat to communism was all too clear, did the Comintern reverse its stance and encourage 'popular fronts'.

What to do about the bourgeoisie has from the beginning been a recurrent bone of contention in Indian communism. Both before and after Independence this has largely been the same question as what the communists' attitude to Congress should be. The parameters of the argument were set in 1920 in a famous disagreement between Lenin and M. N. Roy on the Colonial Thesis (Overstreet & Windmiller, 1960, Ch. 2). Roy, a brilliant

Bengali Brahmin, who, by a carefully staged accident on his part, represented Mexico at the second congress of the Comintern in 1920, stated what has become known as the ultra-left (or sectarian) line: the Communist International should exclusively assist the communist movement and no other in India and in turn the CPI must devote itself exclusively to organizing the masses in their struggle for their class interests. In contradistinction, Lenin's thesis had been that communist movements were simply not strong enough to stand alone in backward colonial countries so they should render assistance to bourgeois-democratic liberation movements. Until 1929 it was the Leninist position which prevailed; from 1929-35 the Royist, though by then Roy had been expelled from the Comintern, and ironically had come round to a Leninist position.

Disciplined observance of such political lines was never anywhere near total, and indeed the lines themselves were never so clear-cut as they appear with hindsight. By 1933 the ultra-left line was being softened but already the CPI leaders on their release from gaol were again participating in non-front organizations. At the local level socialists in contact with the CPI were participants in the newly formed Congress Socialist Party, a ginger group within Congress. In 1936 individual communists were welcomed to membership and by 1937 the CSP became a major vehicle for communist proselytization. P. C. Joshi, the new general secretary of the CPI, was instrumental in seizing the opportunity. Party fractions appeared covertly within the CSP and in some areas, including Kerala, by 1939 the CPI controlled the CSP and the CSP controlled Congress. In 1934 CPI membership in the whole of India had been 150; by 1942 it was 5,000. Later the CPI claimed to have had 20 members on the All-India Congress Committee in 1939 and there is no reason to disbelieve it (Palme Dutt, 1949, p. 397). By 1939 the growth of communist influence was provoking reaction from the dominant Gandhian wing of Congress, especially in the light of the development of a leftish challenge to Gandhi in a contest for the Congress presidency. Determined efforts were made to wrest back control of those Congress units which had come under left or communist influence, including Kerala and West Bengal.

More important, however, was the impact of the CPI's Soviet-ordered dramatic reassessment of the nature of the Second World War in the wake of the German invasion of the Soviet Union in 1941. What, during the period of the Nazi-Soviet Pact, had been an 'imperial war' to be wholeheartedly opposed, now became a 'people's war' to be backed to the hilt. Helpfully the British authorities conveyed the CPSU's message to the many communists in imperial gaols and swiftly released the detainees. In fact, communists combined support for the war effort with anti-British propaganda but to many of the Indian public the communists were placing allegiance to a foreign ideology and foreign power before their own country and its struggle. In the end the people's war was won but in their own way the CPI had paid dearly. A new generation of anti-imperialists saw the communists as the agents of British imperialism. From the end of the war to independence events moved too quickly for the CPI to formulate any coherent policy, particularly since there was no clear guidance from the CPSU. Initially the party returned to the pre-war united-front line. Its response to the British withdrawal was to assert that independence was incomplete. However, by late 1947 sections of the party were arguing that the CPI was becoming at best an appendage of Congress, at worst a spectator. It was neglecting its historic opportunity to lead a mass upsurge against imperialism and feudalism and by its very timidity invited repression. This leftist faction won control of the party's higher counsels and in February–March 1948 the second Congress of the CPI adopted the disastrous Calcutta (or, after its chief protagonist, the Ranadive) Theses. The official CPI history reports that the 'analysis was carried out in the most peculiar manner. Not on the basis of a concrete study of the concrete situation but on the basis of quotations from Lenin and Stalin and later from Mao and the Chinese leaders' (Rao, 1976, p. ix).

Indian independence was dismissed as a chimera. The earlier distinction between progressive and reactionary sections of the bourgeoisie was rejected and with it any collaboration with Congress. The objective now was People's Democracy—socialism and democracy combined—to be achieved by a prolonged struggle using politicized strikes in the urban areas leading to a general rising in the villages. As a revolutionary plan it echoed Russian experience. The only trouble was that Nehru was not Kerensky and August 1947 not February 1917. The CPI lacked the machinery, resources and influence to implement such a revolutionary movement; and they had neither a Lenin nor a Trotsky. The consequence was a series of ill-considered and, except in West Bengal and Tripura, ill-coordinated actions, subsequently labelled 'adventurist' by the party, which led to many deaths, detentions and torture, the exposure of undercover comrades, a split in the peasant organization and widespread demoralization and defection.

At the beginning of 1949 the party in desperation turned to terrorism, sabotage and gaol strikes, which led to even more determined action by the Congress authorities. Only in Telengana Andhra, part of Tripura, and to a degree in West Bengal was there effective organization. In June 1948 the Andhra leadership proposed a quasi-Maoist strategy based on a united front of the entire peasantry and parts of the bourgeoisie under working-class (i.e. the CPI's) leadership, which would sustain a prolonged civil war fought from liberated areas and founded on agrarian revolution. Briefly in 1950-1 the Andhra line prevailed but to avert extinction the CPI turned for authoritative guidance to the CPSU and the CPGB. It was urged to seek rehabilitation.

The ensuing 1951 Party Programme restored the CPI to legality (CPI, 1951, Vol. 8, pp. 1-18). The party proposed to use the forthcoming first Indian general elections to popularize its policies, mobilize and unify democratic forces and expose the Congress Government for what it was. As a secret document circulating among the Politburo, the Tactical Line, made plain, the CPI was not abandoning revolution only postdating it (CPI, Vol. 8, pp. 19-23). The cutting edge of revolution was now the 'maturing economic crisis', which was the inevitable outcome of a regime run by landlords, princes and the reactionary bourgeoisie in collaboration with British imperialism. The election results went some way to vindicating the tactics: although the CPI won only sixteen seats in the Lok Sabha (and 3.3 per cent of the vote), left-wing parties took 20 per cent of the national vote. Congress lost its overall majority in Madras, PEPSU (part of Punjab) and Travancore-Cochin; and the CPI did particularly well in Madras, Hyderabad (Telengana) and Travancore (Kerala).

The situation was however changing fast. Nehru's foreign policy was not pro-Western; American not British imperialism was clearly becoming the main threat to international communism; and the experience of the elections had suggested there were opportunities in united fronts for greater advance. The party's right wing began to challenge the hesitant compromise of the 1951 programme. However at the (third) CPI Congress held at Madurai in December 1953 the majority of the delegates proved to be left inclined and the 1951 line was largely confirmed. The economic crisis continued to mature and signs of a political crisis were discerned. The party's evaluation of Congress was unchanged. As Ajoy Ghosh, the general secretary, put it: there were only two possible courses of action, to cooperate with Nehru's government but criticize specific measures, or to oppose it generally but support particular progressive acts. The CPI continued to do the latter (Ghosh, 1954, p. 4).

Over the next three years there was no escaping the new reality; and a serious party crisis broke. The Soviet Union began to applaud the Indian foreign policy of non-alignment. Khrushchev himself visited Delhi in 1955 and aid for Indian economic development was arranged; and by the so-called Avadi Resolution bourgeois Congress committed itself to bringing about a socialist pattern of society. Meanwhile the CPSU was pressing the CPI leadership to reappraise its negative attitude to Congress: India was a friendly (and progressive) regime in a strategically significant country.

The CPI divided into left, right and centre factions. The left remained adamantly opposed to any truce with Congress because of the class character of its domestic policies. The right took the Soviet part in advocating collaboration with the Congress left in a 'general united front'; and the centre contended that Congress's domestic policies were both progressive and reactionary—which also happened to be the leadership's view. This was a function of the bourgeoisie's contradictory role as both a modernizing and an exploitative force in history. Coincidentally, of course, the centrist position was an expedient compromise between the extreme warring factions.

Debate was launched in advance of the next (fourth) party Congress to be held at Palghat in April 1956. The Congress was, however, overshadowed by the shattering revelations at the 20th Congress of the CPSU at which Khrushchev denigrated Stalin and the CPSU endorsed the concept of the peaceful transition to socialism. At a closed session Ajoy Ghosh explained to delegates that Marx had envisaged such a transition and that it would be possible in India provided: (i) the working class remained the vanguard; (ii) the bureaucracy and police were curbed, and the state apparatus, including the army, was democratized; and (iii) the most reactionary elements were removed. Representative institutions were now to be taken seriously as a battleground for the extension of people's rights and powers rather than as an arena for propaganda as in the 1951 formulation. Cautiously, the text refers to popular elected organs as *'Panchayats*, District Boards, etc.' (CPI, 1951, Vol. 8, pp. 504–11). A few months later that 'etc.' covered the Kerala State legislature.

Over the next two years the position of the centre and right factions strengthened. The CPI assumed office in Kerala, led by a member of the Politburo, and for a year there was something of a honeymoon. Nehru, publicly at least, was sanguine that democracy and communism could coexist. The Moscow Statement of the Twelve Communist Parties in November 1957 spelt out the full implications of peaceful transition; and in April 1958 the CPI held an Extraordinary Party Congress at Amritsar to adopt a new party constitution, which transformed the CPI into a mass party. In some respects the constitution went further than Palghat. The CPI declared its faith in the peaceful parliamentary path as a means of securing full democracy and socialism. Underlining its Indianness, Marxism–Leninism was to be applied to the realities of the Indian situation, its national peculiarities and the best traditions of the Indian people.

A number of commentators have explained the CPI's progress from the parliamentary tactic in 1951 to the parliamentary strategy in 1958 essentially in terms of Soviet pressure on a weak, divided and demoralized party. It would be pointless to deny that the CPSU and the CPGB influenced CPI thinking in the 1950s, as earlier, but the indigenous roots of the new line ran deep. Conversely, the left, which acquiesced in the Palghat–Amritsar programme without conviction, took the Chinese side in growing Sino-Soviet conflict from 1958 onwards because it chimed with its perception of Indian reality. The 1964 split in the CPI was not the result of the shock waves of a central Asian earthquake but a truly Indian fissure. E. M. S. Namboodiripad (1964, pp. 59–60) reflected the view of all sections of the party in asserting that the

> internal differences within the CPI [were] as old as the decision of the British Government ... to create the new independent state of India; they came up in different forms. The leading organs of our Party ... tried to furnish answers ... however, it became clear that there were different trends, different approaches ... This led to a continuous bitter inner-Party struggle, at first of an ideological character,

but subsequently splitting the party asunder.

Two dimensions of conflict stand out: how the party should view the national bourgeoisie and by extension Congress; and how far it was meaningful to work within the existing Indian constitution. After Amritsar, a right minority favoured closer collaboration with Congress, the left even less collaboration, especially after Nehru's dismissal of the Kerala ministry in 1959 on what were political rather than constitutional grounds. For the left, it was further confirmation that one could not trust even the notionally progressive bourgeoisie and that constitutionalism was, in Marxist terms, parliamentary cretinism. In the international context of communism the Chinese rejection of peaceful coexistence between capitalism and socialism and advocacy of national liberation in colonial and semi-colonial countries had an obvious attraction.

With the Chinese occupation of theocratic and feudal Tibet in 1959 and the Sino-Indian border dispute over Longu in the Indian (but imperially defined) North East Frontier Agency in August the differences between the left and right of the Indian communist movement began to crystallize. Following a further clash between Indian and Chinese troops in November the CPI declared for the nation (the border as defined by the McMahon Line) and the left became increasingly disillusioned. Obfuscation by the CPI leadership was increasingly difficult as the World Congress of Communist Parties of November 1960 was bound to force it to indicate its allegiance, CPSU or CPC, no matter how well coded. In the event the CPI's support for the Soviet Union met with strong opposition among the cadre and the National Council agreed to circulate left and right versions of a draft political resolution for the 1961 (6th) party Congress at Vijayawada. A centrist resolution was also circulated. The right saw the biggest threat as emanating from monopoly and foreign capital. Since Congress represented progressive as well as reactionary elements, the CPI should be prepared to work with the former in a national democratic front led, of course, by the working class. The left accused the right of compromising with Congress and underestimating its reactionary character. The CPI must oppose Congress with the utmost vigour. Working-class leadership of democratic forces was underlined in the choice of slogan: People's Democracy. The Centrist draft argued for efforts to win over the anti-imperialist and anti-feudal elements of the bourgeoisie but was in outline closer to the left than the right.

Vijayawada proved inconclusive. After much manœuvring, the official rightist draft was amended to make it more anti-Congress and anti-Nehru in tone but the revision of the long-term programme was remitted to the National Council. Meanwhile Amritsar would stand. How finely balanced opinion was is indicated in the fact that a contemporary estimate was that only 56 members of the 110 National Council were on the right (*Hindustan Times*, 17 April 1961).

Shortly after the Congress in January 1962 the CPI secretary, Ajoy Ghosh, died. The compromise successor was Namboodiripad, slightly to the left of the political centre of party gravity but, to balance this, Shripat Amrit Dange, the leading spokesman of the right, was appointed to the new office of party Chairman, an arrangement that was unlikely to be satisfactory since there was considerable personal antipathy between the two men.

Matters finally came to a head in October–November 1962. The Sino-Indian border conflict took a more serious turn and the CPI National Council declared for the nation against Chinese aggression. Three members of the central party secretariat resigned in protest. Worse was to come. On 22 November the central government swooped, arresting nearly 1,000 leftists under the Defence of India Ordinance, on the basis, it was alleged, of lists supplied by the rightists. The rump then passed rightist and pro-Soviet resolutions and set about 'reorganizing' state units, while the left built parallel party centres. The split, which had been inevitable since 1962, finally came in April 1964 over the affair of the Dange letters. The Chairman of the party was accused of having written to the British authorities in 1924 offering to act for them in exchange for his freedom. When an enquiry was rejected in April 1964 thirty-two members of the National Council walked out and the split was formalized.

Later in the year the rival parties held their congresses, the breakaway group in Calcutta, and the official CPI in Bombay. Their programmes confirmed again that the split was along an Indian fault line. For the right, India's independence was a historic event and India was now on the path of independent development. For the left the transfer of power was only a 'settlement' between British imperialism and Congress and what had happened since was the efforts of the Indian bourgeoisie to establish a compromise with feudalism and imperialism at the expense of the people. For the one, economic progress was real; for the other, illusory. The key group in the CPI's analysis was the national bourgeoisie fulfilling a historically progressive role; for what was soon to become known as the CPI(M) (CPI Marxist) the key class fraction was the monopoly bourgeoisie in league with imperialism. The right's slogan was, then, the establishment of national democracy by means of a front of all patriotic and progressive forces including the national bourgeoisie. The left's slogan was People's Democracy because, they argued, there could be no national democratic road as this was barred by the dominance of the big bourgeoisie and its alliance with imperialism. People's democracy would be formed and led by the working class. Two other distinctions emerged: the CPI emphasized national identity while the CPI(M) tended to underline regional (or sub-national) identity; and the CPI saw the proletariat as the principal force of revolutionary change while the CPI(M) accorded an important place to the peasantry.

The original left programme was modified in the run up to and during the Calcutta Congress in response to the arguments of the centrist leaders, Namboodiripad of Kerala and Jyoti Basu of West Bengal. The party therefore avoided committing itself to an all-out confrontation with Congress on the grounds that the contradictions within the ruling class would lead some sections of it to align themselves ultimately with the People's Democratic Front which was to be a staging post to People's Democracy.

Namboodiripad's part in the events of 1962–5 cannot be overstated. It was the centre under his leadership which enabled the left to mount an effective challenge to the right; and Namboodiripad not only had a significant political following in the party but was rapidly established as the CPI(M)'s principal theoretician. By reason of his long service in the Politburo and his tenure since 1962 of the party secretaryship he also had a virtually unrivalled knowledge of the party machine and its mass base.

The CPI(M)'s revision of the 1958 Amritsar programme omitted the original preamble underlining the possibility of peaceful transition in India but at least by implication it accepted constitutionality for the foreseeable future. The CPI(M) was not to be an anti-system party. In the medium term it would accept the rules of the game but the People's Democratic Front would adopt an altogether more militant strategy than the CPI's National Democratic Front. At the end of December 1964 the Indian government detained some eight hundred CPI(M) cadres alleging that the new party had Chinese links and rejected the parliamentary road but even among non-communists this attempt to tarnish the CPI(M) as anti-national and anti-constitutional was widely seen as a clumsy effort to influence the outcome of the first trial of strength between CPI and CPI(M): the mid-term state poll in Kerala.

The result of this election in 1965 was an unequivocal statement that the real communist party in Kerala was the CPI(M). The rivals put up similar numbers of candidates but the CPI took only 8 per cent of the vote (and three seats) to the CPI(M)'s 20 per cent (and forty seats). Over the country as a whole the 1967 general elections showed that the CPI(M) had a moderate overall lead—5.1 per cent of the Lok Sabha poll to 4.4 per cent. More critically the CPI(M) led where it mattered (see Table 2.1).

Table 2.1 Communist percentage support in state assembly elections, 1967

	CPI	CPI(M)	Total
Kerala	8.6	23.5	32.1
West Bengal	6.5	18.1	24.6
Andhra Pradesh	7.3	7.2	14.5
Punjab	5.2	3.3	8.5
Bihar	6.9	1.3	8.2
Assam	5.1	2.0	7.1
Orissa	5.3	1.2	6.5
Maharashtra	4.9	1.1	6.0
Tamil Nadu	1.8	4.1	5.9
Uttar Pradesh	3.2	1.3	4.5

Source: Baxter, 1969.

In the two states, Kerala and West Bengal, where the communists had a real mass base, the CPI(M) was roughly three times stronger. In Andhra Pradesh, where one in seven voters supported the communists, the parties were evenly balanced. For the rest, with the exception of Tamil Nadu (Madras), the CPI led but there were far too few revolutionary foot soldiers for it to make any difference. At first sight the split might have appeared to be a tragedy for the communist movement but united it had not stood and divided it did not fall. The rift between left and right was unbridgeable and in the long term it was arguably better that the rival lines be put to the test and the proletariat and peasantry make their choice by ballot box and *bandh* (agitation). On that basis the answer is conclusive: between 1967 and 1980 the CPI(M)'s parliamentary vote rose from 4 to 6 per cent and its seats from nineteen to thirty-six whereas the CPI's vote fell from 5 to less than 3 per cent and its seats from twenty-three to eleven. (The 1984 election is discussed later.)

The CPI(M), having established itself as the senior partner by 1967, was soon faced with a severe challenge to its own position from further left: the Naxalites, or, as they became, the CPI (Marxist-Leninist). Capitalizing on the nadir of Congress fortunes, the CPI(M) had led united fronts to office in 1967 in both Kerala and West Bengal. The CPI(M) Central Committee clarified the role of these governments in April 1967. They were to be seen as instruments of struggle rather than agents with real power to give substantial relief to the people, to combine agitation with administration and to unleash discontent (CPI(M), 1967a, p. 70). For some on the far left of the CPI(M) no second invitation was required.

At first the Chinese Communist Party (CPC) had enthusiastically welcomed the formation of the CPI(M); and Maoist propaganda had become available in West Bengal. The CPC's assessment of the 1967 elections was that 'revolutionary flames' were sweeping a country ripe for revolution but within months the CPC was broadcasting and printing virulent condemnations of the revisionist ministries in Kerala and West Bengal, denouncing the CPI(M) and personally attacking Namboodiripad (Ram, 1971, p. 244). In March 1967 in and around Naxalbari, a village in the tribal area of north Bengal, clashes occurred between the labourers and peasants and the Hindu landowners. Aided by some local communist leaders, the tribals temporarily liberated their district. After efforts at negotiation, the inevitable police firings took place but the martyrdoms at the hands of a united front government, of which the CPI(M) was a leading party, gave the dissidents their publicity. By June the CPI(M) Politburo had concluded that 'certain individual Party members especially in West Bengal' were not a legitimate political trend within the party but 'an organized anti-Party group advocating an adventurist line' and challenging party authority and programmes (CPI(M), 1967b). On 27 August the CPI(M) Central Committee unequivocally condemned the Chinese assessment of the Indian situation as utterly wrong and devoid of any relation to reality. This was indubitably true but Naxalitism as an ultra-left deviation had by then appeared in Calcutta,

Andhra, Bihar, Kerala, Uttar Pradesh and Bombay. At a secret meeting in Calcutta in November 1967 an All-Indian Coordination Committee of Communist Revolutionaries was created; and eighteen months later the formation of the Communist Party of India (Marxist-Leninist) (CPI(ML)) was announced on 1 May 1969. The CPI(M) as well as the CPI was dismissed as a social chauvinist bourgeois party, anxious to defend the existing system and faithfully to serve the ruling classes. It was the new party's task to integrate Mao Zedong's thought with the concrete practice of Indian revolution. Firm police and military intervention brought the movement in the countryside under control though sporadic terrorist activity continued into the early 1970s but a more threatening explosion occurred in 1970-1 when Naxalitism became a powerful student movement in Calcutta. However by 1972 the CPI(ML) had ceased to be a significant force. It had fragmented into tiny and often warring factions; Charu Majumdar, the most charismatic leader, was dead; and the CPI(M) had reasserted its hegemony.

For essentially pragmatic reasons the CPI and the CPI(M) had some measure of accommodation in 1967 and 1968; but from 1968 onwards their paths rapidly diverged. In its 1964 programme the CPI had said that 'no National Democratic Front would be real unless the vast mass following of the Congress' especially the progressive sections would have their place (CPI, 1965, p. 43). Mrs Gandhi's support of the communist-backed V. V. Giri—a former union leader—for the Indian presidency against the Congress party machine's candidate, coupled with the nationalization of India's biggest banks, suggested the National Democratic Front was at hand. In Kerala a CPI-led Mini front ministry was being maintained in office with the connivance of Congress. The split in Congress could be read (wrongly) as the differentiation of the bourgeoisie into progressive and reactionary wings. Then in 1971 came the Indo-Soviet Defence Treaty, the socialistic Congress election campaign and in 1972 Congress's entry into the CPI-led Kerala ministry.

As far as the CPI(M) was concerned, the CPI was deluding itself (or being deluded by the CPSU). It interpreted India's growing economic difficulties since the 1960s as serious enough to provoke a major political crisis. The flagrant ballot rigging in the 1972 West Bengal elections by Congress and its tough, if not brutal, police policy, reflected political bankruptcy. The looming crisis could only be resolved by a 'combination of parties and organisations of the left opposition ... powerful and determined enough to reverse' the policies pursued by Congress since independence (Namboodiripad, 1974, pp. 137 and 157). The actual political demands made by the CPI(M) at its 9th Congress at Madurai in 1972 were close to clairvoyant in the light of the Emergency three years later: basic changes in the constitution to eliminate its misuse by the ruling party and the danger of one-party dictatorship and a guarantee of all liberties as well as real autonomy to the states (ibid., pp. 157-8). By 1974 the CPI(M) could point to the popular uprising in Gujarat, which forced a corrupt Congress ministry from office, and the Jayprakash Movement in Bihar, besides economic misery.

The CPI was not entirely uncritical of Mrs Gandhi, and its attitude to Congress varied from state to state and from situation to situation. Nevertheless it could not avoid guilt by association. Discontent within the party grew when Mrs Gandhi arrested communist union leaders and ruthlessly put down the 1974 railway strike: and alarmingly so when Mrs Gandhi assumed plenipotentiary powers in June 1975. In Kerala the CPI–Congress ministry continued in office and the CPI was therefore bound to be held responsible for whatever excesses were committed there. On the mass front, Congress was intensifying its attempt to erode the communist hold on organized labour. With the rise of Sanjay Gandhi, sterilization (of the poor), enforced slum clearance in Delhi and pro-capitalist economic policies proved too much and leading sections of the CPI began to engage in public criticism. On the eve of the 1977 elections, however, the CPI re-endorsed its existing stand of 'unity with struggle' and alliance with Congress wherever possible. Except in Kerala, the result was disastrous. The party's national vote fell from 4.7 per cent to 2.8 per cent and seats were slashed from twenty-three to seven.

Finally at the 11th party Congress (Bhatinda) in April 1978 (and after a further split in Congress), the CPI admitted that its support of the Emergency 'under the belief that it would be used against extreme reaction was wrong' (CPI, 1982, p. 71). The party was beginning to re-evaluate a line which had produced no shift to the left at national level but on the contrary had led to the resurgence of anti-democratic, anti-labour and reactionary forces. How tortuous the process would be is indicated by the fact that in October 1978 a new CPI Chief Minister took office in Kerala and it was not until October the following year that the CPI finally pulled out of a ministry supported by Congress and opposed by the CPI(M) for a decade.

A minority, led by the party chairman, Sripat Dange, resisted the changed attitude to Congress and the normalization of relations with the CPI(M), and Dange was finally expelled to lead with his daughter Mrs Deshpande a pro-Soviet and pro-Congress All-India Communist Party. Its small membership is confined to Dange's long-standing base in Bombay.

By the party congresses of 1982 the political resolutions of the CPI and CPI(M) showed much common ground in advocating a left and democratic front excluding Congress. Differences in emphasis were that for the CPI Mrs

Gandhi's policies were 'retrograde' rather than downright reactionary. The CPI(M), like many non-communist commentators, found Mrs Gandhi, after her return to power in 1980, dangerously inclined to authoritarianism and was prepared to contemplate *ad hoc* alliances with bourgeois opposition parties against Congress whereas the CPI, which regarded communalism and reaction as still greater dangers, was not. Internationally the CPI(M) maintained its traditional independence but was inclined to be more positive towards the Soviet Union and more critical of the CPC. The CPI remained sceptical of what it saw as the CPI(M)'s partial, qualified, and sometimes self-contradictory assessment of the CPC.

The most recent Congresses—of CPI at Patna in March 1986 and the CPI(M) at Calcutta in December 1986—took place in a profoundly changed domestic and international environment. India as well as the Soviet Union and China were all under new management. The CPI, with its special relationship to the CPSU, hailed the 27th Soviet Party Congress as of world significance: the programme and documents opened up 'new vistas in the struggle of world humanity for peace, national liberation and social advance' (CPI, 1986, p. 10). However, domestic developments in the Soviet Union were ignored; and there was certainly no hint that in India as well as communist countries economies could become overly planned. The CPI(M) made no reference to the Soviet Congress in its published Congress proceedings. Soviet peace initiatives were commended and American war-mongering condemned. Both CPI and CPI(M) in particular singled out the destabilizing activities of US imperialism in Punjab and, on this, at least, were at one with many in Indian ruling circles.

The CPI and CPI(M) broadly concurred in their analysis of the new Indian situation but subtle differences of emphasis continued from the 1982 Congress lines. The CPI(M) remained very concerned at the authoritarian tendencies of the Congress regime but acknowledged a 'tendency among certain sections of our Party comrades to underestimate the danger of the growth of communal parties and their fundamentalist character' (CPI(M), 1986, p. 20). The CPI was little exercised by the erosion of (bourgeois) civil liberties and so argues that the left democratic alternative that needs to be built is 'not a permutation and combination of the left parties with the existing bourgeois and petty-bourgeois parties' but 'a radical realignment of political forces ... in favour of the working class, the peasantry and agricultural labour'. 'It is these classes and their alliance ... that can play a pivotal role in drawing other democratic classes to their side and thus building up the left democratic unity.' 'The class essence of our central slogan should never be lost sight of', a fairly explicit indication that it had been. That made clear, the CPI then underlined the 'special national significance' it attached to closer cooperation with the CPI(M). In the end it hoped there would be reunification (CPI, 1986, pp. 11-12).

The CPI(M) concurred in the struggle for a Left Democratic Alternative but aimed at the widest possible combination of 'classes, parties and groups' because the 'most urgent and important task facing the Left and democratic forces [was] the growing threat of authoritarianism'; and such a broad alliance was only sensible when 40 per cent of the votes cast in the 1984 parliamentary elections were for bourgeois Opposition parties. The party was 'fully aware' that some of these allies vacillated and failed to maintain consistent democratic stances but 'the importance of rallying [them] in defence of democracy should not be underestimated' (CPI(M), 1986, p. 36).

In fact the CPI could not afford to stand on its ideological dignity. Notwithstanding its ostensible numerical superiority in terms of membership, the fact is that its independent capacity to mobilize mass support is far less than that of the CPI(M). One indication is the reluctance of the CPI to extend the coordinating machinery down to the grass roots. A national Coordinating Committee had been set up in 1979 in the wake of the CPI's abandonment of its (qualified) support for Mrs Gandhi's domestic policies, but the record of collaboration is chequered. Successes include the organization of peace marches, some *ad hoc* electoral arrangements, and, most importantly, the achievement of all-India opposition conferences especially on the Punjab question. Among failures have been the inability to agree a common stand on Assam, numerous electoral *contretemps* and the CPI's distaste for the re-establishment of fraternal relations between the CPI(M) and the CPC which provoked uncomradely polemics in 1983. Conversely, the CPI(M) was irritated by the Soviet Union's extension of the special relationship with Mrs Gandhi to her son Rajiv, which it took out on the CPI.

While there is no reason to deny that there are ideological differences between the two communist parties, it is probably more meaningful to see the ups and downs in CPI-CPI(M) relations as a complex function of past acrimony with an ever present (and justified) CPI suspicion that the CPI(M) will exploit its upper hand at any, if not quite every, opportunity. Even though the generation at the centre of the original split passes on, it remains hard to see reunification as taking place without strong—and unlikely— pressure from the CPSU, and on terms which concede the CPI(M)'s firm belief in the autonomy of the Indian communist movement. That the Soviet Union would welcome reunification is clear. On General-Secretary Gorbachëv's visit to New Delhi, both CPI and CPI(M) leaders were received by him. The CPI(M)'s warmer view of China is not a problem to the Soviet

Union, but the CPI(M)'s anti-Congressism is far from welcome to a country whose estimation of the importance of Rajiv Gandhi was embodied in his probably unique entertainment at the Soviet leader's own home. The Congress(I) Vice President, Arjun Singh, attended the CPSU meeting recently in Moscow while, ironically, the CPSU sent a delegate to Congress's centenary celebrations but not even a message to the 1986 CPI(M) Congress.

Party Organization

Up until 1958 the CPI had been organized as a cadre party on the democratic centralist lines spelt out in the Comintern's *Principles of Party Organisation*. This was applied in the 1948 (Calcutta) and 1954 (Madurai) constitutions to the Indian context. Following the CPSU 20th Congress of 1956, the CPI adopted a new constitution at Amritsar in 1956, more suited to peaceful transition and to working within a system of representative democracy.

Ideological de-Stalinization and Indianization were coupled with organizational adjustments. Party units, formerly known as cells, central committees and Politburo became, under the mass democratic nomenclature, branches, State and National Councils and Central Executive Committee. The period of probation before becoming a full party member was reduced to six months. There was also some effort to decentralize the power of the party Centre. State Councils, for example, gained the right to constitute lower committees, supervise inner party discussion on state-level affairs, and decide on state-level issues. Participation was encouraged by the enlargement of membership of governing bodies as well as of the rank and file. The National Council was fixed at 101 members and the Central Executive Committee at twenty-five while Congresses were now to be held every two years.

This greater opportunity for democratic involvement by the cadres did little to resolve the fundamental ideological differences within the party and may possibly have contributed to bringing matters finally to a head in the 1964 split. The ideological and tactical conflicts within the party were to some extent reflected in the constitutions of the successor CPI and CPI(M). The CPI, whose leadership saw a purpose in collaborating with the Indian National Congress as a partly progressive creature of the national bourgeoisie, strengthened its own mass character. Democratic centralism was diluted. In major disputes there was to be more open discussion and majority decision. The discretionary powers of state-level units were still further enhanced; and candidate membership was abolished. Essentially the CPI retained the structure of 1958. Currently, there is a nine-member Central

Secretariat—of whom one is General Secretary—which acts as the day-to-day executive of the 31-member Central Executive Committee, the whole elected by the 125-member National Council. In turn the National Council is elected by the party Congress whose 1,000 plus delegates are elected by State Councils on the basis of one representative for 500 members; and so on. The CPI still adheres to 'democratic centralism' but the 1986 report indicates that a price has been paid for the greater flexibility in its interpretation:

Communist values and party forms and norms are indeed well-known ... but they can bear repetition here because they are being ignored or violated ... and the concerned party units appear to be helpless about pulling them up.

We have known days when party forms and norms were fully respected and party discipline and fraternal relations commanded a high premium.... Today many such things go by default so as not to 'alienate some people' ... The leadership intervenes only when there is a 'crisis situation' ... Tendencies of 'non-interference' and 'live and let live' have come to the fore. [CPI, 1986, p. 140]

This reprimand is followed by a reprint of the 1985 Resolution of the National Council *On Certain Harmful Practices in Internal Party Life* (CPI, 1985) and other earlier strictures. Like a bourgeois party some members have leaked 'garbled versions' of National Council and Central Executive Committee discussions to the press; and factional groupings have emerged (pp. 145–6).

In contrast the CPI(M) moved back towards the old cadre style constitution and a more 'traditional' understanding of democratic centralism. It dropped the 'revisionist' preamble of the 1958 Amritsar Constitution; and the terminology of Politburo, General Secretary, Central Committee and State Committees was reintroduced. However, branch did not give way to cell, or mass membership to cadre recruitment, although members do serve a candidate period. Despite the reversion to past language and a firmer party discipline, the organizational differences between the CPI(M) and the CPI are more a matter of degree than of kind at the present time. The CPI(M) may have more hardliners than the CPI but the 1986 resignation of the independent-minded West Bengal Minister, the respected economist Ashok Mitra—on health grounds—was as unexpected as it was undesired. Whether called Central Secretariat or Politburo, both the CPI and CPI(M) need what elsewhere would be accepted as 'collective responsibility'.

Common to both as a deep-rooted problem of organizational structure is the application of 'democratic centralism' to parties which are federal in character in two incontestable respects: the inevitably conflicting experiences, composition and interests of the major state units; and the different arenas and objectives of the parties as mass movements on varied fronts and as electoral machines, governments and oppositions, at state and all-India level. Symptomatic is the fact that both the CPI and the CPI(M) have their headquarters in Delhi, the capital of India, but far from the heartland of either party. The 1982 Political Organizational Report of the CPI(M) censured those who had succumbed to 'federalism', a deviation from party norms described as 'the glorification of the achievements of individual state Party units or decrying their failures without looking at them from the all-India angle'. 'Comrades who are victims of this trend do not realise that without a strong all-India centre and its intervention no strong state Parties ... can continue for long in face of the onslaught from the authoritarianism of the Central Government'. 'The federal outlook which ends up in each state functioning, more or less, as an independent body reduces the all-India centre to a sort of co-ordinating body which periodically meets to adopt some resolutions' (CPI(M), 1982, pp. 140). The implication is clear: only the central leadership is committed to a national breakthrough.

Both party reports complain of the difficulties in persuading state party units to release proven leaders to work at the centre. Regrettable it may be, but understandable it is.

Tensions between leaders of the mass organizations and those whose principal activity is parliamentary and from time to time ministerial are no less predictable. The key figures are likely to have different backgrounds and certainly different experiences. Parliamentary opportunism and 'feudal-bourgeois life-styles' are charges exchanged for accusations that mass leaders run satraps without reference to the party's wider objectives (CPI(M), 1986, p. 70; CPI, 1986, p. 138 ff).

However, it is important not to leave the reader with a misleading impression. Both the CPI, and particularly the CPI(M), are, in the 1980s, far franker in their public self-examination than virtually all Western competitive parties, than almost all their fraternal parties in or outside the Communist bloc. The CPI(M) remains, however, far less certain how far to permit real inner-party discussion. At the 1982 Congress alternative draft resolutions were circulated and discussed but by 1985 there were signs that *glasnost* was frowned on by powerful leaders. Sudhamshu Dasgupta, Gopal Bose and Laxmi Sen were examples of critics dropped from the State Secretariat in West Bengal, while M. V. Raghavan and P. V. Kunnikannan were disciplined in Kerala for protesting at changes in attitude to the Muslim League. For all the individual failings, on average these parties exhibit a moving commitment to their cause, sustained over decades in frequently inauspicious and brutal circumstances. Flawed the communist movement of India may well be, but it has sustained its values far more successfully than

Table 2.2 CPI Membership, 1934–59

1934	150	1946	53,000	1954	75,000
1942	5,000	1947	60,000	1957	125,000
1943	15,563	1948	89,263	1958	218,532
1944	25,000	1950	20,000	1959	178,718
1945	30,000	1952	30,000		

(*Source*: Overstreet & Windmiller, Table II, p. 357; Brass & Franda, p. 22).

any other movement or party in Independent India. Livelihoods and lives themselves are still regularly lost by humble party workers in village and urban slum each year.

Party Membership

Table 2.2 shows the membership of the CPI during the Freedom Struggle and in the years from Independence to the conversion of the party from a cadre-base to a mass organization. It illustrates clearly how far the CPI was distanced from the Liberation Struggle: in 1947 Congress membership was estimated at some 7 million. The price of the 1948 Ranadive line is also evident: membership collapses from nearly 90,000 in 1948 to 20,000 in 1950 and does not reach the previous peak again until the mid-1950s.

At the time of the split in the CPI in 1964, the total membership was around 200,000. Since claimed membership by the rival parties was part of their fratricidal campaigning, it is best to take 1967 as the new baseline. At that time the CPI with 175,000 members was twice as large as the CPI(M) with 83,000 members. Table 2.3 shows the course of membership since then, on the basis of which three observations can be made: first, overall the CPI has grown by around 275 per cent but the CPI(M) by approaching 450 per cent. Second, the CPI appeared to grow steadily throughout the first ten years, 1967–77, but it has since, with the exception of 1980, made no advance in membership. In contrast, the CPI(M)'s real growth has occurred since 1977. In the late 1960s, its membership was somewhat depleted by the impact of Naxalitism and, in the early 1970s, it suffered the effects of repression in West Bengal. Since 1977 however, when the party-led fronts came into office in West Bengal and Tripura, its membership has burgeoned. In the eight years to 1985, the party has increased by 226 per cent compared with the

Table 2.3 CPI and CPI(M) Membership, 1967–85

	CPI	CPI(M)
1967	175,300	82,670
1968	172,902	76,420
1969	172,902	75,390
1970	243,238	84,886
1971	250,000	104,730
1972	280,000	100,125
1973	280,000	103,250
1974	340,000	103,100
1975	340,000	109,610
1976	350,000	102,250
1977	480,000	122,050
1978	459,513	157,030
1979	459,513	197,000
1980	546,000	243,650
1981	467,623	271,500
1982	485,952	326,478
1983	446,429	327,327
1984	478,905	354,265
1985	480,000	367,828

(*Sources*: CPI and CPI(M) Party documents; *New Age; People's Democracy; International Yearbook of Communist Affairs*).

CPI's 4 per cent. The smooth progress of the CPI for much of the period and the roundness of the figures raise some doubts as to their accuracy, but a more important point is that the criteria for admission to the CPI(M) are somewhat more stringent than those into the CPI. It may therefore be wise to treat with caution the presumption that the CPI is really the stronger party. Although the united CPI did become a mass party in 1958, and the successor parties remain mass not cadre in character, it is also fair to note that if the quality control is less than formerly—discipline *has* suffered—membership is not just a question of asking to join and paying the appropriate subscription. Evidence of some commitment is required, particularly in the case of the CPI(M). Allowing for the youthful profile of the Indian population, it can be estimated on the basis of the 1985 figures that around one in 2,000 Indian adults belong to one or other communist parties, one in 1,130 to the CPI and one in 870 to the CPI(M). No figures are available for the minor communist parties to the left and the right but it is certain that their membership does not exceed a few thousand.

The national figures obscure the high degree of regionalization in communist support, particularly in the case of the CPI(M). This had been the pattern throughout the history of the communist movement in India. Commenting on 1956 figures, Overstreet & Windmiller highlighted the importance of the South Indian element. Except for West Bengal, all the big delegations at the 4th Congress were from the south—Andhra, Kerala and Tamil Nadu (p. 359). Recent reports of the CPI(M) include state-wise membership but the CPI publishes only the size of delegations to the National Council, which, however, can be used as a surrogate measure. In 1985 two CPI(M) units—West Bengal (137,000 members) and Kerala (122,000)—made up 70 per cent of the total membership but in 1982 the entire membership in the Hindi belt was only 28,000 (CPI(M), 1982, p. 135). In 1985 the other states with numbers in excess of 10,000 were Tamil Nadu (27,000), Andhra Pradesh (18,700), Bihar (11,600) and Tripura (11,400). Since the size of states varies so much, it is also worth considering the ratio of party members to total population. Kerala (1:245), Tripura (1:312) and West Bengal (1:662) are quite impressive units. Tamil Nadu, Punjab and Assam are around the national average of 1:2,500; but, except for Andhra Pradesh (1:3,600) and Bihar (1:6,300), the ratio is everywhere else very large indeed: in the biggest state of Uttar Pradesh, 1:21,000, in Maharashtra, 1:19,000, in Madhya Pradesh, 1:49,000 and in Gujarat, a dispiriting 1:66,000.

CPI membership, on the basis of delegations to the National Council, is concentrated in four states: Bihar (57,500), Andhra Pradesh (42,000), Kerala (38,000) and West Bengal (34,000). Three other states have significant enrolments: Uttar Pradesh (27,000), Tamil Nadu (23,000) and Punjab (also 23,000). Compared with CPI(M), the CPI is not so heavily dependent on a couple of leading states but conversely there is no outstanding base when measured in terms of the ratio of members to population. Bihar and Andhra offer the best performance of between one member per 1,200 or 1,300 population.

Both parties regularly express reservations about the 'quality' of their memberships. The CPI in 1986 noted a 20 per cent turnover of members at each annual renewal of party cards.

> Reports from state committees indicate that the dropping out is not due to political reasons but due to the inability of the leadership at the local and district levels to educate the members, organise them into suitable party branches, ensure regular functioning of branches and enable them to undertake the day-to-day activities of

the party on their own. As a result vast numbers of branches do not meet at all, except at the time of annual branch conferences ... As a result, many remain 'members at large', who function in fitful fashion and participate only during some big mass campaigns or struggles. And there is a certain percentage which does not become active even [then]. It goes without saying that the consciousness of such members is close to that of the common masses and is subject to the ups and downs in the mood of the masses. [CPI, 1986, p. 131]

Among the reasons cited for this state of affairs are the lack of live and active contact between the district and other intermediate levels of leadership and the actual rank and file. Linked to this is the falling number of branches, down from 25,155 in 1983 to 23,607 in 1985, and the poor circulation of party journals and literature (p. 133). The CPI(M) had already engaged in a tough bout of collective self-criticism as early as 1978; and the 1982 and 1986 Congress reports continue to reiterate the need for more effective organization, coordination and education. As the 1982 survey rightly observed, when only 3 or 4 per cent of those who belonged to the party's various mass front organizations (or 2 or 3 per cent of those who had voted for the party in 1980) were actual members there was no reason for complacency (CPI(M), 1982, p. 132). Similar complaints as those made by the CPI on membership turnover, the circulation of party literature, and branch functioning and supervision appear in CPI(M) documents.

Information on the social composition of membership is not always easy to interpret. In the CPI workers and wage earners constituted 17 per cent of the party membership (CPI, 1986, p. 134) in 1985, yet the 1982 report avers that agricultural workers constitute a sizeable section of the party membership and in some states account for more than 50 per cent of the membership (CPI, 1982, p. 144). The party officially bemoans the long-standing indifference to the task of building mass organizations, particularly trade unions, *kisan sabhas* and agricultural workers' associations (CPI, 1986, p. 135). 'There is an inhibition regarding organising the agricultural labourers because of a fear that it will alienate even the middle peasants' (p. 135) and a failure to enrol the women who have participated in mass struggles. Older comrades are disinclined to bring on younger comrades (CPI, 1982, p. 143). 'A basic weakness is that a large part of the party is disoriented from mass work ... It has become more oriented towards elections to bourgeois parliamentary institutions of all types'. Representation is seen as necessary so as to use these forums for 'mass revolutionary advance. But they cannot become the core and pith of our thoughts and deeds' (CPI, 1986, p. 138).

The character and composition of the CPI party Congress delegates is outlined in the analysis of the Credentials Committee. Around 10 per cent were attending their first congress, about 30 per cent their second or third congress (fifteen stalwart comrades had attended all previous twelve congresses). Although the report concluded that this showed new cadres were joining the leadership, the age of delegates appears to have been rising and a quarter of delegates had joined the party before 1947. Those over 50 years of age were 47 per cent in 1986 compared to 42 per cent four years earlier and in 1986 only 15 per cent of delegates were 35 years old or below. The class origin of delegates was skewed to the middle classes (41 per cent) and almost 50 per cent were university educated. In contrast there were few delegates from agricultural worker backgrounds (3 per cent) and only 16 per cent from working-class origins. Eighteen per cent came from poor peasant homes and 20 per cent from middle-income peasant backgrounds. Although there was a slight improvement on the previous congress, women were still not more than 4 per cent of delegates. The 'economic condition of the cadres continued to be difficult': just over half of those not on a party pension earned less than Rs500 per month (£29) and only one in seven more than Rs1,000 (p. 173). Analysing the mass front on which delegates were primarily active, the largest component was trade-union work (37 per cent), 25 per cent were with the *kisans* and 14 per cent the agricultural labourers. Representation on the women's front was weak and students and youth were not well served.

Like the CPI, data on the CPI(M)'s mass membership is indicative rather than comprehensive. The 1982 Congress report (p. 170) gives detailed information on twelve of West Bengal's sixteen districts. Twenty per cent were working-class, 16 per cent agricultural labour, 36 per cent poor peasants and another 18 per cent 'employees', making 90 per cent of the total. The strength among the peasants is, however, largely confined to West Bengal, Kerala and Tripura. Progress is clearly being made among students and youth. Just over a quarter of Kerala's membership are from these sections but while the party welcomed the intake of youth here and elsewhere, it warns that postgraduate education is not party education. Otherwise students will introduce 'alien trends' into the party. As in the wider Indian society, women are conspicuously absent from any systematic participation in democratic life. Women in 1985 constituted less than 5 per cent of party membership in both West Bengal and Kerala and only 7 per cent in Tripura. In the entirety of CPI(M) state Committees, only 15 women could be identified. Finally, it is worth underscoring the recency of the majority of CPI(M) membership. Nearly two-thirds had enrolled after 1977. The most striking increases were in West Bengal and Tripura (66 and 73 per cent). Kerala, on the other hand, managed a below-average 17 per cent which does not seem to be explicable as a simple function of whether or not the state unit was in office since neighbouring Tamil Nadu grew by 38 per cent in the same period.

Mass front organizations among industrial and agricultural workers, peasants, students and the young, women and minorities are the real wedge that the parties recognize must be driven home by the cadres if the cause is to be advanced; and both CPI and CPI(M) are harsh in their self-criticism. The CPI does not give much detail but is deeply dissatisfied with its work on the rural front. The CPI(M), although more effective in a few states regards the weakness of its *kisan* movement as a patent and grave shortcoming. Of some 2.5 million peasants organized in the All India Kisan Sabha (a joint communist front), over three-quarters are in the one state of West Bengal. Kerala's share is a surprisingly low 7 per cent and, according to the 1986 report, falling (CPI(M), 1986, p. 103). While there are local agricultural workers' unions, and in West Bengal, field labour has been long organized within the *kisan* movement—about 40 per cent of membership—generally the mobilization of agricultural workers has been very poor, partly because their situation is so desperate, partly that there are conflicts of interest even within the communist movement between peasants and their labourers, and partly because the leadership—at each level—has been insufficiently committed. It was not until 1980 that the CPI(M) set up an apex body, the All India Agricultural Workers' Union (AIAWU) and as of 1985 only 1 million of India's estimated 55 million agricultural workers were enrolled. Forty-five per cent of this membership is in Kerala and 30 per cent in Andhra Pradesh. The opportunities are tremendous but as both parties admit they are a long way from being seized. Even in Kerala there were just three full-time cadres to work among 2 million agricultural labourers (CPI(M), 1986, pp. 102-5).

On the industrial front, the official (Registrar of Trade Unions) position is that the CPI(M) trade-union federation, CITU, has 3,000 active unions with a combined membership of 1.3 million (1984) but these figures both under-represent the influence of the CPI(M) unions and underline the failure of the party to convert participation into paid-up membership. West Bengal and Kerala combined have an official membership of around 1 million and elsewhere, apart from Tamil Nadu (130,000), membership is below 100,000 in state units. CITU has a reputation for militancy but it is the heavy industrial and public-service workers who benefit and there are regular complaints within the party of 'semi-feudal' attitudes on the part of trade-union workers and, as in mass organizations at large, a lack of coordination between front workers and party leaders (CPI(M), 1986, pp. 70 and 80).

The one countrywide organization run by the CPI(M) though still dominated by West Bengal and Kerala is the Students' Federation of India

(SFI) which in 1985 had a membership of 1.2 million, a 70 per cent increase on 1981. The student front is volatile, the student community fragmented, and it is extremely vulnerable to communalism, casteism and opportunism. In fact, the student wing of the RSS and BJP remains the biggest college organization; and it is important that in Kerala only 7 per cent of the SFI members are signed up by the CPI(M).

Among the bulk of youth not (currently) in higher education, the national CPI(M) organization (formed in 1980), has a membership around 3 million but again this is dominated by West Bengal (52 per cent) and Kerala (32 per cent). Membership in the Hindi belt remains marginal. Girls are few and far between except in Kerala (30 per cent), and the underclasses are poorly represented. The majority of members are from the middle class or the peasantry and, in Kerala at least, half were unemployed.

The failure in all the front organizations to recruit women has led to the formation of the All India Democratic Women's Association (AIDWA) with a 1984 membership of 1.5 million of whom 1 million are in either West Bengal or Kerala, growing in the former and falling in the latter. The party comments: 'the unfortunate truth is that women's issues are seen to be the concern mainly of its women members' and it continues to be necessary to struggle against the 'feudal and backward attitude among some sections within the Party towards women' (CPI(M), 1986, p. 151).

In conclusion to this survey of mass front activity, it is fair again to redress the balance as in the analysis of the communist parties' organizational problems. Both the CPI and the CPI(M) engage in multifarious mass struggles, which are often unrewarding and, not infrequently, unpleasant for the leaders as well as the led. That there are deficiencies of social vision and implementation is not only evident but recognized by the communists themselves; but it remains true that the communists have over the years more effectively acted as popular tribunes in their key states than other socio-political movements have done elsewhere in India. Their failings are refractions of the wider society but are more appropriately viewed through a microscope than a telescope.

3 History and Political Traditions of Kerala

Kerala occupies a narrow strip of land on the south-west coast of India, 360 miles long and not more than 70 miles wide. In area it is insignificant—four-fifths the size of England; but in terms of its population it is only the scale of India which dwarfs it. Kerala's population is larger than that of several European countries, and of three countries which have caught world imagination in respect of communism; Chile, Cuba and North Vietnam. More people speak Malayalam, the language of Kerala, than Czech, Hungarian or Serbo-Croat.

Kerala is both more 'Indian' and less 'Indian' than virtually any other part of the sub-continent which, as we will see, goes some way to explaining why Kerala has become one of communism's rare outposts in India. The state has, historically, and, often perforce, been outward looking. Inland, the long high chain of mountains known as the Western Ghats effectively separates Kerala from the neighbouring Karnataka (Mysore) and Tamil Nadu (Madras). Only two significant passes penetrate the range. Over the sea, however, Kerala's commercial contacts have existed since the earliest times. Solomon's temple is reputed to have been built with timber from Kerala. Ancient Greece has left its traces. Christians settled and proselytized by the fourth or fifth centuries AD; Muslims within a century of the Prophet; and after Vasco da Gama had landed at Calicut in 1498, the Portuguese, the Dutch and finally the British imposed obligations on the local rulers.

The attraction of Kerala was its pepper, spices and tropical hardwood. The climate is India's nearest approach to equatorial conditions and the coast is of quite striking beauty. Its characteristic scenery is a rich green patchwork of coconut palms and paddy fields, threaded along the littoral by backwaters and lagoons, distantly framed by the Ghats. Temperatures range only between 70° F and 90° F; and unusually there are two monsoons (north-east and south-west), so that it rains more often and, on average, more heavily than in any other Indian state. Although there is a dry period in the first few months of the year—the lean months—the problem in the past had been to drain the water from the land rather than to bring it to the fields. The pre-colonial socio-economic structure was not something akin to the Asiatic Mode of Production but a modified form of feudalism, very probably unique in India. Water is Kerala's major natural resource and, as hydro-electric power, more than compensates for the absence of coal reserves. Geologically, the state's main assets are the rare earths such as titanium and lithium found in the coastal sands.

Kerala is conveniently described in three natural divisions each running from north to south: the coastal lowlands; the midlands; and the highlands. By contrast the pre-independence political divisions ran from east to west: in the north was the Malabar district of Madras Presidency; in the middle, the princely state of Cochin; and in the south, the major native state of Travancore. So, broadly speaking, each unit was a geographical microcosm of the whole, making it possible to focus the impact of differing political systems on the possibilities for a communist movement unusally sharply.

The coast is low-lying—in parts below sea level—alluvial and highly fertile when not saline. It is not only the most densely populated region of Kerala but among the most heavily populated rural areas in the world: 1,500 persons per square mile is not uncommon. The backwaters, often running parallel with the sea, form a maze of islands and lagoons. It was here in the villages of Punnapra and Vayalar in 1946 that the communists attempted a peasant rising precisely because the area seemed to offer the inaccessibility a zone of liberation required.

The midlands zone is a lateritic plateau some 200 to 600 feet high, deeply cut by intensively cultivated valleys. The laterite itself has been graphically dismissed by a leading geographer as 'about as attractive for agriculture as railway ballast' (Spate, 1954, p. 630). What it will grow is tapioca, a near tasteless tuberous vegetable introduced in the 1920s. It has become for the poor of Kerala what the potato was for the nineteenth-century Irish.

The highlands are wet, relatively cool and naturally either forest or downland. Until the late nineteenth century they were inaccessible and sparsely inhabited, and then mainly by tribal peoples; but from 1877 onwards European entrepreneurs experimented with a variety of plantation or garden crops. Rubber now dominates the lower slopes and tea the higher ones. Although there are many small Indian-owned tea gardens, the biggest estate, Kanan Devan, is still British owned. Rubber on the other hand is dominated by the local Syrian Christian community. Large tracts of the Ghats still remain under hardwood forest but over a quarter of the forested area of 1947 has succumbed to the developer's axe or the encroacher's fire. The heavy rainfall and the steep descent to the plains offer excellent opportunities for hydro-electric generation. The biggest scheme at Idikki produces more power than Kerala can use and so the surplus is sold to Tamil Nadu. Unmanaged deforestation however has led to serious problems of soil erosion. The highlands remain thinly populated and still marked by concentrations of scheduled castes and tribes.

Like India as a whole, Kerala is overwhelmingly rural. The official census definition of what constitutes an 'urban' area is generous, but even so only 16 per cent of the 24 million population (1981) live in 'urban' settlements. There are no metropolitan cities—no Calcutta; and there is little of the migration to town and city found in many parts of India and the developing world. There are just three cities with over half a million inhabitants (7 per cent of the total population): Kozhikode in the north, Trivandrum, the state capital in the extreme south, and Cochin-Ernakulam, in between. The Cochin-Ernakulam port-industrial complex is the biggest city with a population of 686,000 but still retains something of its historic past in the Dutch Fort, an eleventh-century synagogue and the Willingdon Island British residency. Ten more towns have populations of more than 50,000 but only three exceed 100,000 and one 200,000. The urban growth rate is actually below the rural average for Kerala. Cultural as well as social and economic factors play their part in minimizing the drawing power of the towns but the demographic vigour of the countryside is clearly related to the central fact that the development process has not been as lop-sided as is commonly the case in South and South-east Asia. Although the communists cannot claim the entire credit for this, their commitment to the nourishing of the grassroots has been important.

In Kerala the centre of political gravity is rural. (Contrasts with West Bengal will be discussed later.) However, the state is not that hybrid of grinding fact and romantic fiction—'village India'. The rural concentration of population is not associated with the nucleated village. Patterns of settlement are ribbon, even cobweb-like; and the village is more of an administrative convenience than a spatially distinct reality. It has been argued that this ancient diffusion of settlement was linked to the development of feudalism in the area (Mencher, 1966).

The peculiar settlement pattern has had implications for the growth and character of the communist movement. During the underground era, party workers were better able to escape detection in the maze of paths and cottages. Conversely the cadre have sometimes been stretched themselves as a legal party because the population is so dispersed. The relative weakness of village social pressures may possibly have contributed to the strain of individualism discernible in modern Kerala. In contrast in West Bengal the communist movement has been able to capitalize on the solidary loyalties of village communities but has also found concentrations of landlord and state power at times overwhelming. The one district in Kerala where nuclear settlement is common is in the Muslim region of southern Malabar. Coupled with the crucial role of the mosque as a communal meeting ground this deviant pattern has helped to buttress the grip of the Muslim League on the local Moplahs—as the Kerala Muslims are known.

Paradoxically, the absence of clearly defined villages has not diminished the Keralite's attachment to his native place. A strong sense of territorial allegiance is felt throughout society though, obviously, most intensely among the more affluent agrarian interests. This is related to the economic and symbolic significance of land but also to the manifold functions of the extended family and sub-caste. By Indian standards Kerala has developed a nascent welfare state but the ultimate safety net even now is the family, its small plot of land, and its connections.

The intensity of the feeling of local roots is matched by the depth of commitment to Kerala's sub-national identity. In the latter part of the first millennium AD there had been a Chera Empire covering much of present-day Kerala but following its disintegration in the course of the eleventh century the region had come to approximate the European feudal system. In the course of the eighteenth century as a result of marriages and wars the multiplicity of kingdoms and principalities was reduced to the three political entities, the princely states of Travancore and Cochin and the Malabar extension of the Madras Presidency, which were to survive to the end of the Raj.

Below the varied historical experience of different parts of Kerala lay some commonalities of social structure and economic organization but the rationale for a Kerala Pradesh (province or state) was primarily language. Keralites are usually known as Malayalis after their language, Malayalam. Dravidians as opposed to Aryans in stock, their language is closely related to the other south Indian languages, especially Tamil. Sanskrit—the root language of the Aryans—has, however, been more influential than on Tamil or Kannada and this fusion is said to explain why Malayalis are so good with languages. The early and sustained development of schools and colleges during the British period is equally important in accounting for the more widespread acquaintance with English than in virtually any other part of India. English is one of the two link languages of India and the link language of Indian communism.

Malayalam itself has its dialects but the standard form is understood, spoken and written throughout the state; and of all Indian states Kerala is the most sharply defined by language: 97 per cent of the people speak Malayalam as their mother tongue and, apart from a few Kannada speakers in the extreme north, virtually all the remaining 3 per cent are bilingual in

Malayalam and Tamil. Except for those who have migrated in search of work, Malayalam is spoken nowhere other than in Kerala. The gulf between Malayalam and its south Indian cousins is at least as great as that between Spanish and Portuguese and this is compounded by the differences in alphabets and scripts. Malayalam has over 450 characters written in a unique and beautiful script.

Two works of the seventeenth century (one in Sanskrit and the other in Malayalam) are the first indications of a 'national' consciousness. They mix history, myth and speculation but by the nineteenth century a strong literary tradition was being established, at that time one marked by political consciousness and in the twentieth century by social realist writing. The rapid growth of literacy gave the writers of Kerala's cultural renaissance a wider audience even than their equivalents in Bengal. By 1947 most villages of any size had a reading room; many were looked after by communist party workers or sympathizers; and by the 1950s it was the proud—and not unjustified—boast of the Malayalis that even the poor in their tea shops had read a daily paper by tiffin (lunch) time. The titles of best-selling novels of the time speak for themselves: *From the Gutter* (1942), *Scavenger's Son* (1947) and *Two Measures of Rice* (1948). It has been estimated that in 1951 alone as many as 2,000 poems and short stories dealing with the struggle for a United People's Democratic Kerala were published in left-wing magazines. Of all this, the communists, committed both to the realization of a united Kerala and to socialism, were the major beneficiaries.

Long before communism had come to Kerala, the Indian National Congress had in 1920 taken a stand on the reorganization of the provinces of an independent India along linguistic lines and established a Kerala Pradesh Congress Committee as a marker. Gandhi however was hostile to political activity in the princely states and the KPCC remained very much a Malabar organization with personal rather than institutional links to political activity in Travancore and Cochin. After independence the Congress rulers of India (for good and bad reasons) sought to renege on their promises to redraw the imperial provincial boundaries. Even after the report of the Linguistic Reorganization Commission (1955), the Kerala Congress Committee proved reluctant converts to a purely Malayali Kerala; and one factor was the fear it would return a communist government, which indeed it shortly did.

Political History: 1792-1918

The Indian sense of history is profound at a family level, at a local level and through the medium of official (and in Kerala and Bengal, party) history. Census collectors take with them calendars of important local events to help villagers reckon their age since rural society tends not to count birthdays. The relevance of history in Kerala is heightened by the distinctive problems inherited from the past in differing parts of the state, by the communists' inclination to characterize history in stages and by the comparative longevity of Malayalis. E. M. S. Namboodiripad, born in 1909 into a traditional Kerala Brahmin family, and now general secretary of the CPI(M) expresses the consciousness of living history in his most famous book, *Kerala, Yesterday, Today and Tomorrow*.

For our purposes we can begin in the mid-eighteenth century. By this time, despite periodic clashes between rival Kerala rulers and intrusions by the mercantilist powers, the Malabar coast was wealthy and prosperous, so much so that the growing conflict for hegemony between the Maharajas of Travancore in the south and the Zamorin of Calicut in the north was cut short by the invasion from neighbouring Mysore of the great Muslim general, Hyder Ali. He and subsequently his still more dreaded son, Tipu Sultan, backed by the French, subjugated the local population, converting to Islam many of those who did not flee south to Cochin and Travancore. At last in 1792 at the Battle of Seringapatam the British and their Hindu allies finally defeated Tipu; and thereafter the British incorporated Malabar into British India with the Hindu princelings restored as puppet rajas and the long-standing as well as neophyte Muslim minority downgraded.

The Mysorean interlude and the character of the British restoration of order were to have profound consequences for the north of Kerala and in the longer term for the possibilities of communist mobilization. From being one of the wealthiest parts of south India, Malabar became one of the most impoverished. Once the initial pacification was over the British neglected this outpost of the Madras Presidency, spending on it little more than was required to ensure law and order. 'Pax Britannica' in India essentially meant the reordering of agrarian relations, what was called the land settlement, so that revenue which very largely came from agriculture would be secure and, as far as they were concerned, painless to collect. In some parts the white man's burden was extended to try to create a prosperous peasantry. In Malabar there was no such altruism and, worse, the nature of the settlement was largely self-defeating if its object was to provide stability in the countryside. The economy of the district could not recover from the devastation of thirty years' war; relations between Hindu landlords and Muslim tenants suppurated; and Hindu tenants by the twentieth century were ripe for communist-led mobilization.

Since almost all the documents of the past were destroyed during the Mysorean Wars, no one can be sure of the earlier system but it appears certain that the *jenmi*, as the 'landlord' was called, had not enjoyed the absolute rights that the British attributed to him. His 'rights' were heavily circumscribed by custom and his cultivators were not 'tenants' in the modern sense. They enjoyed their own inalienable rights subject only to modest 'duties'. The early British administrators either failed to appreciate how subtle a nexus bound *jenmi* and cultivator or they regarded it as evidence of a primitive state of affairs. Under the new system the *jenmi* became an English landowner: absolute proprietor with a contractual title to his land, enforceable in a British court of law, and backed by British might. The malign effects of the rupture in custom were the greater because of the growth of a parasitic, rent collecting class of *kanomdars* between *jenmi* and cultivator. Landlords became absentee; and peasants were quickly reduced to the status of tenants at will—the landlord's will—often on one year leases. After paying land revenue and a variety of quasi-feudal dues, the cultivator was left with no more than a third of his net proceeds. An official report claimed in 1900 that South Malabar had 'earned the unenviable reputation of being the most rack-rented country on the face of the earth' (Varghese, 1970, pp. 192-8). Here agrarian conflict took on a communal colour because most landlords were Hindu and in interior south Malabar many peasants were Muslim. In turn this was a large part of the explanation for the intermittent attacks on landlords and officials dubbed as the Moplah Outrages by the British which punctuated the nineteenth century and culminated in a full-scale Moplah Rebellion in 1921.

A further feature which compounded the misery of the peasants was the treatment of uncultivated land. Normally under British law, land to which there is no valid individual title belongs to the Crown. In Malabar the extensive tracts of waste land were attributed to the nearest *jenmi*; and potential cultivators were further discouraged by the kinds of leases granted for bringing it under the hoe. After seven years the land could be taken back without meaningful compensation for the improvements. As late as 1951 more than one quarter of what was cultivable in Malabar was still unoccupied. In a district where as early as 1911 one quarter of the agricultural population were landless and the vast majority of the tenants insecure and oppressed, the British had foreclosed the obvious safety valve for demographic pressures and agrarian discontent.

The history of Travancore—at independence third most populous of the 562 Indian princely states, and in some but not all respects, one of the most progressive—had been very different. The kingdom of Venad, established in the twelfth century, had expanded by the eighteenth century to cover the land from Cochin to Cape Comorin at the southernmost tip of India. In the process land was appropriated by the state, the traditional feudal aristocracy subjugated, and in a local variant of the 'Enlightened Despot's' attitude to religion, the state dedicated to the household deity of the ruling family. Before the end of the eighteenth century Travancore entered into treaty relations with the (British) East India Company; and in 1805 accepted British suzerainty. The annual tribute of Rs 800,000 did not preclude the company's interference in Travancore's internal affairs but it did speed the growth of royal power at the expense of the local aristocracy and priesthood.

From 1814 the Maharaja's Chief Ministers became non-Malayali Brahmins and in the 1820s and 1830s Travancore began to adopt the features of a modern state: codified law, British-style courts, and (missionary-led) education. From mid-century the pace accelerated. Slavery was abolished—at least in name—in 1855; and under the famous *dewan* (Chief Minister), T. Madhava Rao (1858–72), reform was far reaching: the fundamental reorganization of education; the creation of a Public Works Department; the encouragement of the cash economy; and the enfranchisement of tenant-cultivators, this last in striking contrast to the situation in Malabar. A free market in land was set up in 1865. Travancore in 1888 became the first Native State to inaugurate any kind of Legislative Council. All these developments inevitably engendered a measure of emergent political consciousness: in the 1880s communal and political associations began to surface, three newspapers were founded and in 1891 a petition was presented to the Maharajah protesting against the dominance in government of 'alien' Brahmins. Known as the Malayala Memorial, it was essentially a protest by a group of Western-educated Nairs, the former warrior aristocracy, at being denied bureaucratic opportunity but it also referred to the claims of two other groups, the Syrian Christians and the Hindu Ezhava community. Although this first proto-modern political movement ended with little to show beyond a conciliatory audience with the *dewan*, it symbolized the beginning of a tradition of political activity: caste and communal conflict and rivalry. It is however one of the striking features of Kerala as a whole that with rare exceptions, such as the Moplah Rebellion of 1921–2 which degenerated into communal atrocity, caste and communal conflict has been largely conducted within institutionalized social, economic and political channels.

The Native State of Cochin had been squeezed between the powerful kingdoms to north and south. At the end of the eighteenth century it was less than one-fifth of the area of the Travancore and a quarter of Malabar. Largely overrun by Tipu Sultan, it was forced to conclude unequal treaties first with Travancore and then with the British East India Company until after an abortive rebellion against the company it became in 1808-9 a client state of the British. In more respects than the geographical, Cochin occupied an intermediate position between Malabar and Travancore in the nineteenth century. The Cochin Rajas' efforts to subordinate the feudal aristocracy had been less successful than had the Travancore rulers'. The few thousand *jenmis* who held 60 per cent of the land—mainly in the north—were as unbridled as their peers in Malabar; and many of their tenants were also steadily reduced to a position little better than that of labourers. However on the 40 per cent of land held by the government there was security of tenure but excessive British demands on the Cochin treasury ensured that the peasants' outgoings were onerous. Waste land on the other hand did belong to the state and the port of Cochin offered some hope of relief in casual labour. The pace of administrative modernization was somewhat slower than in Travancore but by the end of the nineteenth century, Cochin had received recognition as one of the better governed and more progressive of the Princely States.

Political History: 1919-1939

Communism came late to Kerala. It was not until late 1939 that a secret party was established and the earliest party fraction was formed in 1937. Apart from the publication (by a non-communist) of a short factual biography of Marx in 1912 and a sympathetic obituary of Lenin in 1924, Marxism attracted little interest anywhere in Kerala until the 1930s. The honour of establishing the first communist organization goes to the six member Trivandrum-based Communist League of 1931. Much more important than this proto-Marxist grouping however was the emergence during the 1930s of Congress 'Socialism' as a body of ideas and of the Congress Socialist Party (CSP) as an affiliated unit of the INC. Those who were to become the core of the Kerala CPI in and after the 1940s had grown with and through the major political movements of the 1930s: from Gandhian Congress into Congress Socialism and finally into communism. The Kerala communist movement had avoided sectarian isolation from the wider struggle for Indian freedom in the late 1920s and early 1930s and been immersed in—and often leaders of— the major indigenous political movements of the 1930s: the agitation against the Raj, the demand for Responsible Government in the Princely State of Travancore, and agrarian discontent in Malabar. Congress socialism was the broad church of the left. Few of those who attended the inaugural meeting of the Kerala CPI in 1939 would have claimed any great theoretical knowledge of Marxism but the ninety leaders enjoyed a more valuable initial asset, the practical experience of the popular causes of Kerala.

Malabar and Agrarian Movements

In Malabar, the early Congress movement had little to do with the great issue of Indian independence, whatever the rhetoric. From 1908, when the first Congress district committee was formed, to the passing of the Malabar Tenancy Act in 1929, Congress meetings were primarily the venue for a tussle between the landlords and intermediary tenant farmers. This Act produced a workable compromise between the *de iure* rights of the former and the *de facto* power of the latter. Thereafter in the wake of the great depression which badly affected the cash crop economy of much of Malabar, the battle lines shifted: was the district committee to represent the Congress of the poor or the (relatively) rich? More important in the area than the civil disobedience agitations of 1930 and 1932 was the campaign in 1931 to open Malabar's most famous temple of Guruvayoor, owned by the biggest landowner in the district, to the four-fifths of the Hindu community denied entry. At Gandhi's insistence, a protest fast was broken in exchange for nothing more than an understanding that the temple would be made available to the lower castes after a decent interval. It was the Guruvayoor confrontation which changed the nature of political struggle in Malabar. Many of the moderate old guard resigned from the Congress executive when the decision to picket the temple was taken. After the *satyagraha* was over, many of the remaining higher caste Congressmen faded from view, some under social pressures from family and community, others because of a realization that it was one thing to seek to replace the British with an Indian ruling class, quite another to undermine the sacerdotal foundations of caste and property. On the other side the young radical activists, many also from the higher castes, became disenchanted with Gandhian methods and Gandhian ideology.

Similar developments at an all-India level led to the founding of the Congress Socialist Party in April 1934 as a left-wing pressure group within Congress. The first leader of the future Kerala CPI, P. Krishna Pillai, was among those who attended and the CSP quickly took root in Malabar. By the end of 1934 the Congress Socialists held five of Kerala's eight places on the

All-India Congress Committee. Within a year CSP activists had established committees in most villages outside the Muslim area with reading rooms where the illiterate were taught to read, and areas outside where socialist dramas and football matches were staged. The CSP joined forces with local unionists and began the crucial long haul to build a peasant movement, a daunting task given the rural power structure described earlier. For a while the CSP had a free hand as moderates drifted away but the prospect of office in the provincial governments to be established in 1937 under the 1935 Government of India Act brought the right back into active politics.

The new Congress ministries, however, were a disillusioning experience. Symbolically, Malabar's representative in the Madras government was Minister for Courts and Prisons—and there was no change in either. In Kerala, as in south India generally, the left made giant strides in 1938. The All-Malabar Peasants Union, for example, enjoyed a paid-up membership of 30,000 by the end of the year; and in the contested election for the national Congress presidency in 1939 between the socialist Subhas Chandra Bose and the Gandhian Pattabhi, Kerala voted as overwhelmingly for Bose as Bengal did for its own favourite son. The CSP's success in part stemmed from the more disciplined organization introduced through contact with the CPI. Krishna Pillai and Namboodiripad had detailed discussions with Sundarayya, the Andhra CPI leader; a party faction was formed at Calicut in 1937; and it was becoming difficult to distinguish CPI from CSP in Kerala. When the CPI was finally and secretly launched at the end of 1939, virtually the entire CSP leadership was present and with them the guts of Congress organization in Malabar.

Travancore, Responsible Government and Communal Rivalry

In Malabar socialism developed within the organizational framework of the Freedom Struggle; in Travancore and Cochin it developed within the framework of the struggle for responsible government. In Malabar the key issue was the extreme concentration of agrarian rights; and political parties from Congress, through the CSP to the CPI, grew in the context of feudal landlordism. In Travancore land was a less important issue to the degree that rights were more diffused. The central question was the democratic control of the executive but since communalism ran deep the issue was transformed into one of communal control of the executive. Did citizenship extend to low-caste helots or to non-Hindus in a state dedicated to a Hindu god? On the answers turned not only jobs in government service but the distribution of resources in a modernizing state.

Socially, Travancore was a paradox. It was on the one hand a bastion of Hindu orthodoxy and on the other contained (in 1931) a 1 million-strong community of Syrian Christians, the oldest surviving branch of Christianity east of Persia, as well as some half a million non-Syrian Christians, chiefly low-caste Catholics. Swami Vivekananda, the famous Hindu reformer, who visited south India in 1892, dismissed Kerala as a madhouse of caste; and the British took Travancore as a benchmark for caste differentiation. There were of the order of 500 castes and sub-castes but the structure was unusual. Of the four basic *varnas*—priest, warrior, businessman and service—the Vaisya (business) category was non-existent, and Kshatriya (warrior) rare. The martial role had been performed by the Nairs, who were regarded as *sudra* (service) by the local Brahmins, while money-lending and trade were undertaken by Christians. Actual cultivation was performed by the Ezhava community; and although they should therefore have been *sudra*, they were defined by the Brahmins as untouchable and so denied temple entry and temple approach.

Kerala's particular lunacy was to extend the concept of pollution from touch to sight. The lowly Pulaya must remain not less than 96 feet from the Brahmin, 64 feet from a Nair and 30 feet from an Ezhava. Language itself was repugnant in its debasements. For those who could approach close enough to communicate with a Brahmin, the Brahminical residence was a palace but their own at best a hovel, at worst a 'shithouse'.

The Syrian Christians faced no such social inconveniences; and indeed not infrequently expected the low castes to efface themselves as they would to the Hindu high castes. As late as 1957 when the communists had come to power a British journalist (Zinkin, 1962, p. 152) reported:

Paul (a wealthy Christian) stopped to curse, his handsome face turning a slow red. 'You saw that fellow. He did not get off the path for us ... Of course, we have done away with unseeability a long time ago and that's only right. But until six months ago that fellow knew his place; when he saw me he would get off the path; today he nearly brushed me aside. That is what they call equality ...

The origins of the Syrians are a matter of speculation but there was already a flourishing church in Kerala by the sixth century and conversions appear to have been primarily from the Nair warrior caste, and also from the Namboodiri Brahmins.

After the vicissitudes of the Portuguese era, the Syrians came into their own with British ascendancy. The patrilineal and nuclear family system was well adapted to the new environment; and the Syrians took early advantage of the new educational and commercial opportunities. Taking all Christians in

1901, their literacy rate (15.8 per cent) was well ahead of all Hindus in Travancore (11.7 per cent); nearly half of the 15,000 Travancoreans then literate in English were Christian; and six out of the seven newspapers in the mid-1890s were Christian-owned. The Syrians were pioneers in banking and large-scale agricultural and commercial activity and the 1920s and 1930s they were powerful competitors to the once dominant Nairs. By 1931 the Syrians had overtaken the high-caste Nairs in average annual income per family (*Census of India*, *1931*, Vol. xxviii, Part 1, App. IV).

Among the Hindu castes it was not the Nairs but the Ezhavas who first began to break out of the constraints of orthodoxy. In fact Ezhava status had been somewhat variable. Although their historic occupation was 'toddy tapping' (extracting resin from the palm for fermentation), and their common occupation in the nineteenth century field labour or coir-weaving, there had been occasional Ezhava rajas while the Ezhavas of Malabar, the Tiyyas, had always claimed a higher ritual ranking. Ezhava social customs were less irksome than those of the higher castes; and, as low castes, they had little to lose and much to gain by participating in economic and social change. By the 1880s there was a small educated and professional elite and in 1903 ten of the most wealthy Ezhavas established Kerala's first caste association, the SNDP *yogam* named after Sree Narayana Gura (1857–1928), an Ezhava divine comparable locally to Vivekananda. The society numbered 50,000 by 1928 and in 1974 its 60,000 membership was twice that of the combined communist parties, both of which drew disproportionate support from the same caste.

In its early years the SNDP in its secular aspect preached the gospel of self-help which to the ordinary Ezhava was something of an irrelevance since he had no capital or qualifications; and in the 1930s in the wake of the Great Depression, which hit coir badly, the SNDP became increasingly politicized, torn between moderate and militant factions. Entry to temples and government service was achieved in the mid-1930s but the *yogam* lost many actual and potential members to the emerging communist movement. Only in the 1950s under the fiercely anti-communist R. Sankar (1909–72) did it recover influence by means of a network of educational institutions and shrewd political pressure on government.

The Nair equivalent, the Nair Service Society (NSS), was founded in 1914 with three aims: to liberate the Nairs from superstition and taboo; to establish a chain of educational and welfare organizations; and to defend and advance Nair interests in the political arena. Of all pressure groups in Kerala it has probably been the most consistently successful.

The Church, SNDP and NSS were expressions of caste and communal rivalry not national or class mobilization. The Indian Congress's self-denying ordinance of not interfering in the affairs of the princely states was to delay the intrusion of cross-cutting secular forces until the late 1930s; and the conflicting elites rarely had occasion to mobilize the people at large. By the early 1930s, however, radical strains were evident in student and popular consciousness and the well-informed Dewan began to fear the growth of socialism and communism.

Apart from a major temple *satyagraha* at Vaikom in 1924 there was little significant political activity in the 1920s. Politics chiefly consisted of jockeying for the ear of the Dewan and members of the royal family. The continued high-caste Hindu near-monopoly of jobs in government service and the overwhelmingly Nair composition of the Legislative Council, however, increasingly disaffected Christian and Ezhava communities. Capitalizing on a power struggle within the palace in 1931-2 they, together with the smaller Muslim community, launched a Joint Political Congress (JPC) to pressurize for change. By 1935 the Dewan, Sir C. P. Ramaswamy Aiyar, a figure of all-India stature, Machiavellian intrigue and Whiggish views, had decided that concession would have to be made, the better to maintain royal, Hindu and, in that order, Nair ascendancy in the state. The SNDP had formally threatened to convert (*sic*) to Christianity *en masse* (Nossiter, 1982, p. 80). Temple entry was conceded and, with more reluctance, communal representation was granted in the legislature.

Sir C. P. had, however, by now alienated the Nairs by his autocratic bearing and conduct. Gandhi was no longer so hostile to meddling in the affairs of princely states; and a new generation of more secular politicians had appeared. The JPC was supplanted by Travancore State Congress (TSC), which brought all communities together on a common platform whose minimum demand was the resignation of Aiyar and real aim the introduction of responsible government. A strike of 40,000 coir workers in 1938 increased the Dewan's troubles. Sir C. P., however, survived with the help of bribes, bullets and the rumour mill, central to which were his hints that further constitutional change could only lead to Christian ascendancy.

The hard core of the TSC remained united despite this humiliation till Aiyar was finally ousted after independence and Congress had won Travancore's first democratic elections in February 1948. Thereafter, however, elite politics reverted to its old communal channels. Ramaswami Aiyar had—not without justification—tried to pillory TSC as 'Christian Congress'; and in the late 1940s the uneasy 'nationalist coalition' was damaged by the formation of a short-lived Hindu Mahasabha or Hindu alliance of Nair and Ezhava at the instigation of the NSS and SNDP leaders. Caste and communalism were further acerbated by the formation of the combined state of Travancore-Cochin in 1949 which increased the Christian presence. In the seven years of its existence Travancore-Cochin had five different governments, as first one community and then another brought down ministries, allegedly dominated by rival communities.

Travancore and subsequently Travancore-Cochin had, however, meanwhile developed a powerful socialist and popular movement, whose origins lay with the interaction of young high-caste drop-outs and depressed and oppressed low-caste coir workers. The official Unemployment Enquiry Committee of 1928 prophesied that the 'burgeoning intellectual proletariat' seeking white-collar posts and not finding them constituted a 'menace to good government' and noted with alarm 'the growing fascination which socialistic and communistic ideas ... exercise upon the minds of the young men educated in our colleges' (Government of Travancore, 1928, pp. 47–8). Those so fascinated, actually, included some of the best minds of their generation. Two years later the even less sympathetic British agent in residence wrote to his superiors of the 'considerable political and social activity in [the coir district] for the last eight years since the Vaikkom Temple entry Satyagraha. During the past 8 months, mushroom political organisations have risen ... the Atheistic League, Revolutionary League, Youth League, Labour Association, etc., all sponsored by local Congress Extremists' (Nossiter, 1982, p. 32).

The first record of any self-styled communist organization appears in early 1931 when a printed pamphlet entitled *The Communist Party* circulated in Trivandrum citing N. P. Kurukkal as Organizing Secretary of the Indian Communist Party (Kerala Provincial Organization). So far as is known it was unconnected with the party nationally. It was, however, the basis of the Youth League reconstituted in Trivandrum in 1933 which played an active part in the agitations against Sir C. P., resisted communalism, and fed into the CSP and ultimately the CPI.

The labour movement appeared first in Alleppey in 1922. Essentially moderate in character the Travancore Labour Association (TLA) maintained strong links with the SNDP during the 1920s. With the onset of the Depression, the TLA became more militant and by May 1934 a police note of a meeting of 2,000 labourers reported that 'the principles of communism are taking root in the minds of the labourers' (Chandiakaryll, 1985, p. 118). Neither the exploitation of communal differences in the work-force nor labour legislation had much effect in countering this. Deteriorating conditions in the Alleppey district coir industry led in 1938 to a strike of some 40,000 workers; and in the following year to an Agricultural Labourers Union in the adjacent rice growing area of Kuttanad where capital intensive technology was reducing the demand for labour. In both cases there was clear evidence of the radicalization of the work-force by the CSP-Marxists. It was here in 1946 that the CPI was able to mount its Punnapra-Vayalar Rising.

In contrast to Malabar and Travancore, Cochin experienced little political disturbance during the 1930s. The agrarian question was tackled early and by 1943 virtually all tenants had been given security of tenure. Prior to 1925 Cochin had no legislative council but thereafter it advanced quickly to diarchy and in 1938 it became the first princely state to concede a measure of responsible government. The development of the port of Cochin by the British gave a boost to the economy and public opinion was characteristically moderate perhaps as a result of the large and prosperous Christian population and the dominance in the Hindu community of the Menon sub-caste of Nairs, whose aptitude for administration and practical politics led after Independence to a dreadful joke that Delhi was afflicted with 'menonghitis', because there were so many Menons in government. Chetty, the Dewan, was also an altogether more accommodating politician than Aiyar.

Although a communist cell operated in Ernakulam (the industrial sector of Cochin) from at least 1938 onwards, the CPI appears to have been content to confine its operations there to the labour front. A CSP unit existed and after 1941 some communists operated through the relatively militant Praja Mandal; but for the communists Cochin was a small prize and a useful shelter from the wrath of the Raj to the north and Sir C. P. to the south. Both the Christian community and Chetty, who had no reason to love Ramaswamy Aiyar and did not suffer from his obsession with the threat of communism, were happy to connive at his embarassment.

Communism in Kerala, 1940-50

The secret formation of the Kerala CPI in October 1939 was announced with tarred slogans on walls and government buildings on 26 January 1940—Independence Day—but the CPI continued to operate through the Kerala Congress party until the Raj began to arrest its leaders and the Congress nationally purged the Kerala Congress of its non-Gandhian elements. Compared with many units, the CPI in Kerala survived the ignominy of siding with the British during the People's War period fairly well. A Madras official reported wryly that the 'Malabar comrades were 10 per cent anti-Nazi and 90 per cent anti-British Government ... intolerable friends' (Nossiter, 1982, p. 86). It is undeniable that the years were a setback but party membership did treble to 600 by 1945, and the party was able to stage its attempted rising in 1946 and agrarian protest movements in Malabar in 1946–7. More serious than the war was the adventurist era of 1948–50 when over 3,000 party workers and sympathizers were imprisoned. Nevertheless the CPI was on the evidence of the election results of 1951–2 stronger than ever when it returned to legality. Through thick and thin it had worked for the workers and peasants' causes; the simplicity and integrity of these latter-day secular *sanyasi* (holy men) was in marked contrast to the bourgeois life styles of many of their opponents; Congress was increasingly identified with communalism and corruption especially in Travancore–Cochin; and the CPI had involved itself with the state-wide movement for a united Kerala. In few other parts of India could the communist movement be so confident of the outcome of taking the legal road.

4 Social Structure of Kerala

Population and Employment

In 1901 the population of Kerala was 6.5 million; by 1951 it was 13.5 million, by 1971 it was 21.3 million; and by 1981 it was 25.5 million. In the last two decades the population has grown by 26 per cent and 19 per cent respectively. With a population density three times that of Indian as a whole, Kerala is one of the most densely populated parts of the world (1981): 655 person per square km. overall, 558 in rural areas, and as much as 1,128 in the rural parts of the coastal district of Alleppey. The demographic pressures on land, food and employment are a desperate exaggeration of all-India trends, yet the fourfold increase in population in eighty years is testimony to the quality of social provision. The high growth rates in the first fifty years occurred in the native states where early attention had been paid to medical and public health services, complemented by education and higher status for women than is usual in India. As important in recent years has been the development of an effective distribution of food through ration shops. As of 1982 there were 4.1 million family ration cards extant covering over 90 per cent of all households. In the mid-1950s infant mortality in Kerala was already down to 50 per thousand compared with an official 113 for India as a whole. By 1980 even rural infant mortality rates were down to 39 per thousand. Birth rates have fallen in tandem, now estimated at 24 per thousand compared with the Indian figure of 33. Most revealing of all considering the low incomes of the bulk of the population is life expectancy, 15 years longer than the Indian average and favouring women (67) over men (64). Kerala is also the only Indian state with a preponderance of females over males (1,032:1,000 in 1981).

In an agrarian society the principal resource to support the population is land. By 1974 the per capita availability of land was down to a quarter of an acre (India three-quarters of an acre) when two acres of standard fertility was taken as the minimum requirement for family subsistence. As early as 1962 a third of all rural households were landless, two and a half times the Indian average. By 1971 the agricultural labourers (with no land or minimal land) had risen to 63 per cent of the agricultural population (India, 38 per cent) and exceeded 70 per cent in the coastal areas. Further, the farm labourer generally lacks continuous employment owing to the seasonality of the farmer's need for additional workers. Probably not more than a quarter of the field labourers work more than 200 days a year and alternative employment in the off season is rare. There has also been a tendency for the number of days worked to fall, in part because there are more potential workers chasing the available hirings but also because the labourers' unions have been almost too successful in raising wage rates. Kerala has the highest daily wage rates in the agricultural sector of any Indian state. Farmers have therefore economized on labour and latterly begun to transfer their operations to the neighbouring states of Kernataka and Tamil Nadu.

Employment figures are indicative and far from exact but the trends are clear. The percentage of the population engaged in economic activity has steadily fallen this century. In 1901 it was 45 per cent. By 1981 it was less than 30 per cent. The change is only marginally a function of the shift in the age structure of the population. More important are the decline in female participation in the primary economy and extended schooling. The burden on the working population of supporting 70 per cent dependants needs no emphasis.

Unemployment has likewise grown steadily. By 1954 10 per cent of adult and able-bodied men were seeking employment; and as many as a quarter were classed as casually employed. The most recent (1980) survey shows that as many as 18 per cent of the labour force had no employment whatsoever in the preceding year; and national estimates suggest that Kerala's unemployment and underemployment may be as high as 10 per cent of the Indian total when its share of the population is not even 4 per cent. In round figures 2 million Keralites were seeking work through employment exchanges in 1982. The most remarkable feature of the unemployment situation, however, is that half the job seekers are educated to, at least, the Indian Secondary School Leaving Certificate standard (16+ examination). Of these 80,000 are graduates and 7,000 postgraduates.

The state is still industrially backwards. Industry absorbs only a fifth of the labour force. Average daily employment in registered factories in the late 1970s was less than 300,000. The private sector as a whole in 1982 provided only 520,000 jobs and the proportion of jobs in the private sector fell eight percentage points between 1970 and 1982. Conversely the public sector share has risen from 42 to 50 per cent of the total. Some relief has been given since the mid-1970s by temporary migration to the Gulf to work in construction. At any one time in the last decade there would have been around 200,000 Malayalis in the Middle East. However this boom appears to be coming to an end and the returning migrants will only add to Kerala's unemployment problem.

Education

The population explosion, the pressure on land and the search for jobs are all-India phenomena even if Kerala varies in degree. It is education which has given the state its distinctive qualities. Of all the changes destructive of the highly traditional order in Kerala, education has been the most important. The achievement is remarkable. By 1981 the general literacy rate (including babies) was 70 per cent, almost exactly twice the all-India figure. Still more striking was the general female literacy rate of 66 per cent as compared to 25 per cent for India. Excluding those below five years of age, the effective literacy rates become: 87 per cent for males; 76 per cent for females; and 81 per cent overall. Not even the Indian capital of Delhi (general rate 61 per cent) compares; and of the states the nearest competitor is Maharashtra at a general rate of 47 per cent. High rates of school enrolment in Kerala are complemented by low rates of drop out in school. Significantly, the effort and expenditure have been on primary and secondary education rather than higher education. Although Kerala's spending on colleges and universities and its output of graduates are above the national average, degrees have not been prioritized to the extent visible in much of India. Education has been for the masses not just an elite. Although there is a sizeable cultured group, Kerala, for better and worse, does not have an intelligentsia in the sense, for example, of the *bhadralok* of West Bengal.

To a greater extent than anywhere else in Asia, education has been provided by private agencies. In 1981-2, 61 per cent of all lower primary schools were privately run, rising at degree level to 84 per cent. Since the schools and colleges are run by communal managements—Christian, NSS, SNDP and Muslim—the implications for the communist movement, bearing in mind the old Jesuit maxim of 'give me the child till seven, and I will give you the man', are profound. As will be shown later, the communists have found it very difficult to alter the situation at all substantially. On the one hand, on average the better educational institutions (as well as the worst) are more often privately than publicly managed. Communists have frequently not only themselves been educated in Christian colleges but also sent their children there. On the other hand education is big business and the vested interests deeply entrenched. In a communally articulated society and in a fragmented political system, private ownership of education is, surely, here to stay.

Two important consequences have followed from the massive expenditure on basic education; the poor are almost as literate as the privileged; and a greater degree of social mobility has taken place in Kerala than anywhere else in India. The early literacy of the lower castes and backward communities has been an important factor in the development of the society and, through the medium of newspapers and magazines, of the high degree of politicization. However the belief that because Kerala's literacy levels have been so much higher than elsewhere, there must be some kind of causal link to the rise of communism is fallacious. There is no strong correlation at local level in any case. The CPI successfully mobilized the poor because its message chimed with inchoate popular aspirations; and oral communications from public meetings through socialist 'street theatre' to gossip round the village well and in the tea shop were just as important as the outpouring of progressive writings. The radically minded schoolmaster possessed the pamphlet and disseminated it through the study class.

Education may in fact prove in the longer term to be an obstacle to the communist movement's advance in Kerala. The daily press is more widely read than in any other state. Apart from English and Hindu newspapers, the circulation of Malayalam daily papers (1.3 million in 1978-9) is greater than in any other Indian language despite the small size of the language community. The circulation of the communist papers is insignificant as compared to the non- and more often anti-communist press. Only one of the twelve major papers, *Kerala Kaumudi*, shows editorial sympathy to the left; and a good part of the press takes every opportunity to magnify the real and imagined failings of the communists. The cinema, a kind of south Indian Hollywood, is also a major mass medium in Kerala. Twenty per cent of all Indian films currently (1980) produced are in the Malayalam language. Latterly, television and video—paid for with Gulf expatriate earnings—have become a new status symbol. Like radio (for many years known as All Indira [Gandhi] Radio), television in India gives little or no opportunity for minority parties to make their case. It is now largely financed by commercial advertisements.

A second way in which educational advance has begun to work against the left is in communally sponsored social mobility. It is no longer the case that communal managements recruit students exclusively from their own kind but preference is usually given to members of that community or caste and that is also true in the hiring of staff (usually, however, subject to a 'donation' to the foundation). Further, in the public sector an elaborate system of job reservation has been evolved so that some 40 per cent of all posts are filled in complex rotation from communities which have been classed as 'backward'. (Once on the list, it is of course highly unlikely they would be removed.) This historical accommodation between the different communities has done something to equalize opportunity but it has at the same time institutionalized caste and communal segmentation and tended to legitimate the existing system. If enough individuals (often the more ambitious) escape 'backwardness', there is that much less incentive to challenge the dynamics of backwardness itself. For the communists there is an acute dilemma here: as the equation between caste and class loosens, can reservation on a caste basis be defended?

An official enquiry in 1968 (Backward Classes Reservation Commission Report, 1970, vol. 2, appendices 14–17) gave some indication of both progress and its limitations. The three 'forward' communities—Brahmin, Nair and Syrian Christian—formed one-third of the population. By the tenth standard of schooling (Secondary School Leaving Certificate year), they constituted 52 per cent of students on course rising to 67 per cent at graduate level in arts and sciences. Disparities in employment were decidedly greater although to some extent this is presumably a function of the fact that the older generations in public service were recruited on simple merit basis. In Government service proper the highest grades (Gazetted officers) were two-thirds drawn from forward communities falling through executive and clerical grades to 46 per cent in the lowest (porter) grades.

Another, and perhaps more powerful solvent in the last decade, has been the impact of the remittances of Gulf migrants on income and status. No one knows the flow of funds but it has been not less than Rs 2,200 million ($220 million) annually and may have been twice as much. (Total state income in 1980-1 was Rs 33,000 and per capita income around Rs 1,300 ($130)). For 200,000 plus Keralites in the Middle East and their families at home, the boost in income was staggering. Hardly a village in Kerala has been untouched: lavish modern houses, cars, scooters and the white and electronic goods of a consumer age can be observed. Kerala has rapidly gone from a deeply traditional society to something approaching a materialist one. The effect has been the more striking because the chief beneficiaries have been the formerly disadvantaged: Moplahs (Muslims), Ezhavas and Latin Christians. The high-caste Nairs, whose economic situation has been steadily deteriorating for three-quarters of a century, are still reluctant to engage in (degrading) manual work and are relatively rare in the Gulf. As former tenants and even, in a few instances, agricultural labourers bought up their erstwhile landlords' homes or built a fine new property opposite his decaying residence, communal tensions developed with political consequences, which will be dealt with later. Property prices soared. Equally significant, the traditional marital market was disrupted. And 'black money' was a cancer in the body politic.

Comparatively speaking, Kerala's justly famed land reforms, widely regarded as the most far-reaching in non-communist Asia have had more limited effects on the social structure. Landlordism has been virtually eliminated (though not capitalist farming) and feudal and rentier relations abolished but the long-drawn-out process of legislation and implementation and the fine print of the acts enabled landowning families to spread their surplus above the land ceiling among their extended kin. The transfer of proprietorial right has significantly benefited all classes of *tenants* but tenants were themselves differentially drawn from the favoured castes and communities. Those who toiled in the fields as labourers gained the absolute right to their hut and a few cents (hundredths of an acre) surrounding it—at least where there was no subterfuge—and, if for some half a million such families, the change was millennial, it did not fundamentally alter their place at the bottom of the social and economic hierarchy.

In the first twelve years since the definitive land reform act of 1970 just over 50,000 acres of surplus land originating from landlords has been redistributed. Far more significant was the 500,000 acres of *puramboke* (land which had been reserved for public purposes) assigned to half a million families. The achievement is a very major one but again it cannot more than marginally redress the historic imbalance in access to land between the castes and communities.

The three religious communities are roughly divided in Kerala in the ratio 60:20:20. Punjab apart, Kerala is the least Hindu of all the India states; and it is becoming steadily less Hindu as a result of differential birth rates. In 1911 'Kerala' was 67 per cent Hindu; by 1971 it was 59 per cent Hindu. In the 1960s the Muslim population grew by 37 per cent, the Christian by 25 per cent but the Hindu population by only 23 per cent. Inter alia from a communist perspective this is critical since the communists in Kerala have never enjoyed much support from the minority communities. The Christians and Muslims of Kerala are distinct from their co-religionists in the north. They are not the descendants of past imperial conversions, although among the Latin Catholic and south Malabar Muslims, the present size of the communities is not just a function of natural increase over time. Conversion to Islam and Christianity has been in the last three hundred years a means of escape from an oppressive Hindu caste system and, for Christians especially, an avenue of social mobility.

The different religious communities are not evenly distributed through the state. Muslims are concentrated in the north (Malabar) especially in the Malappuram district; and Christians are strongest in south central Kerala (Ernakulam, Kottayam and Idukki districts). Politically this distribution is important in two ways: first it tends to create communal pocket boroughs; and second in constituencies of significant but not preponderant minorities, they can hold the electoral balance of power. Where Muslims are particularly concentrated, then the area is represented by one or other wing of the Muslim League, while the Christians divide between the mainstream Congress (Indira) and the various congress splinters of the 'plantation party', Kerala Congress.

Kerala is a unique instance of large numbers of three major world religions living peaceably in one territory. Indeed, if one regards communism as making similar, if secular, truth claims to those of religion, then the state has four faiths. Hindu, Christian, Muslim and Communist interact daily and tolerance has been the norm. Inevitably there are communally coloured incidents but the only major clash this century was in the later stages of the Moplah Rising of 1921-2. At the Partition of India in 1947 there were no disturbances. However since the late 1970s there has been a marked rise in tension which appears to stem from the rapid change in wealth of some Muslims through working in the Middle East at the same time as the Hindu chauvinist organization, the Rashtriya Sevak Sangh (RSS), began to take form in the state. Particularly susceptible are the Nair community, traditional villages bosses, whose income continues to decline in relative terms. The RSS has proselytized among all sections of Hindu society in Kerala, even, and unusually, among the untouchables. Its membership is not certainly known but informed local estimates in 1984 put it at around 60,000. As an organization the RSS is disciplined and it has given young Hindus quasi-military training as well as a pride in religious observance. Whether or not the RSS was behind the incident in late 1983, when a Trivandrum (and largely Muslim) bazaar was burnt down, is unclear but the suspicion that they were is as significant as the fact of the matter. For the communists who have fought communalism bravely the growth of fundamentalism among both Muslims and Hindus is dangerous.

Under the British, the censuses recorded not only religious community but also caste or church. Since independence, as a matter of policy, the Indian government has not enumerated caste except for those designated as 'scheduled'—the untouchables. An official sample survey in 1968 does however give sound estimates for Kerala. The Brahmins, chiefly Namboodiris, constituted just 1.8 per cent; the biggest high-caste group, the Nairs, formed 14.5 per cent; Syrian Christians, the Christian equivalent in ranking of the Nairs, were 16 per cent. The largest single group was the Ezhavas at 22.2 per cent, followed by the Muslims at 19 per cent. The Muslims, it should be noted, are themselves broken into more or less hierarchical and endogamous groups but the bulk are drawn from the poorer sections of agricultural society. Latin Catholics (as distinct from the so-called Romo-Syrians, who recognize the Pope but practise Syrian rites) are some 3.6 per cent of the population and typically are converts from menial castes. Scheduled castes (8 per cent Hindu; 1.5 per cent Christian converts) at 10 per cent are half the India average and scheduled tribes are only 1.3 per cent of the Kerala population. The one real concentration of scheduled castes is in the southern highland *taluk* of Peermade (26 per cent) and of tribes in the small and formerly malarial district of Wynad in interior Malabar (30 per cent). As in India as a whole, positive discrimination has officially operated and in Kerala land reform has helped but the disparity in condition and prospects between the castes and outcastes remains. Recent official evidence shows that particular groups among the scheduled have disproportionately benefited from positive discrimination.

Absolute degradation does exist in Kerala along with the indignity of (primitive) labour. Nevertheless, relative to the *bustees* and slums of the major cities of India and the deprivation of caste-ridden villages in drought-prone regions, Kerala has on average a higher quality of life, though not standard of living. Kinship, sub-caste and even village networks of welfare and support are supplemented by large-scale intervention to provide basic needs from food through education to dispensaries and electricity. Kerala's per capita income may be as much as 30 per cent below the all-India figure but on a recent physical quality of life index it was 69 per cent above the norm. Averages, however, conceal much and the results of an extensive 1980 survey of housing sketch the disparities that still exist. Nearly one quarter of all 'houses' in Kerala were huts and another 5 per cent 'old and dilapidated units'. The material of these huts—mud, bamboo and reed for the most part—does not last and they would better be described as shelters. In Alleppey, historically a communist centre, and two other districts, the percentage reached 40 per cent or more. Of the *pukka* houses half have a floor area of less than 500 square feet and 80 per cent less than 1,000 square feet. Only 18 per cent of all houses in the state have water-sealed lavatories (Government of Kerala, *Survey on Housing*, 1980).

There is no doubt that economic and social inequality between castes and communities has been more eroded in Kerala than virtually anywhere else in India but within each group, including to some extent among the higher castes there are enormous variations. The last figures available (1968) report that 1.6 per cent of all Keralites had what was then a high annual income (Rs 8,000): among Ezhavas 1 per cent, Latin Catholics 1.1 per cent; but among Nairs 2.8 per cent, Syrians 3.1 per cent and Brahmins 10.4 per cent.

Land reform and Gulf money may have slightly redressed the balance in favour of the lower castes but the existence of elites among the formerly disadvantaged does not betoken fundamental change. Social mobility for the few masks the continued inequality of the many.

It seemed possible in the 1950s and 1960s that class might be gradually supplanting caste and community as the basis of Kerala politics, but the late 1970s and the early 1980s have seen a resurgence of caste as the dynamic of politics. When in the early days of the communist movement there was an almost one-for-one correlation between caste status and class position, the mobilization of the unprivileged masses through class conscious political movements was paradoxically easier, given a dedicated communist cadre, than it is in the 1980s when social uplift exists in theory.

5 The First Communist Government, 1957-9

Formation of the 'Regime'

From a Marxist-Leninist perspective, theory and practice should interact. When the CPI forsook the adventurist line in 1951, the Kerala comrades already had a good deal of experience of electoral competition, which, on the whole, had been profitable. With one exception (Cochin, 1948), they had contested elections at every opportunity. Namboodiripad had been elected to the Madras legislature as early as 1939; and Gopalakrishna Menon had been returned for the working-class constituency of Cranganore in 1949 when the Calcutta line was dominant. Tranvancore had been the first Indian state to hold mass suffrage elections (in February 1948) at a time of immense Congress popularity. Yet, standing as independents because the party was illegal and despite bitter repression, the CPI won 10 per cent of the votes. In the first Travancore-Cochin elections the CPI-led United Front of Leftists took 23 per cent of the poll. The CPI (18 per cent of the vote) won 29 of 122 seats and its socialist allies another 7. The turnout of voters at 71 per cent, far higher than in any other state, reflected levels of literacy and indicated the ability of the left to mobilize the poor. Analysis of the geographical distribution of party support showed that the left was well entrenched in the densely populated coastal areas, disproportionately peopled by Ezhavas and other low castes (Nossiter, 1982, p. 112). Mid-term elections in 1954 confirmed that the communists, working within a left front, were making such progress (51 out of 118 seats) that Congress hegemony was threatened.

Likewise in Malabar, the CPI's performance in the 1951-2 assembly elections and the District Board elections in 1954 suggested that Congress had more to fear from canvassing the popular vote than the communists had. An electoral deal with the Peasant-Workers Party (KMPP) worked well. The CPI mainly contested in the north and the KMPP in the south, together taking twice the number of seats won by Congress. When, soon afterwards, the KMPP merged with the moderate Praja Socialist Party and its admired Gandhian leader retired from politics, the CPI was able to inherit much of its following in the south.

Two years later the CPI scored a spectacular success—in the District Board elections. An excellent grassroots organization coupled with disarray among its Congress and socialist opponents enabled the CPI for the first time to win outright control of a sizeable local government body. With twenty-four seats to Congress's fifteen on the forty-eight member board, the communists had beaten Congress at its own game. Further, in subsequently winning Nehru awards for their model administration, the comrades could claim to have governed more honestly and more democratically than their rivals. When in 1956 after the Palghat Congress the Kerala CPI held a provincial conference to consider its attitude to the forthcoming all-Kerala elections, there was only muted opposition to a real bid for office.

The resulting resolution, the *Communist Proposal for Building a Democratic and Prosperous Kerala*, was significant for four reasons. It promised to build not to destroy. It saw as its objective not just 'true democracy' but prosperity. The platform was to be a practical 'minimum programme' aimed at political stability, social justice and economic reconstruction; and the leftish partners would share the platform. When the election manifesto was published in January 1957 it was certainly a far cry from the original Communist Manifesto. It bore a decided resemblance to the basic outline of the central government's Second Five Year Plan—more Congress socialist than communist. Alone among the contestants, the CPI put forward a detailed and workmanlike plan for the regeneration of Kerala. Key points included: a rise of 130 per cent in Kerala's plan allocation; the establishment of new industries; an impartial police policy; education reform; and, above all, a comprehensive Agrarian Relations Bill. Queues formed to buy the manifesto and reprints were ordered and consumed. It was the logical extension of the Kerala party's past involvement in specific popular grievances and an expression of the non-sectarian, broad-based approach recommended at Palghat rather than a ripple from the 20th Congress of the CPSU.

Amidst great popular euphoria the communists won—with the aid of a handful of party-backed independents. Contesting 100 of the 126 seats, they took 60 on 35 per cent of the poll. The world's press carried, according to their inclination, 'Red Star' or 'Red Peril over India' headlines. Among the factors most often cited to explain the victory were: the sorry state of the corrupt, communal and demoralized provincial Congress; the contrast with the well-organized, secular and enthusiastic CPI, at once movement and machine; the transfer to Madras of the Tamil Congress southern *taluks* of Travancore and the gain from Madras of communist Malabar; Indo-Soviet friendship; and the adoption by Congress itself of a socialist goal in December 1954. In Kerala, it was said, non-communists came to believe that if socialism was the pattern prescribed for India by Nehru, then the CPI would make a better job of it than the local Congress party. Interestingly, the CPI was surprised by the scale of its success whereas the central government's Intelligence Bureau regarded Congress's defeat as a foregone conclusion. Efforts have been made to interpret the communist victory in communal terms; and certainly the CPI's campaign managers did match candidates to constituencies with a watchful eye on caste considerations (Zinkin, 1962, p. 155); but in the last resort there is no denying the communists won because there was a mass surge in their favour. Quite simply, they deserved to win.

Both at the time and since, there has been no agreement as to whether the communists were to be taken at face value or not. The American authors of *Communism in India*, published in 1958, thought that Kerala posed a clear challenge to Marxist-Leninist orthodoxy (Overstreet & Windmiller, p. 481-2). The Bombay-based Democratic Research Service (1959) had no such illusions: the communists were doing their best to transform Kerala into a communist dictatorship. Malaviya, a left Congressman who acted as press attaché to the CPI government, and (recently) Leiten have, on the contrary, argued that communists were entirely genuine, achieved a good deal of their manifesto and were undemocratically ousted from office by the Congress central government (Malaviya, 1958; Leiten, 1979).

In point of fact the Kerala CPI was not entirely sure itself what it was embarking upon, for very good reasons. First the idea of peaceful transition was contingent on an imponderable. What in Indian conditions would the response of the ruling class and its state apparatus be? Could Congress and the social forces behind it be trusted to abide by their own rules? Second, the communists had won office in one state of the Union. Did the parliamentary road wind from there to the capital or was the Kerala Secretariat, simply a more palatial version of the District Board office? Third, the Kerala comrades were not just men (and occasionally women) of *the* (abstract) people but leaders of *their* people, the Malayalis, whose expectations were high and more pressing than those of the Politburo, some 2,000 miles away. Indeed, there are signs during the ministry that loyalties were sometimes still more particularistic. The Malabar and Travancore-Cochin units had different traditions and had only recently been formally integrated. To the north the greatest issue was land reform; to the south educational reform. Lastly, the comrades had developed different skills through working on different fronts. The world could look very different to those who worked daily on the mass front than it did to those who debated in chambers and argued in law courts.

There was no single understanding in the party of its wider programme. It was twice necessary for the national party secretary to intervene to resolve conflict within the State Committee. However the dominant view was that of the Chief Minister and leading Politburo member, E. M. S. Namboodiripad. In part author of the emergence of the party's line from 1953 onwards, E.M.S., as he is universally known, had a subtle grasp of the realities as well as the theory of the situation: the vested interests in Kerala; the powers of the centre; the pressures from below, within and without the party for legislative reform and executive action; the need to succour weaker comrades after their years in the wilderness; and the importance of using power, however limited, to strengthen the party.

The provincial decision-making centre of the party was the State Committee. Under the discipline of democratic centralism it set the framework for the operation of the various wings of the party. In practice there was more flexibility than this formal description implies. The State Committee was often a reconciliatory body, papering over unresolved conflict with ambiguous formulae. It could hardly be called to decide on each and every issue that arose; and, inevitably, the party secretary, M. N. Govindan Nair, was of great significance in the day-to-day interpretation of the party line. Govindan Nair, urbane and shrewd, was himself sceptical of the parliamentary road, quipping to a Western journalist friend that communism with a democratic constitution was like capitalism without private enterprise (Zinkin, 1962, p. 154). Nair had legislative experience in the Travancore-Cochin assembly. In the nature of the division of labour between agitators and administrators, his position entailed integrating the urgent interests of the field workers with the painstaking procedures of parliament and goverment. Similar considerations applied at district and local levels and on specific fronts such as peasant, labour and student. These polycentric tendencies help to explain some of the inconsistencies of the communist record both in 1957-9 and thereafter.

From the beginning there was within the Kerala party a dissident minority, which argued that what was taking place was tantamount to parliamentary cretinism. The majority, however, was not prepared to dismiss the chance to probe the bourgeois democratic defences. At the time no one, not even Nehru, had any real idea what room for manœuvre a non-Congress state government might have. Apart from the doubtfully relevant 1937 provincial Congress governments of the Raj, there was no past precedent; and the Indian constitution was essentially latitudinarian on the point. At sub-state level, in Kerala, the CPI had experimented with some success already. The pressures on the party to try its hand were irresistible: the Soviet Union wanted it; the Indian Politburo willed it; and most important of all the labouring poor yearned for it. One of the radical minority reported—with pride—hearing the police upbraided by the crowd: 'Now you daren't attack us because our government is in power. Namboodiripad is our leader. We are ruling' (Damodaran, 1975, p. 47).

The formation of the ministerial team strongly suggested the CPI meant business. Namboodiripad, preferred by the Politburo to other aspirants, was an intellectual and organizer of all-India stature, and a Brahmin who had given everything, including his property, to serve the commonfolk (Namboodiripad, 1987). The ten departmental ministers (eight CPI and two independent) were as impressive an array of talent as any state council in India at the time. The non-party ministers, both heavyweights, were noteworthy. Dr A. R. Menon, Minister of Health and Welfare, was an Edinburgh-trained doctor, whose political record included membership of the All India Congress Committee and office as Minister for Rural Development in Cochin (1938-42). By nature a blunt man, he had a fearsome reputation as a critic of administrative incompetence. Menon was not the person to include in the cabinet unless there was the intention to do what was promised. The law portfolio also went to an independent, V. R. Krishna Iyer, one of the country's front-rank lawyers, who subsequently served in the Indian Supreme Court. If the government was to wrestle with the centre, few could be more useful. The CPI had formed a ministry which was strong, capable and honest, with, in stark contrast to what had gone before and what was to come, little or no reference to communal or regional factors. The parliamentarians, too, were more than a match for their opponents and earned a reputation for extensive preparation and forensic skill in dissecting the arguments of the Congress opposition in the assembly.

All was not quite so well, however, with the body of the party supporting this fine head. Already in 1956 it was showing signs of obesity. When in June the Malabar and Travancore-Cochin units were amalgamated, there were 25,000 members, of whom only some 2,000 were long-standing and unquestionably committed comrades. In 'many parts of Kerala' there were very few and even no party units (*New Age*, January 1960, p. 1). After the election victory, membership began to rise, especially after the conversion of the CPI in April 1958 from cadre to mass party. By 1960 membership stood at 60,000 of whom 18,000 were candidate members. Significantly, after the ministry was dismissed the numbers fell quickly: to 41,000 in 1961 and 23,000 in 1963-4. Some of those who joined from 1957 onwards were, of course, sympathizers, whose jobs or family situation had previously precluded open commitment but more appear to have been opportunists. The 1957-8 membership drive undermined the party's greatest asset, its disciplined organization. 'I have to boost the party up to 50,000 cardmembers' the party secretary complained at the time, 'They think I am a magician. I can increase membership only at the cost of discipline' (Zinkin, 1962, p. 155). Later senior party leaders were privately inclined to blame whatever excesses were committed in the name of the party on anti-social elements who jumped on the bandwagon. The argument is not merely a convenient one: there is some truth in it.

Agrarian Reform

The most important reform attempted by the ministry was the Agrarian Relations Bill, which Namboodiripad rightly regarded as the government's greatest achievement. It was the first comprehensive measure of its kind undertaken in India, and tackled tenurial relations of greater complexity than anywhere else in the country. After Independence a variety of measures had been enacted in Kerala as partial and ineffectual remedies for particular problems. The CPI's first step within a week of taking office was to proclaim a Stay of Eviction Ordinance to protect tenants and hutment dwellers till the full reform was on the statute book. Work on the main measure started immediately but the bill did not pass its third reading until June 1959, only days before the government was removed. By the time the bill returned from Delhi where it had to be sent for official comment, a Congress–PSP Ministry was in power and the final version of January 1961 was much modified to accommodate landlord interests. The act was, however, soon emasculated in the courts and had no practical impact. The bill is none the less of central importance to an assessment of the regime.

Two features of the ministry's approach to land reform stand out: its very moderation, which is not to denigrate it; and the assiduous efforts to anticipate the difficulties encountered elsewhere through bureaucratic inertia and judicial review. The bill aimed to create a free peasantry but provided for compensation to the landlords, which was inevitable within the Indian constitutional framework. In fact the draft follows the outlines of the Congress Agrarian Committee report of 1949 as did the definitive Kerala act of 1970. The political constraints did not, however, conflict with the party's intentions. Namboodiripad had argued (1952; 1954) that land reform should first be addressed to the abolition of feudalism and the generation of capitalist relations in agriculture. Achutha Menon, the Finance Minister, who later presided over the implementation of the 1970 land reform, added a further practical justification. Treating farmers who supervised cultivation as if they were truly tillers of the soil was necessary in the interests of production; and in any case, he noted, given the low per capita availability of land, no possible redistribution would materially benefit the labourers (1958, p. 20). Really radical solutions such as state ownership or collective farming had already been ruled out on the grounds that the best revolutionaries try to help the peasants carry out their own schemes whether or not they appeal to intellectuals 'from a scientific point of view' (Namboodiripad, 1954, p. 81). Certainly the Kerala Peasants' Union was a more influential pressure group within the CPI than the labourers' union. Nevertheless, it would be unfair to leave the impression that the ministry neglected the agricultural labourer. He was given security of tenure to his hutment and daily wage rates rose more—relative to productivity—than anywhere else in India. The farm *worker* was treated as such: a proletarian on the land. His uplift was to be through security of employment, better working conditions and enhanced wages, which led logically forward to the field labourer's 'Magna Carta', the CPI–Congress Agricultural Workers Act of 1974.

The second important feature of the land reform bill was the ministry's efforts to circumvent the problems of adjudication and execution. Courts had struck down much of the agrarian reform thus far attempted in South Asia. The government therefore removed as much as possible from the purview of the courts and charged the Land Board and Land Tribunals, backed by advisory People's Committees, with the reform's implementation. Naturally the opposition complained that these would be packed with communists but that does not appear to have been generally the case; and in Kerala at least partisan considerations were often transcended by village consciousness of natural justice (Gough, 1968, p. 197). One puzzle remains. The ministry could have sought to barricade the whole bill from challenge in the courts by using the 9th Schedule of the constitution which debars judicial review of state legislation on land reform. It did not request this; and it remains unknown why not.

The Agrarian Relations Bill's major provisions showed the concern with making the act workable. Security of tenure was conferred on tenants and those 'deemed' to be tenants. The fact of cultivation was sufficient proof, irrespective of whether any deed or document could be produced. Landlords were allowed to resume land for personal use, subject to conditions and to the payment of compensation; but unless the landlord had less than five acres himself, he could not deprive his erstwhile tenant of a subsistence holding. Rent arrears were drastically reduced. On the appointed day, all cultivating tenants would be deemed to have bought their holdings and the landlords' rights would be henceforth vested in the government. It was to be the state that was responsible for the collection of compensation. This was to be paid in instalments and based on sixteen times a clearly defined 'fair rent'. The land ceiling was variable but at, for example, only 15 acres for double cropping paddy land, it was the lowest set in India. The exemptions included plantations and lands held by public, religious and charitable bodies but not the large-scale farms or *kayals* of the Kuttanad rice bowl. Here two-thirds of the anti-communist Liberation Struggle Committee members who fought to oust the government in 1958-9 owned at least 1,000 acres of *kayal* each. The contrast between their wealth and the serf-like poverty of their labourers was obscene.

Fully aware of the dangers of potent opposition, the ministry sought the widest possible consensus among the interests affected. The peasants' union lobbied for speedy progress but the government took a broader view. There was extensive discussion in Delhi and consultation locally before the bill was introduced; and the final draft rested on seven or eight earlier versions. The second reading alone lasted 124 hours and more than 1,000 amendments were debated. Nearly a year elapsed in committee. This slow progress was only partly explicable in terms of the complexity of the issues and the efforts to allay opposition. Within the communist party there were profound differences on tactics. The Travancorean communists, some of them with personal or family connections with the predominantly Nair landlords, feared provoking a Nair-Christian anti-government confederation which they rightly expected would doom the ministry. Malabar comrades, on the other hand, had few such links and no such fears. Their political experience was largely of peasant mobilization; and compromise with landlord interests at this stage was unthinkable. Gradually as the committee stage of the bill proceeded, the 'radicals' wore down their 'pragmatic' comrades. And what the Travancore comrades feared, happened. The Nairs linked arms with the Christians to launch the Liberation Struggle.

Christian antipathy to the communists was both general and particular. It was general in that the church in Kerala was profoundly conservative and its Romo-Syrian and Latin Catholic sections bitterly anti-communist. This was the papacy of Pius XII and the era of persecution of Christians in Eastern Europe. It was particular because the complete control of children's education was jealously guarded and because the provision of school and college education—to Hindus as well as their own flock—was one of the most remunerative of the church's (and their managers') activities. Education was big business. Within weeks of the formation of the ministry, the Vicar General of the Changanacherry Archdiocese was publicly asserting that educational institutions were as sacred to Catholics as the churches themselves, and that they were prepared to lay down their lives for the cause of educational freedom (*Deepika*, 18 June 1957).

Kerala's outstanding educational record could mainly be attributed to the work of private, communally based institutions, led by the Catholic Church, though enjoying financial support from government. However, all but the entrenched interests conceded that reform was necessary to eradicate corruption, communal bias, malpractice and maladministration and to give the state a measure of control commensurate with its subsidies. Both Sir C. P. Ramaswami Aiyar and the last Congress Chief Minister of Travancore-Cochin had tried to bring the private managements to heel but been beaten. As with agrarian reform, there was widespread agreement that something had to be done.

The CPI's commitment to immediate action stemmed from a variety of sources: they too recognized the importance of shaping the minds of the young; the party enjoyed much support among the educationally disadvantaged Ezhavas; and teachers were among their commonest village leaders. The Education Minister was himself a former teacher and a man with a burning grievance. Joseph Mundasserry had been dismissed from his Christian college after 27 years' service because he had visited (communist) China. Whether or not, as was alleged by the Opposition, it was personal animus which drove Mundasserry, it soon became clear that from the party's point of view it was a tactical error to have confronted the two major vested interests in Kerala simultaneously.

For all the hostility of the Catholic Church, the bill introduced in July 1957 was modest enough. In thirty-six clauses, prepared in the Secretariat and later approved by the party, the government sought to regulate the appointment and conditions of teachers, ensure proper records, establish local educational authorities with a mixture of official, elected and nominated members and provided for temporary or permanent supercession of managements which failed to comply with the act but in exchange for compensation. Non-communists need only have been troubled by its provisions on the improbable assumption that the communists would rule for ever; and, in fact, the bill was initially generally welcomed, even by the (non-Christian) Malabar wing of Congress. The communists did not have a majority on the Select Committee which devoted most of its time to clarification and modification (not the rejection) of the bill's clauses. Only one of four dissenting minutes from the committee emanated from its six Congress members. Opposition to the bill in principle was essentially Christian and extraparliamentary. By September the bill had passed all its stages and was despatched to Delhi. It was here that the battle commenced in earnest. The Christian contribution to the Congress party in Kerala was fully appreciated by the all-India Congress leadership. There was genuine doubt whether the bill might infringe the rights of minority communities as enshrined in the constitution; and on the advice of the Union cabinet it was referred to the Supreme Court for an opinion. The court did find difficulties but the ministry accepted its Opinion and by February 1959 a revised version of the bill had secured presidential assent.

Having lost the democratic contest, the Catholic Church now turned to unconstitutional techniques, in alliance with the Nairs. The Nair Service Society, led by the veteran but charismatic Mannath Padmanabha Pillai, was increasingly fearful of the consequences for its community of land reform as the communist 'radicals' stiffened the bill but it also had grievances in education. Mannath, who claimed that NSS backing for CPI candidates had determined the election outcome, believed that an understanding had been reached that the Nairs' reward would be an NSS engineering college near Palghat. Late in 1958 the Education Minister informed Mannath that the money was now more urgently needed for Ezhava education. Lastly, the revision of the education bill to safeguard minority rights meant that the NSS colleges would suffer more from reform than their Christian rivals. Facing a pincer movement, the ministry offered concessions to the Church but negotiations failed in March 1959 and the Catholic hierarchy announced that it would close its schools unless and until the Education Act and its rules were still further amended. Meanwhile Mannath, in a well-publicized and atavistic gesture, let loose a splendidly caparisoned white horse as the traditional challenge of Nair warriors to whomsoever might dare to ride it. The symbolism was not lost on the ministry.

The churches now prepared to defy the rule of law, the very crime of which they accused their enemies. *Deepika*, the semi-official Catholic organ, quoted St Luke's Gospel: 'he that hath a purse, let him take it . . . and he that hath not, let him sell his coat and buy a sword' (17 May 1959). The so-called Liberation struggle was launched; and the civil war, which, in 1958, Namboodiripad had been unbraided for publicly fearing, commenced in all but name. Congress kept its distance: some shared Nehru's reservations about the constitutional proprieties; some disliked alignment with communal forces; but others were happy to let the Liberationists do the dirty work. When the Kerala provincial Congress Committee begged advice from the national leadership, it was Mrs Gandhi who visited Kerala openly to endorse the demands of the private school managements and the right of the people to seek to thwart the legislation of their duly elected government, to which the President of India, advised by the Union Cabinet, had given his assent. This was the very stance which the communists had forsworn in adopting the parliamentary road.

Law and Order

As the Liberation Struggle gathered momentum, the opposition increasingly justified their actions on the grounds that the government had surrendered its democratic legitimacy, acting in a flagrantly partisan and lawless way. The cry that law and order was flouted by the communists was the ultimate case for the ministry's dismissal. The charge sheet indicted the CPI on two counts: that the ministry's police policy of neutrality in labour, property and political disputes was actually the neutralization of capital and opposition; and that the party was interfering at all levels in due legal process. As Panampilly Govinda Menon, former Congress Chief Minister, somewhat illogically summarized it: 'If the Communists violated laws, they would not be arrested; if they were arrested, they would not be prosecuted; if they were prosecuted, the cases would be withdrawn; and if the cases ended in conviction, the sentences would be remitted' (*Indian Express*, 30 July 1958).

That there were excesses such as the so-called cell courts—summary justice handed out by party officials—or justice denied through pressures on the local police is not privately denied by party leaders. There was also in communist strongholds such as Alleppey and Trichur an unsurprising settling of old scores in the class war; but rightly communists deny that revolutionary justice was ever party policy. After the experience of 1948–51, it would have been foolhardy in the extreme. Namboodiripad defining the new police policy when taking office, emphasized that while the police must no longer be used to break up strikes and agitations or to side with property against poverty, there was a definite limit to how far collective bargaining and direct action could go. The personal life and property of the employer or landowner was inviolable (*New Age*, 18 August 1957). The CPI's position on the role of mass struggle was a defensive not an offensive one. The 1958 Amritsar resolution dealing with Kerala warned that vested interests might not respect the verdict of the ballot box and the party could be driven to mass action (CPI, 1958 p. 15). It was the Catholics who first formed a militia, the Christophers, and the communist equivalent existed more on paper than in reality. The staunchly conservative London *Daily Telegraph*'s correspondent and the British owned pro-Congress Calcutta *Statesman* certainly treated the claims of the church with great scepticism. Fairly hard evidence is provided by the State Administration Reports which for the material period were prepared after the communists had been removed. Crime generally did rise more than in neighbouring states but not to the degree that would suggest a communist-inspired breakdown in law and order. Murders, for instance, grew from 167 in 1956 to 294 in 1959; riotous assembly—liberationists rather than communists—from 500 to 2,000; and detection rates declined from 41 to 27 per cent. Cognizable crimes in general did not fall markedly after the communist period except for riotous and unlawful assemblies. When all the possible qualifications are made the Kerala crime rate of roughly one per thousand persons is scarcely an indication that law and order had broken down (Nossiter, 1982, pp. 158-8). In a society chronically afflicted by poverty, debt, unemployment and landlessness, it is a remarkably low figure. In Britain even before the recent rise in unemployment the crime rate was ten times that in Kerala. Govindan Nair explicitly attributed excesses to the party centre's loss of control over a membership which doubled during the life of the ministry. 'The [new] comrades were too impatient, too undisciplined, too stupid' or not genuine aspiring comrades at all but hooligans (Zinkin, 1962, p. 164).

When in the summer and autumn of 1958 a wave of violent clashes erupted between communist and non-communist workers and it became clear that the NSS and Catholic Church were prepared to take the offensive, the CPI held meetings at state and national levels to determine the party and ministry's response to the rapidly deteriorating situation. The conclusion was that there would be no mass action in defence of the regime; the police were to be instructed to ignore pressures from local communist cadres; and in exchange for the subservience of the party's organizational wing to the ministry in matters of law and order, the government would consult more closely with activists on policy by means of a special joint committee. Shorn of the window-dressing the party in the countryside was to be distanced, if not actually separated, from the state apparatus.

In November the argument was renewed at a special Kerala party conference. A variety of solutions was canvassed: to expand the ministry into a united front of leftists; a massive popular mobilization to overwhelm the reactionaries; and immediate resignation. The reaffirmation of the decision to soldier on is said to have been approved when Namboodiripad attended the 21st CPSU Congress two months later. As the Liberation Struggle gained momentum, Achutha Menon, Finance Minister and next in seniority to the Chief Minister, took over the law portfolio from the non-party Krishna Iyer. All arms licences were rescinded in the four most troubled districts; and Menon announced the recruitment of 10,000 special police officers. At the invitation of Namboodiripad, Nehru was invited to see for himself what was happening in the state. 'How', he is reported to have asked the CPI State Committee somewhat ingenuously, 'did you manage to so wonderfully isolate yourself from the people in such a short space of time?'; and recommended a negotiated solution to the educational imbroglio and thereafter fresh elections (Zinkin, 1962, p. 159). Privately, Nehru was thought to be content to watch the CPI struggle on the hook. Govindan Nair in particular was for resignation and, after the Liberationists turned down an offer to negotiate in June, the State Committee agreed, only to be overruled by the CPI's National Council which preferred downright dismissal for its propaganda value. In the course of the next few weeks 17 people died in police firings, 300 were seriously injured in *lathi* (cane) charges and some 150,000 people arrested. News that the Liberationists intended to storm the Kerala Secretariat on 9 August finally enabled Namboodiripad to prevail on the centre to intervene (Mullick, 1972, pp. 351-7); and on 31 July 1959 the 28-month experiment came to an end with the long-sought Presidential dismissal of the government under Article 356 of the constitution. In retrospect, on the main charge against the ministry that it had subverted the rule of law, it is hard to avoid the conclusion that the communists were more sinned against than sinning.

Administration

In a communist state proper, state and party are fused; in a liberal democratic system, the theory is that state and party are distinct. In practice the public interest is conflated in many ways with partisan ends and legitimated through such conventions as ministerial discretion. In India where one party was dominant, the political elite none too scrupulous, and the mass electorate little schooled in the 'civic culture', Congress had not been setting an example in distinguishing sectional advantage from the general good. In Travancore-Cochin administration had been scarred by communalism, nepotism and patronage and marred by simple inefficiency. The CPI had promised in its manifesto to abide by the spirit of the constitution not its letter by restoring honesty and economy to government and also to decentralize decision-making.

In fact, the opposition claimed, the CPI placed the interests of the party before those of the state, of its supporters before those of the citizens at large and even tolerated individual aggrandizement. It would be impossible to check the many allegations and in view of the politically charged atmosphere unwise to assume that where there was smoke there must be fire. However there is evidence that party interest intruded into administration. In September 1958 the Law Minister assured a conference of District Collectors and police officials that interference by local cadres in their work would be checked. There was one major scandal, the so-called Andhra Rice Deal, in which the state incurred an avoidable loss of Rs 153,000 on urgent grain purchases; and grave suspicions that the party had benefited. It must be noted though that the Chief Minister instituted an official commission of enquiry. Whatever the truth of the matter, far greater losses were incurred through the government's use of cooperative societies for the construction of public works and the running of the toddy (a country liquor) industry. The Public Works Department of Travancore-Cochin, as almost all public works departments throughout India then and now, was a byword for inefficiency if not synonymous with corruption. The CPI blamed this on the use of private contractors, and established instead a chain of Labour Contract Societies to whom work was to be given at cost (as estimated by government engineers) plus 50 per cent. In 1957-8, 400 items of work were undertaken at an outlay of Rs 2.3 million. Several societies failed and the monies advanced were lost. Financial arrangements were decidedly obscure; and the opposition alleged that much of the money found its way into party funds. Similar complaints were laid when the new cooperative system in the distribution of toddy led to a substantial drop in excise revenue and an increase in illicit trafficking. It was also said that 'only communist-led societies' need apply.

Such evidence must nevertheless be viewed in an all-India context. The Chief Secretary, head of the Kerala civil service, and no communist sympathizer, asserted that the communists were neither better nor worse than their predecessors or peers. The one difference was that the communists were new to power and more dependent on local party officials who, unlike the ministers, were often uneducated, ill-informed and vindictive. The Chief Minister *per contra* was very anxious to put his house in order. Namboodiripad's own aims were captured in his address to senior Secretariat staff on taking office: a firm but sympathetic appeal for mutual cooperation:

Our experience and approach to conducting affairs and yours are of two different types. Both of them should be combined for the good of the people and the state ... It is true that in administrative affairs, excepting [Dr Menon] none of us have any experience. In this we have a lot to learn from you. Similarly we have opportunities to feel the pulse of the people. You will have a lot to learn from us ... The old social order is changing. You must correctly understand this change ... Only if we exchange our views ... can we succeed in building a Socialist order ... let us be partners. [*New Age*, 21 April 1957]

Twelve years on, after another period in office, Namboodiripad was disillusioned: IAS officers 'are recruited and trained by the Congress Party government at the Centre, and posted to states' with non-Congress governments. 'What shall I do with them?' (Potter, 1986, p. 165).

Theoretically the CPI was of course committed to the view that senior officials were agents of the ruling class not servants of the people. The party introduced non-official personal assistants for the Chief Minister and three others—hardly in principle objectionable or unusual; and party cells were formed in some departments ostensibly to expedite administration. Whatever the reality there is no evidence these changes materially affected the working of the government machine. Relations between ministers and top civil servants were in fact quite good for the first eighteen months. One or two of the more unbending secretaries were transferred but officials generally found their new masters no worse than the old and in some cases much better: full of ideas, ready to listen, and aware of the sensitivity of civil servants to partisan interference with proper procedure. Relations only began to deteriorate towards the end of 1958: first, it was impossible to insulate the Secretariat from the turmoil outside; second, it was claimed the Chief Secretary was increasingly acting on the orders of Delhi not the Chief Minister; and third, a group of young officers, close to a rising Christian Congress leader, P. T. Chacko, were almost certainly behaving in a way incompatible with their 'service' obligations. By 1959 the line between those for and those against the communists ran right through the Secretariat.

The party secretary later stated that the main weakness of the ministry had been its failure to improve the *efficiency* of the administrative machine and his evidence to the Administrative Reforms Committee set up by the communist government in 1957 makes it clear that efficiency was not a euphemism for something more sinister (Report of the Administrative Reforms Committee, 1960, vol. iii, pp. 121-2). The Committee, chaired by Namboodiripad himself, was far from a propaganda exercise. Its membership alone is inconsistent with such a view: the Chief Secretary; a retired Chief Secretary, the founder of the Indian Institute of Public Administration; a former Travancore-Cochin Congress minister; the government's press attaché; and the least 'party man' of the CPI ministers, Mundasserry. A thousand detailed questionnaires were sent out, 158 witnesses examined, and Part I of the three-part report required sixty-two days of sittings. To all intents and purposes the committee was unanimous and the ministry embarked on the necessary legislation for *panchayats* and district boards, although the bills lapsed when the assembly was dissolved. The CPI government did take its twin objectives of more democratic and more efficient administration very seriously even if party pressures, especially at local level, and opposition within the Secretariat, frustrated its intentions.

The history of the first CPI government was not simply a titanic battle between the forces of good and evil. The acrimonious polemics of the time neglected the fact that for the most part until the final months business went on pretty much as usual in the Assembly and the Secretariat. A great deal of time went on routine and non-controversial legislation to promote 'modernization'. New communist legislators discovered that access to the corridors of power could be used to tackle the problems and grievances of their constituents and constituencies. In sum the party developed an appreciation of both the possibilities and the limitations of work on the parliamentary front; and many MLAs became adept at waging this form of warfare, even though many remained uncertain and ambivalent as to its ultimate importance in Indian communist strategy.

Assembly work did not exist in isolation from representational office in lower elective bodies or in trade unions and other mass organizations. Panchayat boards, elected by universal suffrage with some powers, had existed in Kerala since 1950. They provided a training ground for class struggle, electoral mobilization, and administration as well as a ladder to more senior office. Unlike most of India at the time, *panchayats* were politicized in Kerala; but even so the class struggle rarely completely polarized. Whether consciously or not, communist members of politically mixed local bodies sought to insulate their board work from the wider political battle, to keep discussions concrete, and to avoid putting matters to a divisive vote (Gough, 1968, p. 197). Local government, reflecting Kerala's subtly complex society, nourished a reconciliation of revolutionary and constitutional politics.

MLAs frequently held union office and this helped to link parliament and agitation and the ministerial and organizational wings of the party. Although Kerala was industrially underdeveloped the working class was a fairly well-organized and a growing political force. In 1956-7 there were nearly 800 registered trade unions with a claimed membership of 130,000 which had risen by 1959-60 to 1,650 unions with a claimed membership of 320,000. These small unions were aggregated into one of the three national federations, the Congress INTUC, and CPI AITUC and the RSP UTUC. In 1957-8 some 80 per cent of all Kerala's trade unionists belonged to the CPI federation compared with about 30 per cent nationally.

Just as the CPI had effected a historic compromise with the system in the 1950s, so AITUC had become less confrontationist, seeking to encourage Indian economic development even at the price sometimes of the short-term interests of the working class. This moderate stance emphasized that there was no need for every struggle to end in a strike and that 'strikes must be peaceful in order to secure the largest measure of popular support. Non-proletarian forms of mass action such as the traditional Gandhian *satyagraha* and the hunger strike were now admissible as well as collective bargaining, wage boards and parliamentary work' (Crouch, 1966, p. 179).

The formation of a communist ministry was an especially interesting test of the new strategy. The Labour Minister, T. V. Thomas, the senior AITUC leader in Kerala, quickly committed the government to AITUC policy and Namboodiripad spoke of the need for a long-term solution of capital-labour relations. Unless, the Chief Minister told the silver jubilee session of the AITUC, there was close cooperation of workers and owners and:

> unless the resources of the State, private capitalists as well as the financial resources even of the smaller man were tapped in order that all the existing industrial units were not only maintained but further expanded ... and new industrial units were established, the working class in Kerala had no salvation ... [Malaviya, 1958, pp. 39–40]

As already noted, the new police policy was not a licence for industrial anarchy. Notwithstanding some partiality in its administration, the CPI's labour policy was essentially constructive. Thomas, a powerful figure in the government, was a long-time advocate of negotiation and conciliation. Civil servants received wage increases; the scope of minimum wages legislation was extended; and an earlier Congress-sponsored report on wages and conditions in the coir industry, Kerala's largest work-force outside agriculture, was implemented. The foundation of a range of conciliation bodies led up to the introduction of a comprehensive Industrial Relations Bill in 1959, which, however, was a casualty of the imposition of Presidential Rule. At the heart of the measure was the adoption of a one-industry-one-union formula. The rival trade-union federations, however, suspected—not without reason—that such a *prima facie* sensible step would be yet further excuse to favour CPI unionism.

If the government used its discretionary powers to favour its own union affiliates, the opposition parties went out of their way to cause embarrassment by stirring up industrial discontent. Days lost through strike action during the ministry's term remained far higher than in the neighbouring states but the only major strike in which the CPI's AITUC was involved was the 1958 plantation strike which was directed against foreign monopoly in the shape of the British tea company, Kanan Devan. In sum, the CPI seriously and responsibly attempted to implement current AITUC policy while none the less exploiting (or allowing line management to exploit) government influence to strengthen its own section of the union movement. The tension between the CPI as vanguard of the organized working class irrespective of specific party allegiance and the CPI as a competitive political party fighting to extend its purview was sadly illustrated in July 1958 when two workers belonging to the Revolutionary Socialist Party's UTUC were shot by police, following an attack on a factory manager. A State Committee debated how to react. Workers had been shot dead by a communist government. By a process of syllogistic reasoning—to condemn the police would lower their morale, so strengthen the anti-communist forces and could lead to the overthrow of the government, which would be the greatest blow to the working class—the conclusion was to defend the police action.

Perhaps the soundest verdict on the government and on the relevance of the parliamentary road as a way forward was the result of the 1960 election. The major anti-communist parties, Congress, PSP and Muslim League forged an electoral alliance, backed by the churches, the NSS and the SNDP, which to some extent was funded by American agencies. Once the divided opposition parties and communities united, the CPI was bound to lose seats since in 1957 they had won only twenty-six seats with more than half the votes cast; but the CPI did improve its share of the poll—including party-supported independents from 41 to 44 per cent. The two elections are not strictly comparable for a variety of reasons—the registered electorate rose by 8 per cent, turnout by 18 per cent, and separate (party) ballot boxes were replaced by a common box (Nossiter, 1982, pp. 127–34). In Malabar the CPI's vote improved by about the same percentage as it fell in Travancore-Cochin. Overall two interpretations are possible: the electors of the north were more satisfied with the ministry's performance than those of the south, where the loss of party discipline in the localities had been most obvious; and/or that caste and communalism was a more persuasive force in the erstwhile princely states than in Malabar. The one contemporaneous survey of voting reports that three-quarters of the harijans voted communist, three-fiths of the Ezhavas but only one-quarter of the Nairs and one-tenth of Catholics and Syrian Christians (*Times of India*, 2 September 1960). We may conclude that the electoral impact of the CPI's term of office was the extension of its mass base among the 'have nots' of the Hindu community, including the poorer Nairs, but a loss of support among the better off of all communities and little progress among the poor of the Christian community, threatened incidentally with excommunication if they dared vote for the communists, and the Muslims. In the light of the size of the minority communities it was clearly imperative for the communists' advance to make the humbler Christians and Muslims aware of their class position.

6 From United to Disunited Front

The CPI Split in Kerala

By the early 1960s it was clear that the two states where communism had taken real root were Kerala and West Bengal. Whichever wing of the divided party controlled them would in the long term emerge as the dominant force in Indian communism. Among party functionaries, including the State Council and the parliamentary party, the right commanded a two-to-one majority, and initially it dominated the Kerala unit of the AITUC; but the left enjoyed an overwhelming majority among the organized peasantry and agricultural labour; and since the rural poor was the power base of most district and constituency committees, the left controlled many local organizations. In Malabar full-time workers and party members with surprisingly few exceptions aligned themselves with the left, whose leaders in the state were their own best-known and loved leaders, E. M. S. Namboodiripad and A. K. Gopalan. In Travancore, Quilon was under right-wing control and in Cochin the same was true of Trichur but even in the south the left preponderated.

Mid-term elections soon tested the rival claims in Kerala. In 1964 the state Congress party had also split when rivalries between Ezhavas on the one hand and Christians and Nairs on the other for control of the Congress ministry and organization had led to the breakaway of a Christian and Nair plantation faction which adopted the name of Kerala Congress. The Congress ministry collapsed and new elections were held in March 1965. National interest in the first test of strength between right and left communists was intensified by the maladroit arrest under the Defence of India rules of some 800 leading left cadres only weeks before the poll, 120 from Kerala. A further complication for the communists was the pitch by Congress for Ezhava support. The rival wings of the CPI joined battle not only with each other but with Congress for the allegiance of the lower castes who were, to all intents and purposes, the lower classes.

Despite the recency of the split the campaign began with serious but abortive efforts by the CPI(M), CPI and Revolutionary Socialists to form a united front of leftists. Ostensibly the reason for the collapse was the CPI's insistence that the United Front should declare its unequivocal opposition to the communalist Muslim League but the CPI(M) wished to leave itself room for electoral manœuvre in Malabar on the grounds that any fissures in the bourgeois edifice should be exploited even if that meant a temporary, vacillating, unreliable and conditional ally. Muslim 'independents' were worth a trip to the mosque to avert a Congress victory. The CPI(M) turned to two minor parties, the Samyukta Socialists and the Kerala Socialists, and also reached accommodation with the League in six constituencies, while the CPI concluded an alliance with the Revolutionary Socialists, of local importance in Quilon.

The result was calamitous for the CPI: a humiliating three seats in a 133 member assembly and 8 per cent of the total poll from seventy-eight contests; sixty-seven candidates lost their deposits. In contrast the CPI(M) on a 75 per cent turnout emerged as the biggest single party with forty seats, followed by Congress with thirty-six. Of the forty left communists elected, twenty-nine were in detention. Seventy-three candidates took 20 per cent of the total poll; and in the forty-five constituencies where the CPI and CPI(M) clashed directly the CPI(M) won twenty-four and the CPI none. There were only two out of nine districts where the CPI won more of the poll than the CPI(M): Quilon and Trichur.

The left's victory is simply explained. Its leaders, Namboodiripad and Gopalan, were not merely state-wide charismatic figures; they articulated the ordinary communist villager's beliefs. The CPI's cadre had predominantly been involved with working-class not peasant activity but the proletariat were few in number. At the grass roots the CPI was perceived as revisionist and prepared to compromise with Congress which in Kerala meant the party which had brought about the downfall of the communist ministry and, by the 1963 Agrarian Relations Act, surrendered to landed interests. Congress propaganda that the CPI(M) was unpatriotically pro-Chinese on the Sino-Indian border dispute found little support. For one, the Himalayas were a long way away; for another, the central government appeared to recall the existence of Kerala only when it suited its political convenience. It arrested the state's heroic figures on trumped-up charges of subversion but did little to solve its food crisis. The degree to which Namboodiripad and Gopalan reflected the hopes and fears of the poor explained the contrast in organizational efficiency of the rival parties. The CPI had the officers but the CPI(M) had the field marshalls, and NCOs and troops in the people's army. The exception to the pattern, Quilon, arose from the predominance of the CPI and RSP in the heavily unionized cashew factories of the district, their mutual alliance, and the personal influence of Govindan Nair.

The CPI(M) was established as the 'real' communist party in Kerala in 1965 and knocked the stuffing out of the CPI nationally. No less importantly there was a dramatic fall in the communist vote. The combined vote was under 28 per cent; or if all thirty party-supported independents are included 32 per cent, substantially below the 1960 peak of 44 per cent. Conversely the 'total' Congress vote at 45.6 per cent compares very favourably with the 37.8 per cent poll when the united Congress stood alone in 1957. As in 1960 there are technical difficulties in arriving at a precise estimate of the decline in communist support and a more accurate measure overall may be 3 per cent. This average, however, obscures the fact that while the communists maintained or improved their position in Malabar they suffered sharp setbacks in Travancore. The split (and the detentions) damaged the movement's ability to maximize its vote; but the unevenness of communist performance suggests other factors were operating. Two stand out: the revival of communalism, in part associated with the fragmentation of the party system; and, second, the determined effort of Sankar, SNDP leader, and the first Ezhava Chief Minister of Kerala, to build his community into the very foundations of Congress in the state. For thirty months he had been dispensing favours and patronage designed to make the Ezhavas safe from communism in line with the national Congress policy of extending its following into the lower castes. Ironically Sankar lost his own seat to the CPI(M) in the election but Congress's progress in Alleppey and Quilon testified to his success in consolidating Congress support among the increasing number of middle-class Ezhavas and in winning over new adherents among the humbler members of the community through the expansion of educational, and occupational, opportunity.

The break up of the party system and the revival of communalism ensured that neither communists nor Congress could ever again hope to gain a working majority alone. Government must be by coalition; but, whereas in the past, communist-led united fronts had been predicated on the alliance of left and progressive forces, any such advanced configuration would be increasingly difficult after 1965. A winning coalition would perforce include either Congress or the Congress enemy's enemies, whether or not they were socialistically desirable bedfellows. Growing economic differentiation combined with the declining ability of the Indian and Kerala economies to satisfy rising and competing aspirations by caste, class and region shattered the party system. This profound challenge to the communist movement in Kerala occurred precisely at the point when its own failure to agree on the class (and, by extension, party) analysis of Indian society had come to a head in the split.

Formation of the United Front, 1965-67

The reader may be surprised to learn that those who were divorced in 1964 were living in sin by 1967; but so it was. The CPI rout in 1965 stunned the Soviet Union which had taken the CPI's own assessment of its strength at face value. It was clear that the CPI(M) was far more capable of exploiting mass discontent. The CPSU also realized that its assumption that the CPI(M) was pro-Chinese was inaccurate. Soviet analysts had no desire to see 'their' party humiliated at the forthcoming general elections and so recommended the construction of at least a bailey bridge between the CPI and the CPI(M). The CPI now needed little encouragement to explore the possibilities of cooperation without prejudice to ideology. If the party was to survive at all, there was no alternative. Conversely, the CPI(M) could be magnanimous: everybody knew who was boss. In any case the desperate food crisis in Kerala in 1965-6 has already brought the entire left together in joint agitation. By early 1966 the CPI(M) had appreciated that the conversion of the *ad hoc* alliance for agitation into a united electoral front at a time of national anti-Congressism and deep Malayali resentment of Delhi and its fellow-travelling provincial Congress could secure victory. The key was the Muslim League, with its pocket boroughs in southern Malabar and influence elsewhere. It was willing to cooperate on the basis of a minimum programme. The League's position was, as always, dictated by an uninhibitedly instrumental view of politics; business with anyone if the price was right: two portfolios and the rectification of the Muslims' under-representation in government service. Marxist thinking in offering a generous deal was, however, more than opportunist. Younger Muslims were proving responsive to communist influence; and in time a communist Muslim constituency might be built up.

Once the League has been incorporated into the front, agreement on the distribution of candidacies and on the common programme was quite straightforward. In keeping with the spirit of its political line of building the broadest anti-Congress front, the CPI(M) did not overplay its hand despite being the dominant partner. The smaller parties were fairly treated in the seat allocation. Out of 127 constituencies the CPI(M) was awarded 61, the CPI 24, the Samyukta Socialists 23, the League 15 and the RSP, KSP and KTP 10 in all. The minimum programme, which did not preclude separate manifestos, was in fact the maximum programme on which agreement could be reached, omitting references to all divisive issues. Unlike the 1957 CPI manifesto it was heavy with panaceas but light on practicalities. In deference to the League, the preamble did not mention socialism and justified the front entirely in terms of defeating Congress and restoring political stability to the state. Bland the document may have been but it served its purpose well enough in highlighting all those regional problems—poverty, education, employment and centre-state relations—which were the lowest common denominator of anti-Congressism.

The inevitable result was defeat for Congress but its scale in terms of seats masked surprising resilience in terms of percentage vote, not least because, on the eve of the election, rice virtually disappeared from both markets and ration shops. Congress had contested all 133 seats but won only 9 and ignominiously failed to qualify as an opposition party in the assembly. Kerala Congress also slumped badly to 5 seats. Had Congress been united another 20 seats would have been won. In contrast the Front took 113 seats (plus four independents). The CPI(M) improved its position to 52 representatives, the CPI to 19, the SSP to 19 and the League to 14. Clearly the left communists were the dominant partner but—and it had not been their intention—they lacked an overall majority within the front, which was soon to be a source of difficulty.

Congress's share of the vote actually rose from 33 per cent in 1965 to 35 per cent, in part because of a halving of the Kerala Congress vote but the combined Congress vote fell by only 3 per cent which, in all the circumstances—national as well as local—was hardly a poor result. A better test of trends in voter alignment is the longer-term comparison of the share of the poll in 1957 and 1967. Over the decade Congress's own percentage vote fell by 3 per cent—about half the national average—but the total Congress vote had actually risen nearly 5 per cent. When all the qualifications are made, it appears that total Congress support had fallen by some 3 per cent in Malabar and risen by 8 to 9 per cent in Travancore-Cochin. Importantly, this was not because of shifts in Christian support which were maintained at previously high levels but movements in predominantly Hindu areas. Congress was not finished but it was becoming more clearly a Travancore-Cochin party and inevitably therefore more likely to be entangled in the caste and communal politics of the south, the more so, as the party system fragmented into particularistic groupings based on community and constituency. Like the CPI(M) the Congress party in future could only hope to come to power as part of a coalition.

The United Front in Office, 1967-9

The disintegration of the Congress-dominated party system was a national phenomenon. For the communists it was a double challenge: they were themselves split—largely over their attitudes to Congress as an historical force; and they were not faced with a situation in which there was a sizeable non-left, even non-progressive opposition to Congress. In the past 'united fronts' has been more or less synonymous with 'left fronts'; and the question of what to do when reactionary or communal parties might make the difference between Congress victory or defeat had scarcely arisen. In India ideology informs communist thinking but party lines are not formulated in a vacuum. They are intellectual constructions abstracted from developments in a range of individual and widely differing states, informed to some extent in the case of the united and residual CPI by the geopolitical interests of the CPSU. Inevitably provincial (and personal) factors count; and it is difficult to make sense of the actions of either the CPI(M) or the CPI without reference to the interaction of party ideology, state-level political problems and the logic of electoral competition. Clearly it is a fine line which separates the principled pursuit of power from the pursuit of power for its own sake. Mathew Kurian, a CPI(M) theorist, put it well: 'Any political party, however revolutionary, if it understands real politics functioning within the bourgeois system, must play the game of the system, but though sometimes compromise may be necessary, a revolutionary party cannot build its programme on bourgeois methods like horse-trading' (Hardgrave, 1970, p. 1002).

The United Front was a matter of substance for the communists in three states: Andhra, West Bengal and Kerala, the areas where the movement could expect to do well. In Andhra so bitter was the conflict between the CPI(M) and CPI that not even a limited front was achieved; and in a fratricidal contest, the communists ended up with a mere 12 seats in a 186 member assembly. Communism in Andhra never recovered and today a regional party, Telugu Desam, forms the anti-Congress government of the state. In West Bengal a post-election United Front emerged but though it took power, it lasted only months. Only in Kerala was the breakthrough made but, though the ministry lasted thirty months, and passed one momentous piece of legislation on land reform, it proved a disastrous experience for the CPI(M).

A communist-led *left* front presumes a measure of like-mindedness. Some of the partners are further down the socialist path than others but all share a similar orientation. In a united front no such assumptions can be made. For the Kerala non-left participants, the coalition is quite simply a marriage of convenience. The United Front's essential problem rose from such interparty rivalries, exacerbated by the impact on the state of India's economic crisis, in turn provoking conflicts within as well as between parties.

The initial struggle over the allocation of portfolios indicated the shape of things to come. The CPI(M) as the leading partner took the key departments: Chief Minister, Home, Revenue and Law as well as Transport and Harijan Welfare; the CPI was given three potentially important 'nation-building' departments—Agriculture, Electricity and Industry—but their success mainly depended on the goodwill of the Marxist-controlled supervisory departments. The League secured Education and Finance and the remainder were distributed among the minor parties.

The names of the actual ministers were supplied by the individual parties themselves and rubber-stamped by the Chief Minister, which in practice meant some nominees who were unworthy of office either on grounds of integrity or ability. It was inevitable that some parties who had never expected to share in government took their chance to pillage the treasury for the constituency and themselves.

Technically, the ministry was a front not a coalition and machinery had to be established to ensure a measure of collective responsibility and collective discipline. There was, of course, the council of ministers, but the cabinet itself was an inappropriate body for the reconciliation of differences. It was designed for other purposes than general coordination; its members could hardly meet frequently enough or long enough to deal with the press of business; and perhaps most important of all, it excluded the crucial party organizations from discussion. Namboodiripad's solution to the problem was the coordination committee. This was a multi-party liaison committee composed of one representative from each party, normally a key organizational figure such as the party secretary. The Chief Minister presided *ex officio* and the committee was serviced by Azhikodan Raghavan, CPI(M) state secretary. The hope was that the liaison group would link mass party to cabinet, agree broad lines of policy before ministers put detailed proposals to cabinet, and facilitate backstairs bargaining between front parties. After a few months, however, the committee had begun to inflame conflict rather than douse it. Its frequently fraught proceedings were leaked to the press, decisions were flouted and by mid-1969 it had ceased to meet. The ministry's majority was too great; its political spectrum too broad; and it misrepresented the actual balance of power in the cabinet and at the ballot box in its one-party-one-voice membership. The CPI(M) was 'big brother' but in the liaison committee little brothers were tempted to gang up against it and within six months commentators were reporting of a front within the front, initially composed of the CPI, League and SSP.

The formation of an Inner Front chiefly stemmed from the souring of CPI(M)–CPI relations. In West Bengal the collapse of the United Front ministry had been accompanied by mutual communist recriminations. In Kerala there were public disagreements over the handling of the alarming food crisis with the CPI(M) Food Minister in one corner and the CPI Agriculture Minister in the other; and worst of all the CPI(M)'s decision not to support an industrial policy for Kerala promulgated by the CPI Industry Minister and already agreed in cabinet. The CPI was also anxious that the CPI(M) was abusing its ministerial powers to favour its partisan interests beyond an acceptable level. The strains and stresses of everyday politics including the CPI's own need to repair fortunes were magnified by the CPI(M)'s reconceptualization of the meaning of state 'government' by serious differences within the CPI(M) which threatened for a time even that new position.

The CPI(M)'s view of the purpose of participating in state ministries and Namboodiripad's own account of party thinking in 1967 were stamped with the marks of the experience of 1957–9. The party's Programme of People's Democracy argued that such People's Democratic governments gave the revolutionary movement a fillip and could strengthen mass mobilization but did nothing to solve the fundamental economic and political problems of the nation. All they could hope to achieve was to bring some 'immediate relief to the people', which might include agrarian reform and popular participation in state and lower level administration. In April 1967, after the installation of UF governments in Kerala and West Bengal, the CPI(M) Central Committee opined that the new governments should be seen as instruments of struggle rather than agents with real power to give substantial relief. Ambiguously it added that there was 'an ocean of difference between declaring them straight away as instruments of struggle and the direction to strive' so to use them.

Government as 'struggle' might be interpreted in three ways: the use of state patronage to strengthen the party; class struggle both through legislation and agitation against propertied interests; and conflict with central government. The partisan deployment of patronage is a well-established convention in Indian politics; and the communists might well argue that there was a case for redressing the balance; but in a united front there were bound to be conflicts of interest especially when one partner controlled the core departments. Class struggle also led to difficulties. The CPI Industry Minister was accused of anti-labour tendencies because he sought to commit the government to preferential recognition of trade unions 'having constitutions with adequate provisions for maintaining industrial peace'. How else could foreign and domestic investment be encouraged? In 1968 Kerala topped the all-India league table for days lost per thousand workers, through strikes and lockouts totalling 2.5 million man days. CPI(M) Minister Imbichi Bava's astonishing statement that Kerala would not be washed into the sea if the giant hydro electric scheme at Idikki was not finished was the kind of comment calculated to alienate the floating vote of the towns which had helped to return the UF in 1967. Agitation against the Central Government raised fewer problems but even here the front partners suspected that they were being used by the CPI(M) for its own ends.

The slogan 'agitation and administration' which came to be used by the CPI(M) to epitomize its line originated in a centre-state context as the CPI(M) riposte to the Congress President's bluntly indiscreet comment that the Namboodiripad ministry would be thrown out if necessary. The choice of V. Viswanathan as governor of Kerala, a known anti-communist, hardly allayed Marxist fears. The CPI(M)'s post-election *The New Situation and the Party's Tasks* (1967) spoke of 'the crisis that has gripped the capitalist path of development', projecting itself into 'the political superstructure ... of the Indian Union' (1967, p. 70); the Kerala High Court reprimanded the Chief Minister for pursuing a policy—agitation and administration—which was contrary to law and was deliberately designed to foment violence in the state; and in 1970 the Indian Supreme Court found Namboodiripad guilty of contempt of court for having asserted that judges were guided by class hatred, class interests and class prejudices (Nossiter, 1982, p. 260, n. 15). Whether tongue in cheek or not, the Supreme Court also held that the defendant's interpretation of Marx, Engels and Lenin was erroneous; the founding fathers were acquitted. Whatever the theoretical consistency of the dialectic of agitation and administration and its value in beating off the challenge from the far left, Govindan Nair of the CPI was right in warning that the contradictions would destroy the ministry (Namboodiripad, 1968, p. 7). To the partners in the front, agitation appeared designed to assert one party's hegemony while some in the electorate were beginning to seek relief from the unleashing of discontent.

Growing divisions within CPI(M) ranks made the job of convincing the public of the necessity for simultaneous agitation and administration that much more difficult. During the election campaign there had been evidence of conflict in the CPI(M). Wallposters appeared signed by the Kerala Red Guard denouncing Namboodiripad as an agent of the bourgeoisie, rich peasants and decadent reactionaries and parallel party centres began to form in different parts of the state. The CPC commenced to broadcast and print vitriolic denunciations of the Kerala (and West Bengal) ministries and in August mounted a virulent personal attack on Namboodiripad himself. In Cannanore, the original heartland of communism in Malabar, the Left Extremists, or Ultras as they were usually known in Kerala, gained control of the district party and by the beginning of 1968 it was claimed that only three of the nine district committees were securely in official CPI(M) hands. Meanwhile in Andhra the state plenum had rejected the national leadership's draft ideological programme for the forthcoming national plenum and in West Bengal (wisely) no state plenum took place. The fate of Kerala and its ministry was clearly critical.

Soon after the election Namboodiripad had resigned as state party secretary to be replaced by one of the few ranking Muslim cadres, Imbichi Bava. Bava proved soft on the Ultras and in any case lacked the personal or party stature to handle the situation. In 1968 backed by the national leadership, Namboodiripad, A. K. Gopalan and C. H. Kanaran, the Marxist heavyweights of Kerala, produced a package of organizational measures to combat the threat of a takeover. A. K. Gopalan was to take over as party secretary; the state committee was to be halved in size to twenty-four members; and the national leadership was to produce a slate of nominations to the restructured body. Informed estimates reported that the new committee contained six Ultras and five waiverers. The Kerala state plenum overwhelmingly endorsed the draft ideological resolution. In the event it was estimated that 5 per cent of CPI(M) membership left to join the Ultras' party of Communist Revolutionaries; and by February 1969 five CPI(M) MLAs had either resigned or been expelled from the party. In party terms Namboodiripad's position had been transformed by early 1969. Kerala was the one major CPI(M) unit which could be guaranteed to follow the national leadership's line. The United Front ministry had survived despite premature obituaries in the press. The inter-party and intra-party disputes had, however, impaired the government's effectiveness, undermined its public standing and now threatened its existence at a time when the land reform bill was some months from completing its legislative stages.

The Front's growing weakness was reflected in a marked deterioration in law and order and in burgeoning charges of corruption. The continuing economic crisis, party clashes at local level and the police force's uncertainty as to what role it was expected to play under a CPI(M) Home Minister contributed to a sharp rise in registered criminal cases: 46 per cent up between 1966 and 1969 and 23 per cent up between 1967 and 1969. Murders has risen from 247 in 1966 to 297 in 1967 and reached 390 in 1969, few of which were perpetrated by Naxalites. Another complaint against the ministry was that it tolerated a novel and nasty form of industrial agitation, the *gherao*. This involved surrounding the manager (and often the college principal) till the demands were conceded. In fact Namboodiripad issued a formal directive in June 1967 outlawing the practice. The Labour Minister (of the Kerala Socialist Party), however, disagreed. As in 1957-9 there were widespread allegations that communists interfered with the administration of law and order. From late 1968 Naxalism reached Kerala but though there was fear as individuals received intimidatory communications—often for no obvious political reason—only sixteen deaths in the late 1960s can properly be attributed to Naxalites. As quasi-political violence became commoner both the Opposition and the CPI(M) established volunteer vigilante corps but apart from the Jana Sangh RSS their importance can be wildly exaggerated.

It was the issue of corruption not, as in 1959, law and order which was the focus of party conflict and the immediate cause of the ministry's collapse. The UF election manifesto had promised that corrupt legislators would be brought to book and anti-corruption measures would be implemented on as extensive a scale as was possible for a state government. The government was, however, widely regarded as corrupt and specific allegations were made in the assembly against every single minister. Whatever the merits of the individual charges, there was no doubt that ministers by-passed many of the proper routines. One of the most widely criticized deviations was the irregular appointment of some 200 alleged CPI(M) supporters to posts in the state transport corporation by the CPI(M) Transport Minister, Imbichi Bava.

One of the curious features of Indian public life is that the machinery for the investigation of allegations of corruption is so limited and so unwieldy: namely, the government's own Vigilance Department and recourse to the Commissions of Enquiries Act. The UF ministry did seek to strengthen the provision but differences over the detail of the legislation between the CPI(M) and CPI delayed its introduction into the assembly and it was still in committee when the ministry fell. In any case since it excluded the prime suspects from its provisions—ministers and MLAs—it was marginal to the problem.

In contrast to the situation in 1959 the ministry collapsed from within. There was no liberation struggle; an insignificant opposition in the assembly; and a central government which was happy to stand aloof as the UF tore itself to pieces. In April 1969 the CPI presented the CPI(M) with a thirteen-point ultimatum on behalf of the Inner Front, of which the essence was the charge that 'only the CPI(M) rules . . . all others have either to fall in line or get out' (Menon, 1969, pp. 51-4). Serving three months notice, the CPI warned that if the CPI(M) did not mend its ways, it would have to reconsider its participation in the government. As the Muslim League had been the key to the formation of a winning electoral coalition, so it was the key to the continuance of the ministry. The CPI(M)'s hope that concessions to the League would isolate the CPI proved false. The League took the bait—a Muslim majority district in Malappuram and a new university at Calicut—and spat out the hook. Its leader, Bafaki Thangal, was both utterly hostile to communism and scheming. The Inner Front already had reason to believe that if the ministry fell, Congress might support an alternative; and the League's greatest aim was recognition by Congress as a legitimate non-communal party.

The occasion—not the cause—of the ministry's resignation was the demand for an inquiry into corruption charges against CPI(M) ministers. Namboodiripad declined and challenged the Inner Front to move a motion of no confidence. It was carried and Namboodiripad resigned. His calculation that the Governor would impose presidential rule, however, proved unfounded; and the CPI leader, Achutha Menon, was invited to form a minority ministry made up of the League, Indian Socialist Party and Kerala Congress (hitherto an opposition party), supported by the RSP and implicitly by Congress. It was an initiative which was to have far-reaching consequences: ministerial stability; the exclusion of the CPI(M) from power for a decade; and the institutionalization of programmatic 'socialist' government. Namboodiripad's UF Ministry had however one great achievement to its credit: the definitive Kerala land reform. The first communist ministry's act had been effectively struck down in the courts; and in 1963 it had been replaced by an act of a fundamentally different character. Whereas the earlier legislation rested on a presumption in favour of the cultivator, the Congress-sponsored measure reversed the onus of proof. It was up to the tenant to apply to purchase the landlord's rights through the agency of the Land Tribunal. By means of other changes of detail the 1963 act shifted the balance towards the existing vested interests and halved the estimated surplus of land available for redistribution.

In their election manifesto the UF partners had committed themselves to the amendment of the act in favour of tenants, small landlords without alternative means of subsistence and hutment dwellers. In effect the result was virtually a new piece of legislation. The central features of the measure were the abolition of landlordism by compulsorily vesting proprietorial rights in the government and their subsequent assignment to the actual cultivators; the transfer of the burden of proof in disputed cases from tenant to landlord; the widening of the definition of tenancy to include those with no title, to several kinds of sharecroppers and to the victims of legal subterfuge by simply 'deeming' them to be tenants. Hutment dwellers were granted security of tenure; rent arrears were reduced to one year and future annual rent fixed at as little as two days' wages. The right to resume land was heavily circumscribed and was to lapse six months after vesting date. Compensation was fixed at levels which were admittedly expropriatory; and it was to be paid in instalments to the government who then paid the landlord. Default did not however prejudice the former tenant's rights. Hutment dwellers were granted the right to purchase their plots at one-quarter the market value, half to be paid by the government, and the remainder in twelve annual instalments. The ceilings on land-holding were the lowest in the sub-continent. For a family with three minor children the maximum was twenty acres; and the range of exemptions radically pruned. *Kayal* land was brought into the net as well as pepper, arecanut, cashew and coconut plantations.

The bill was not actually introduced into the assembly until August 1968 and did not complete its progress till days before the ministry fell. The slow pace of drafting was partly a result of the determination to make the legislation absolutely watertight and partly that the CPI(M) minister concerned, Mrs Gouri, first had to cope with the food crisis and then suffered a heart attack. The explanation of the delayed passage through the assembly is more controversial. The UF partners blamed it on the centre's unhelpfulness while Congress and Kerala Congress attributed it to the reservations of the League, whose leaders were also significant landlords.

Land reform was one of the two specific measures of 'immediate relief to the people' contained in the CPI(M)'s *Programme of People's Democracy*. No such progress was made with the other—increasing popular participation in administration. The one major bill to extend considerably greater powers to the *panchayats* failed to reach the statute book. Scarcely any party wanted to give more power to the people whatever their rhetoric; and shifts in public opinion from mid-1968 rendered the CPI(M) still less enthusiastic since in new elections it stood to lose its existing domination of *panchayat* boards. The party of democratic centralism was as ambivalent as its bourgeois rivals towards the devolution of power downwards.

7 National Democracy: CPI and Congress, 1969-79

The year 1969 saw a dramatic turnaround in the state's politics for Kerala; ministerial stability; for the CPI, an entirely unexpected come-back; for the CPI(M), an unanticipated decade in the wilderness; and for Congress, its first collaboration in government with communists. In the aftermath of the communist split the tactical lines of the CPI and CPI(M) had become increasingly differentiated. Nationally, the CPI's line was the united front from above and its slogan the establishment of a National Democratic Front. In 1964 the party had argued that 'no National Democratic Front would be real unless the vast mass following of the Congress and the progressive sections of the Congress at various levels take their place in it' (CPI, 1965, p. 43). The CPI's historic mission was to forge this alliance. In 1969 Mrs Gandhi, fighting the old guard in Congress, supported the communist-backed candidate for the Indian presidency against her party's official nominee. The outsider, V. V. Giri, one time labour leader and during the early 1960s a popular Governor of Kerala, won. Shortly afterwards Mrs Gandhi nationalized India's largest domestic banks. Could the National Democratic Front become a reality?

In 1968 the CPI Central Executive had agreed to allow state units flexibility in interpreting the party line in the light of the objective possibilities in each state. In West Bengal the CPI adopted a relatively militant stance; in Kerala the party maximized the possibilities of peaceful transition. After all in any agitation in Kerala the CPI(M) was the easy victor. CPI ministers had been conspicuous in their constructive approach to their task and adamant that their failures were the fault of the big brotherly tendencies of the CPI(M). The decision to form a Mini Front in 1969 was approved by the national leadership but it was a still state-level initiative. Kerala offered the opportunity to experiment with national democracy without a formal commitment to sharing power with Congress. The Chief Minister declared that he would resign rather than be dependent on Congress votes but it was the benevolent neutrality of the New (Indira) Congress which sustained the minority government.

The CPI(M) regarded the CPI's position as self-delusion. India's economic problems had matured to the stage of political crisis. The Congress split in 1969 and Mrs Gandhi's leftist sloganizing was merely a manœuvre by the country's ruling class. At a practical level the CPI(M) had strong reasons to seek to bring down the Kerala government. There was a real danger that the CPI(M) would be excluded from the benefits of implementing the hard-won agrarian reform act. The CPI, though modestly claiming only to be fulfilling the 1967 election manifesto and restoring law, order and administrative impartiality, was equally determined to destroy the CPI(M)'s hegemony on the left of Kerala politics.

In the assembly and on the streets battle royal commenced. Obligingly the central government expedited the presidential approval of the agrarian reform bill which became law on 1 January 1970. By a series of parliamentary strategems the Mini Front survived until on 2 April Achutha Menon coolly announced that the Governor had granted him a dissolution, and that he would remain in office until the election. The former gold medallist in law had relied on British precedents which no one had thought obtained in India.

Although public opinion was shifting towards the Mini Front, there was still no chance of defeating the CPI(M) without some kind of deal with New Congress. Neither the CPI nor the RSP was yet ready for a formal alliance. Mrs Gandhi was adamant that there must be an electoral understanding. The CPI(M) must be defeated at all costs; and New Congress's progressive credentials demonstrated in what was the first Indian election after the Congress split. In turn the CPI(M)'s assessment of New Congress as the main political expression of bourgeois control of India led it to an arrangement with Old Congress and its right-wing allies, the Democratic Front.

Despite the choice of twenty-two parties, the only parties that really counted were the CPI(M) and New Congress. The Mini Front won 36 of the 133 seats—the CPI 16 and the Muslim League 11; the CPI(M)-led People's Democratic Front took 41; the CPI(M) alone 28 seats; but New Congress, clearly emerging as the dominant wing of Congress in Kerala, won 32 seats and the rightist Democratic Front 15. As the electoral arrangements were highly complex, percentage votes do not reveal much. The CPI(M)'s 23 per cent (from seventy-two contests) was not a sign that it was losing its mass base (Nossiter, 1982, p. 224). It is also clear that New Congress was heir to virtually all Congress support in Kerala and especially among youth and labour.

Achutha Menon's second ministry—four CPI ministers, two from the Muslim League, two RSP and one from the PSP—took office on 4 October 1970. National democracy was recognized by the inclusion of four New Congress representatives in the nine-member co-ordination committee; and by what Achutha Menon called a 'humble attempt to reconstruct the state and make a modern Kerala' (*Hindu*, 5 October 1970). In contrast to the agitation and administration philosophy of the CPI(M) 'textbook revolutionaries' (*Link*, 12 July 1970).

The 1971 Lok Sabha elections were a further stage in the development of the special relationship between Congress and the CPI. While ruling out national alliances, Mrs Gandhi encouraged agreements at state level; and in Kerala the Mini Front divided seats not only with New Congress but with the rightist Kerala Congress. The CPI(M) retained only two of its nine parliamentary seats but it did secure 43 per cent of the poll from eleven contests. The most important feature of the parliamentary battle, however, was the success of Youth Congress candidates. Congress was being rejuvenated both literally and figuratively.

In the wake of the general election a joint meeting of the Congress MLAs and the KPCC agreed to give the party's central Parliamentary Board—often known as High Command—freedom to decide when the time was ripe to request an invitation to join the Mini Front government. Shortly after the signing of the Indo-Soviet Defence Treaty in August 1971, the Mini Front tendered the invitation of its own volition. After some hard bargaining the expansion of the government into a Maxi Front was agreed on 13 September: the cabinet increased from nine to thirteen, with the Mini Front partners holding eight ministries to the New Congress's five. Congress abandoned its claim to a post of Deputy Chief Ministership but took the Home portfolio. The senior partners in the Mini Front were well content. They had ensured the ministry's long-term future. For a modest price they had established an all-India precedent: New Congress, by joining them in government, had signalled an end to their political untouchability. There was just one problem. Youth Congress, particularly its volatile student wing, had declined to join. Instead, its leader, the increasingly powerful A. K. Antony, became convenor of the co-ordination committee. Youth Congress was not to be shackled by ministerial responsibility. The Marxists were happy that the CPI and Congress had at last consummated their union. By sustained agitation on the mass front and pressure in the Assembly, they hoped to discredit National Democracy thoroughly and so the CPI and Indira Congress. 'The issue ... today', Namboodiripad asserted, 'is not Government but development of the people's struggle for the problems they are facing' (*Hindustan Times*, 13 October 1971). The CPI(M) was not the prime mover in all the agitation which affected and inflicted Kerala in the next thirty-three months prior to the 1975 Emergency. Indeed it behaved with restraint on crucial questions. Nor did it manufacture strikes and demonstrations out of nothing. Nevertheless it endeavoured to orchestrate popular struggle consistently with its tactical line.

For the first year, the Maxi Front ministry coped adequately with the rising tide of agitation if at some cost in terms of time, energy and, through pay settlements, money to secure adequate remuneration for those in work rather than the creation of jobs for those without it. Thereafter national and local developments conspired to give the ministry the roughest possible ride; and the survival of the government was a tribute to the considerable political skills of the CPI Chief Minister.

From 1971-2 onwards the Indian economy rapidly deteriorated: the monsoons were erratic and harvests poor; the Bangladesh war (1971) and the oil price increase (1973) intensified inflationary pressures; and the increase in the cost of living far outstripped the rise in incomes. In Kerala the problem was accentuated by the state's chronic food deficit and falling demand for some of its cash crops. By 1973 the economic situation was desperate. The general index of prices rose by almost a quarter. Agricultural production slumped badly and industrial growth continued to decline. By July and August rice could not be bought at any price and the coastal areas were officially designated famine zones. Inflation provoked a rash of strikes but since the state was living on overdraft there was little option but to resist the workers' demands. The state was paralysed by a transport strike and a leading minister for the first time spoke of a political crisis which was only resolved by an ultimatum to the CPI and Congress unions to meet the government half-way. The ministerialists rarely controlled their labour and mass fronts. The Youth Congress convenor of the co—ordination committee had resigned his post; CPI members were picketing state offices; and the Congress union federation, INTUC, was preparing to censure its own ministry. Unsurprisingly, within the ministry there were tensions and conflicts, notably between the League and Congress; and after the death of the League strong man, Bafaki Thangal, in January 1973 the prospect of a split within the hitherto monolithic League. Forecasts of the 1974 food situation in Kerala were as bleak as the economic prognosis generally and all the opposition parties met in January to embark on a programme of comprehensive agitation.

The Maxi Front had a record of constructive legislation, especially the Agricultural Workers Act and the several University bills, but the ministry had had little chance to make much progress on the basic economic issues. Increasingly, it was driven to punitive action to contain popular discontent. In August 1974, the CPI(M) launched a new 'liberation struggle', a phrase which echoed not only demonstrations against the first communist government in 1959 but also the movement led by Jayprakash Narayanan, the veteran Gandhian, against the corrupt and incompetent Congress governments of Bihar and Gujarat earlier in 1974. Finally, on the eve of the annual budget session in February 1975 the CPI(M) announced that the five opposition parties would boycott the assembly altogether. The following month the ministry technically lost its overall majority in the assembly when the League finally split.

With elections due by September the ministry was teetering and the CPI more and more divided on the merits of the alliance with Congress. After initial gestures Mrs Gandhi had proved singularly unprogressive. A coterie of communist sympathizers in her inner councils had fallen from favour; she had dealt summarily with a CPI-led national rail strike in the autumn of 1974; and the CPI found itself identified with an exceptionally unpopular national government. In Kerala itself Congress was deeply divided between the Youth Congress organization and the ministerial elders and tormented by a resurgence of communalism within and without the party.

The Emergency, 1975-7

The government was saved by the declaration of a national state of emergency in June 1975. Elections were postponed. No threat to security actually existed in Kerala, yet hundreds of party activitists from the CPI(M) and Socialist Party were detained. By and large it was the middle-rank cadres who were removed from circulation. The government did not want to make a martyr out of Namboodiripad. As far as the CPI(M) was concerned it was the fulfilment of their expectations. The economic crisis had brought about political crisis. Indeed the political demands outlined in the party's 1972 9th Congress were remarkably prescient in the light of the Emergency three years later: changes in the constitution to prevent its misuse by the ruling party, avert the danger of one party dictatorship and to guarantee civil liberties.

Reaction in Kerala was muted. There was heavy rain and flooding; the opposition was taken by surprise; and the middle classes, at least, were delighted at the prospect of a holiday from agitation. In governing circles there were more mixed feelings. The election was averted but increased central intervention was unwelcome while the CPI and the other junior partners presumed Congress would be more assertive in the coalition. For the Chief Minister the Emergency offered the opportunity to press ahead with constructive measures but also the real danger that the senior Congress minister, Karunakaran, in charge of the Home portfolio, would become *de facto* the real Chief Minister.

In one important sense the declaration of Emergency changed nothing in

Kerala. The political problem was still how to construct a coalition capable of beating off the CPI(M)'s challenge to which the key was the rebel Kerala Congress, loosely aligned with the CPI(M) since 1970.

For the Marxists the alliance was mildly embarrassing but not inconsistent with its stance that 'my enemy's enemy is my friend'; but for the CPI matters were more awkward. Kerala Congress, backed by sections of the Christian Church, was 'communal' and, compared with Indira Congress, a decidedly reactionary plantation interest. However, since the League was an honorary member of the national bourgeoisie, there was no real reason why Kerala Congress should not be accorded the same status. The fundamental difficulty lay in fact with the youth wing of Congress, which unlike its counterpart in north India, was relatively progressive and had waged a long-running battle with a party that was a front for the hated Christian college proprietors. Youth Congress, however, was now no more capable than the CPI(M) of conducting agitation and many of its educational demands had been conceded shortly before the Emergency began. Thus on 26 December 1975 Kerala Congress joined the ministry, though factionalism within KC caused continuing difficulties. Considering the circumstances, the Kerala Congress leadership played its hand skilfully: it gained two ministries, Finance from Congress, and Transport from the CPI, the vacant Speakership of the Assembly, and the promise of twenty-five good candidacies at the next election. The finance portfolio was a great coup. It was not only a ministry which could intervene in virtually any other's affairs but, no less important, it could insulate the interests that paid for KC from taxation.

Despite the cessation of mass politics for the duration of the Emergency, ministerial manœuvring continued. The ruling front as a whole took the opportunity to repair its fortunes in a steadily improving economic and food situation; and with Youth Congress under wraps and the CPI(M) under lock and key the Congress elders, led by Karunakaran, re-established their command over the Congress party. There was growing resentment at the burgeoning power of the senior Congress chief, well placed as Home Minister to hire and fire. A tough political operator at any time, he was a man to avoid in an Emergency. Without the pressure to build broad-based mass constituencies, politics settled back into communal channels. Karunakaran was a Nair; his Youth Congress rivals disproportionately Ezhavas and Latin Catholics.

Mrs Gandhi's announcement of parliamentary elections in March 1977 was swiftly followed by the news that Kerala would hold its delayed assembly elections simultaneously. The coincidence of elections enabled a convenient arrangement to be concluded. It was the Lok Sabha result which mattered most in Delhi and Congress was given a preponderance of candidacies in that election in exchange for a lion's share for the partners in the Assembly contest. Ranged against the powerful Ruling Front was a seven-party opposition alliance led by the CPI(M). The partners—Janata (in Kerala a mixture of long-time socialists and old Congressmen), the Congress Radicals (expelled in 1973), the Opposition Muslim League, the RSP National, the KSP and the Kerala Congress (Pillai) faction were an ill-assorted bunch and united only in their hostility to Mrs Gandhi. The opposition campaign was in fact fought almost entirely on the issue of liberty versus dictatorship. The Ruling Front, after so long in government, fought on the basis of its record— but a record which antedated the Emergency: land reform housing for the poor, the agricultural workers act, and above all stability and steady progress. The guidelines for the future were simply more of the same plus promises directed at key interests and minorities. In this vein the (privileged) minority, the high caste Nairs, were placated with the granting of Ruling Front tickets to six members of its (Nair) National Democratic Party.

Commentators, perhaps influenced by the unpopularity of the Emergency nationally, expected a close contest. In fact the Ruling Front won handsomely with 53 per cent of the vote and 111 of the 140 seats in the Assembly elections and a clean sweep in the parliamentary poll. The CPI(M) was reduced to seventeen seats in the assembly but fighting only sixty-eight constituencies it still managed 22 per cent of the vote, just 1 per cent less than in 1970. In the circumstances it was not a bad performance overall but there was alarm in the party at the major setbacks in two of its three historic heartlands, Palghat and Alleppey.

The Ruling Front's success can be explained partly by reference to trends in southern India as a whole where the Janata Wave which brought the first non-Congress government to power nationally had little effect. The worst excesses of the Emergency—forcible sterilization, brutal slum clearance and the like—had been little evident in the South. The Chief Minister of Kerala and A. K. Antony, the state Youth Congress leader, had effectively vetoed even a visit from Sanjay Gandhi to Kerala. No less important, however, were state-level factors. The Ruling Front constituted the most powerful combination of communal and sectional interests ever put together in Kerala. Politicized Kerala may be by Indian standards, but allegiance to community leaders who perform individual services in times of need remains strong. Nor can it be denied that the ministry was again popular. Land reform had been implemented; houses had been provided for the homeless; a start had been made on ensuring a fair deal for the agricultural labourers; prices were under control; and the availability of food was for once not an electoral issue. It may well be that the CPI(M)'s failures in Palghat and Alleppey could be attributed to the ministry's erosion of rural support for the CPI(M) through this package of progressive measures. That said, we should not forget that the CPI(M) with 2 million out of 8.8 million votes was the largest single party in the election.

Despite and because of the scale of the victory, the Ruling Front quickly ran into trouble. The victors fell out over the distribution of the spoils—the portfolios—particularly now that Achutha Menon, the elder statesman, had retired. The non-Congress partners actually enjoyed a majority in the assembly without Congress support. What had happened during the Emergency became more widely known, increasing reservations in the CPI and Youth Congress. In Kerala, this meant the Rajan affair. Within days of the new ministry taking office Karunakaran, the new Congress Chief Minister and erstwhile Home Minister, was accused of complicity in the fate of an unfortunate young student, P. Rajan, who was believed to have died under torture during the Emergency. Karunakaran was, of course, then responsible for the conduct of the police. Youth Congress, deeply hostile to Karunakaran, led the attack, and on the advice of Congress High Command, he resigned to be replaced by the YC leader, A. K. Antony.

After nearly a decade of ministerial stability, Kerala now reverted to its earlier pattern. Antony, who had sided with the anti-Gandhi official Congress when Congress split after the post-mortem on the Emergency, resigned as Chief Minister in October 1978 because his party declined to contest parliamentary by-elections against Mrs Gandhi's candidates. P. K. Vasudevan Nair of the CPI took over only to be a casualty a year later of the CPI's national reappraisal of Mrs Gandhi when the CPI withdrew from the ministry. The Governor then made a final effort to patch up an alternative cabinet but this three-man ministry lasted only forty days and on 1 December 1979 Kerala came under presidential rule.

8 Left and Democratic Fronts

The state's elections which the CPI(M)-led Left and Democratic Front won were held in January 1980 at the same time as the seventh parliamentary elections, when Mrs Gandhi triumphantly returned to power. The temptation to contrast the two has to be resisted however. For all the theoretical discussions of national and left democratic fronts during the 1970s, what the Kerala assembly election exemplified was how far communist victory at the polls had come to depend on the composition of electoral coalitions. Of the votes cast 94 per cent went to the LDF or its rival, the Congress-led UDF. Besides the three Marxist parties, CPI(M), CPI and the maverick RSP, the LDF included the Mani and Pillai factions of the Kerala Congress and the rebel All-India Muslim League, none of which qualified for the labels 'democratic' or 'left' in communist terms, while the Congress (Urs) might be both but was to prove a vacillitating ally.

The UDF was an even more heterogeneous collection: the official Indian Union Muslim League, a third faction of Kerala Congress, Janata, the Praja Socialist Party and two quasi-communal parties the (Nair) National Democratic Party and the (Ezhava) Socialist Revolutionary Party.

In terms of the number and distribution of potential votes, the LDF was the more powerful grouping. For the first time since 1967 the Marxist parties' support was pooled which made victory in several areas of Travancore-Cochin highly likely. Congress (Urs)—largely the former Youth Congress—both divided the Congress vote and gave the CPI(M) access to the votes of radicalized young people. Scarcely less important was the contribution of the Mani faction of Kerala Congress which represented many of the Christian and Nair farmers in central Kerala.

The CPI(M)'s motives in building a winning coalition were mixed. The party wanted to win the election, perhaps at some cost in doctrinal purity, but not at any cost. Very broadly speaking, the alliances reflected a left-right split. The CPI(M)'s realignments took account of the party line nationally, the inclinations of the party locally, and shifting trends in voter opinion as registered in by-elections and local elections. Namboodiripad had consistently advocated isolating Indira Congress; and the CPI(M) had never once allied itself with mainstream Congress. As the party system had fragmented, the CPI(M)'s unity ensured its continued role in state politics despite the slow contraction of its electoral base.

Overall the LDF won 93 of the 140 seats in the assembly and 50 per cent of the vote. The UDF took 46 seats and 44 per cent of the vote. The CPI(M)'s performance—35 seats from 50 contests—cannot be taken too literally as a measure of its standing. The Marxists fought some hopeless seats and stood down elsewhere in the interests of the alliance as a whole. However, the fact that the CPI(M) did not seek hegemony in terms of winnable seats, in contrast to West Bengal, reflects its relative weakness. Its margin of victory was reduced throughout the state. The outcome in Palghat was particularly disappointing. Taken together with the 1977 and 1980 election results in Palghat and the generally poor turnouts by Kerala standards in both the state and national polls, it seemed that the Marxists were still losing ground.

Three factors may explain this: first the alienation of the middle and rich peasantry. Land reform had tended to make 'landlords' of former tenants who were increasingly locked in conflict with the agricultural labourers, bidding, with CPI(M) support, for better wages at the expense of farmers' hitherto underprivileged families. The campaign itself was less than full-blooded, indicating reservations among the cadre at the nature of the company they were keeping. The party's 1982 Congress report points out that the (prized) characterization of the alliance as a Left and Democratic Front was given by 'a consensus of allied parties' and did not reflect any necessary fit with the concept as visualized in the CPI(M) programme. In the party's official thinking it was akin to the United Front formed with Bangla Congress and others in West Bengal in 1967-8.

The composition of the ministry precluded bold initiatives. The six parties had little in common. The CPI(M) Chief Minister, E. K. Nayanar, though a fine comrade with a long record of sacrifice, was not of the stature of Achutha Menon, E. M. S. Namboodiripad, or—in West Bengal—Jyoti Basu. He had been State Secretary since 1972, edited the party organ, *Deshabhimani*, and had sat in the Lok Sabha as well as the Kerala Assembly but he had never held ministerial office nor established real ascendancy in the state unit. Of the three other CPI(M) ministers only one, the Home Minister T. K. Ramakrishnan, held senior office. With a rugged union career he was unlikely to be an emollient influence. Mrs Gouri, the ablest and most experienced of the CPI(M) team, was relegated to Agriculture and Social Welfare. The strong man in the ministry was K. C. Mani of the Kerala Congress who was powerfully placed as Minister of Finance and Law. Apart from the establishment of district councils as a non-controversial act of administrative decentralization, the work of the LDF ministry centred on a series of welfare and social security measures for the least well off, increased emoluments for state employees, and a 'new' police policy—one reminiscent of the 1957-9 communist government. The social advances included improvements to, and extensions of the food distribution system, already the best in the country. Despite price rises in the market, this kept the rationed price within bounds and ensured adequate and cheap supplies of other essentials.

Two initiatives attracted the hostile attention of the Congress-led opposition who charged the ministry with looting the Treasury: pensions for farm labourers and unemployment assistance. Pensions were given to agricultural workers over the age of 60 (whose annual income was below Rs 500) at the rate of Rs 45 ($4.5 per month). Unfortunately, the initial applications were inadequately scrutinized and verification in the second year (1981–2) showed that 41 per cent of those to whom pensions had been sanctioned were actually ineligible. It was expected that some 300,000 retired workers would benefit by 1983 at a cost of Rs 10 million ($1 million). Equally important as an act of social justice was unemployment assistance inaugurated in 1980–1 at the rate of Rs 50 per month. The unemployed qualified if they had been registered as unemployed for three years and had an annual family income of less than Rs 4,000 ($400). Nearly a quarter of a million applications were sanctioned in the first year alone. After the LDF fell from power, the scheme was modified to apply only to the young and educated unemployed and was coupled with a grant-aided self-employment scheme. Whatever the cost to the Treasury, and the possibility of partial administration, such schemes are unlikely to be reversed by future administrations.

Rather more controversial was the police policy of neutrality as between labour and capital. The incidence of strikes escalated and in February 1981 the government bowed to the demand of public employees—largely belonging to unions organized by the ruling parties—for the abandonment of the 'no work, no pay' system introduced by Achutha Menon's governments in 1973. There was now no personal cost to strike action by workers in the government sector. In the event, the issue came to a head over the conduct of the headload workers, the universal porters of India. Many were organized by the CPI(M). Historically an urban underclass, the headload workers felt still more estranged by the task of carrying the newly won consumer spoils of wealthy Gulf workers. The CPI(M) Home Minister, T. K. Ramakrishnan, directed the police not to intervene when the porters massively increased their charges and enforced a monopoly with strong-arm tactics. The reaction of the 20 per cent of the population who in income might be termed 'middle-class' was intense. 'Law and order', as in 1959 and 1969, was again the stick with which to beat the Marxists.

It was the alleged failure of the CPI(M) Home Minister to maintain law and order which was the ostensible cause of the collapse of the ministry. In October 1981 first the twenty-two-member Congress (Urs) and then the nine-member Kerala Congress (Mani) withdrew from the front. Clashes between rival party supporters had become common although most of the deaths occurred in affrays between CPI(M) followers and Hindu (RSS) extremists. The CPI(M) was also accused of partisanship in the use of government machinery, favouring CPI(M) trade unions and 'big brotherly conduct' towards its front partners. It was a situation that Indira Congress was happy to exploit by indicating that the door was open, if Congress (Urs) and Kerala Congress cared to walk through it.

On 26 October Nayanar tendered his resignation. After two months of presidential rule, K. Karunakaran, who had been Chief Minister in 1977 before the Rajan affair broke, again took office. His six-party ministry survived only weeks despite frantic manœuvring before Kerala again went to the polls in 1982.

The battle was still between the LDF and UDF but with a switch of former LDF members to the UDF. Congress (Urs) had split. The majority—Congress (Antony)—changed sides and the rump—Congress (S)—stayed with the LDF. Kerala Congress (Mani) merged with KC (Pillai) to join the UDF; and a section of the Revolutionary Socialists also moved over. How fragmented the party system had become is reflected in the fact that the UDF contained eleven parties and the LDF seven. On a 73 per cent poll, and with generous financial and other support from Mrs Gandhi, the UDF won a working majority with 77 out of 140 seats but in terms of votes cast, it scraped home by just 100,000 votes, 1 per cent of the total. The CPI(M) was the biggest single party with 1.8 million votes (from fifty-one contests) but this represented only 19 per cent of the poll. Independents backing the party brought the total up to 21.6 per cent; and if the CPI and the official RSP are included the putative Marxist vote might amount to 30 per cent. The resulting ministry was the first prolonged ministry since 1964 to include no communists.

Even more dispiriting for the CPI(M) and the LDF was the outcome of the 1984 Lok Sabha election in the wake of Mrs Gandhi's assassination. In Tripura, the CPI(M) retained both its seats. In West Bengal there were some setbacks but the Left Front remained the largest force. Only in Kerala did the Left haemorrhage. The UDF won seventeen of the state's twenty seats and, with a little more careful planning and execution, could have swept the board. Of the twelve seats won by the LDF in the general election of 1980, six had been held by the CPI(M). In 1984 the party lost all its sitting members and it gained one seat from Kerala Congress (Mani). The CPI(M)'s losses included a Politburo member, and the widow of the legendary Kerala peasant leader, A. K. Gopalan. The CPI lost all its four seats, including one which it had held ever since 1957. In a state with a deserved reputation for political volatility, governments are supposed to lose support not gain it. Yet the gap between the LDF and the UDF had grown in nineteen months from 100,000 votes to 1 million; and the state, normally at variance with the country as a whole, had at last fallen into line with national trends. State elections were not to be held 'tomorrow' (in the language of the pollsters) but, on the basis of the assembly segment declarations in the parliamentary poll, the ruling UDF's tally of seats would hypothetically have risen from 77 to 113 out of 140.

Assessing the Kerala result in the CPI(M) weekly, *People's Democracy* (20 January 1985), E. M. S. Namboodiripad argued that while the sympathy vote for Rajiv Gandhi and the surge of national feeling played a part in the LDF débâcle the unique political situation developing in the state was equally important. The evidence does suggest that the national factor was powerful. The electorate had risen by 6 per cent since 1980 but turnout increased by 14 per cent. Women outpolled men in many constituencies and young people, including first-time voters, often preponderated over older voters. More persuasive still is the outcome of three assembly by-elections held only a month after the parliamentary election. With high turnouts the LDF won all three with varying degrees of ease whereas on the disaggregated assembly segment voting in December they would have lost.

The Karunakaran Ministry of 1982 to 1987, made up of nineteen cabinet ministers, drawn from seven parties and two independents, is perhaps the most extraordinary in Kerala's tortuous political history. From its inception it was riven with dissension, infected by communalism, and widely accused of venality. It skidded, not merely slipped, on as many banana skins as there are varieties of this prolific fruit in Kerala. That it survived to full term says as much about the CPI(M)'s determination to see it hung with adequate electoral rope as about the indubitable political agility of the Chief Minister.

Again the elections in 1987 were fought with a multiplicity of parties, organized into a CPI(M)-led LDF and a Congress-led UDF. The chief difference was that now it was possible to see a much clearer distinction between the fronts in left–right terms. The CPI(M) had finally decided that it would no longer compromise its position by electoral deals with the Muslim League, provoking a minor breakaway in the Malabar wing of the party. That part of the dissident Congress of 1978 which was progressive allied with the LDF so that the final line up was no longer 'United Front' but a higher stage of socialist coalition-building, a fairly genuine LDF, if not yet the straightforward Left Front of West Bengal. On balance the loss of Muslim League support may have been counteracted by the national decline in Rajiv Gandhi's popularity. Certainly, the outcome was far closer than in the contemporaneous elections in West Bengal: the LDF won 76 seats—the CPI(M) 36—to the UDF's 60—Congress 33—but with a 1 per cent margin of percentage votes (44.91 to 43.70). The remaining two seats were taken by the far right of Indian politics with a disturbing 11.37 per cent of the poll, once an unthinkable phenomenon in Kerala. For comparison the gross CPI(M) vote was 22.32 per cent, its party-supported independents 3 per cent, and the CPI and supporters 8.55 per cent, a total of just short of 34 per cent. The interpretation of Kerala election results is hazardous but it is striking that in only three of the state's fourteen districts was the LDF percentage higher than in 1982. ('Kerala at the polls 1987', *Frontline* of 18 April-1 May 1987) The lost Muslim League votes, in any case concentrated in Malabar, ought to have been far outweighed by CPI(M) capitalization on UDF performance. E. K. Nayanar formed his second ministry, this time with every expectation of a full term of office. What is less clear is whether the CPI(M) unit in Kerala has the programme or the personnel to advance the popular cause.

9   West Bengal: History and Political Traditions

Both in India and abroad, West Bengal is often confused with the great—and grotesque—city of Calcutta, a presumption at once both true and false. Only 17 per cent of the state's current population live in the Calcutta 'Urban Agglomeration', a fitting label for a degenerate metropolis. Yet Calcutta was, until 1911, the capital of India, on the eve of Independence the largest city, after London, in the British Empire, and in the twentieth century not so much the gateway to India's wealth as it had been in the nineteenth century but a turnstile between East and West. Paradoxically, while Bengal had more justification for reviling imperialism than almost anywhere else in India, Britain irreversibly changed Bengali political institutions and culture. Bengal was the microcosm of British rule in India and the base from which the British East India Company subjugated the sub-continent. The Bengalis, fusing oriental and occidental thought, created in the late nineteenth and early twentieth century much of what is justly called the Indian Renaissance, a movement which included such different world figures as Rabindranath Tagore and M. N. Roy. As a people, the Bengalis were the first to absorb and the first to reject Western hegemony. It was here that Indian national consciousness was formed; and it was here, as the freedom struggle took shape, that a rival movement to that of Gandhi emerged: violent, impatient, incipiently class-conscious and leftist. Virtually every 'ism' has had its exponents in Bengal but Marxian socialism has proved the most enduring: and, in contrast to Kerala, communism appears to be winning the war with communalism.

West Bengal is, in area, close to the size of England and a little larger than Kerala. Its population—but not for long—is almost exactly that of Britain. Tucked away in the north-east corner of India, it stretches from the Bay of Bengal where it has a broad base in the Ganges-Brahmaputra delta northwards in a narrow ribbon to the foothills of the Himalayas, Darjeeling and Kalimpong before turning eastwards round the north of Bangladesh. Geographically it is, quite simply, a nonsense, the tragic result of the Hindu-Muslim partition of British India in 1947. Like Kerala, Bengal is peripheral to the Hindi heartland but from the 1750s till 1912 it could more properly be held that the Hindi heartland was peripheral to Bengal.

The region is very distinctive: the great deltas of the Ganges and Brahmaputra, a fertile, shifting land of alluvium and floods. Here in contrast

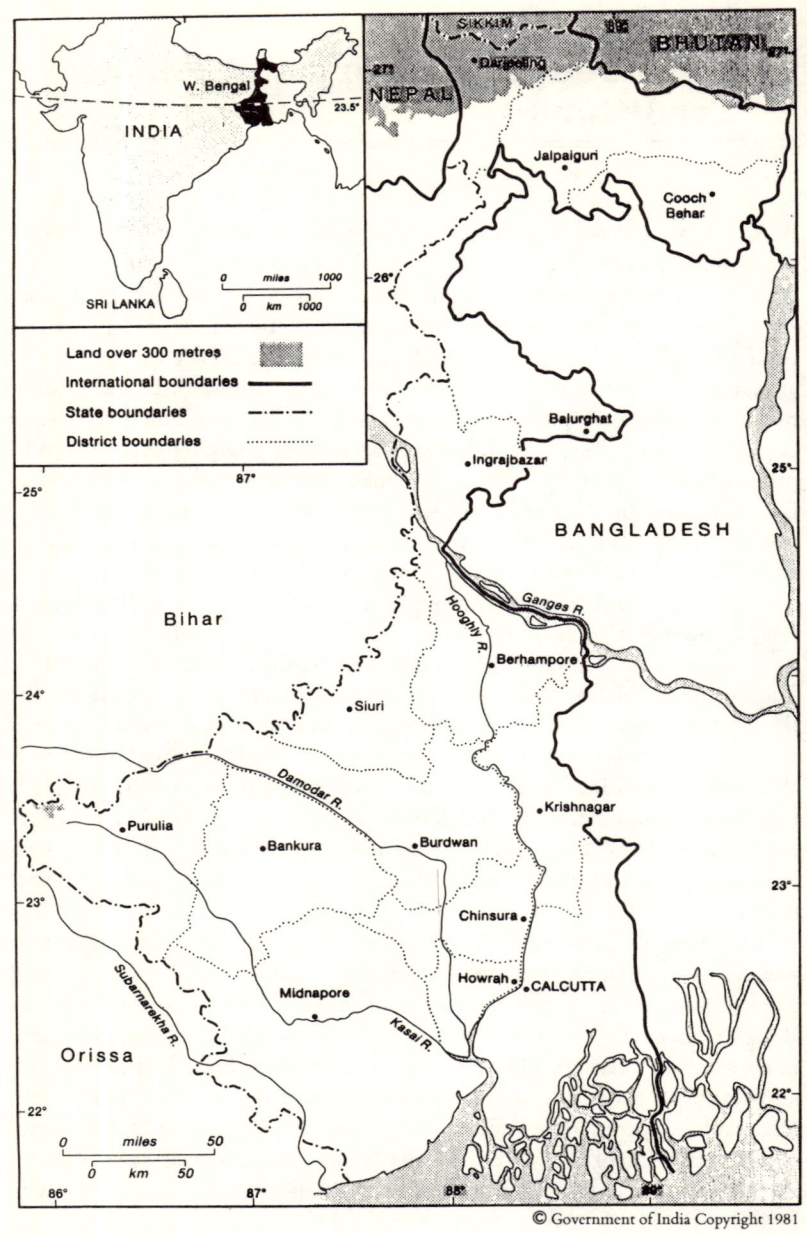

Map 2: West Bengal

to the Indo-Gangetic plain to the west, the aboriginal inhabitants, from whom modern Bengalis are descended, had adapted to their environment with its moving river systems and frequent inundations with a decentralized and relatively undifferentiated form of society. Communications were unreliable and the division of labour less developed than in the heartland. In part because of the symbiosis of man and nature and in part simply because the region was at the limits of the imperial reach of Aryans and Mughals, the alien elites—Brahmins after the fifth century consolidation of the Gupta empire and the Mughals from the thirteenth century—did not succeed in completely imposing their socio-religious orthodoxies on Bengal. It was the British who came nearest to the transformation of Bengali society with their 'Permanent' Settlement of agrarian relations, the introduction of a Western system of administration, and capitalist development. More than anywhere else in India the British fulfilled their destructive and constructive roles as envisaged by Marx and came nearest to creating the conditions for a successful communist movement.

The Background

In the mid-eighteenth century Bengal was the richest province in India. The Mughal empire received an annual levy of $1.5 million (Rs 5.3 million) without Bengal much noticing it. The British East India Company had been trading peacefully for more than fifty years in conditions of free trade for a trivial annual payment to the Nawab of Rs 3,000. Alivardi Khan was, however, old; the designated successor, his grandson Seraja, was a youth of 20, who on succeeding to power in 1756 proved to be not only headstrong but fearful and vacillating. The Mughal empire itself was collapsing and the fiefs including Bengal were increasingly able to pursue their own wayward policies. The Nawabs however were dependent on the financial goodwill of the merchant families of Bengal, and in particular of the Hindu banking house of Seth which financed government activities. Seraja's first act was to attack and take the East India Company's trading settlement of Calcutta, the occasion of the much exaggerated Black Hole of Calcutta episode. By chance the British had just previously been reinforcing their forces in India in preparation for war with France. By January 1757 Clive had recovered Calcutta, concluded a more favourable alliance with and discredited Seraja with his bankers and laid the way open for the Nawab's palace rivals to supersede him. The outcome was the Battle of Plassey on 26 June 1757, a damp squib of a military affair but a turning point in Indian history. It was not so much a battle as a transaction by which the merchants and bankers of Bengal led by Jagath Seth sold the Nawab to the East India Company. Clive installed as governor of Bengal the ageing Mir Jafar, one of Seraja's own generals who had stood aside till the battle was decided, and Bengal became a client state of the British even though it is doubtful if that had been the intention.

The price for installing and maintaining the puppet regime was truly terrible. The agreement with Mir Jafar, besides confirming the Company's privileges, required the payment of $3 million to the Company as compensation for the temporary loss of Calcutta, $1.5 million to its European inhabitants and among a host of other payments $700,000 to Clive in cash and an estate worth nearly $100,000 a year to keep him in the state worthy of the fancy Mughal title he had been given. These payments have to be set in the context of a Bengal treasury which contained less than $5 million. Worse still was the privilege accorded to British merchants. Trading on their own account within India had long been a recognized perquisite of Company servants but they had done so on a more or less equal basis with their Indian competitors. Now they were to trade duty free. There ensued what can fairly be described as the gang rape of the most attractive province of India. Clive was no angel but he was disinclined to tolerate in others what he thought fit for himself. During his five years absence the open, shameless plunder and corruption was such that it gave a new word of contumely to the English language, 'nabob', a corruption of 'nawab', originally used to describe the retired servants of the company who returned to England with immense fortunes and 'orientalized ways' and coming to mean *nouveau riche* ostentation.

Within twenty years famine had carried off an estimated 10 million people in Bengal, about a third of the population. Elite opinion in Britain was growing increasingly alarmed at the conduct of the Company Bahadur (valiant and exalted). By 1770 the enemies of the company found their opportunity: it was teetering on the edge of bankruptcy and was compelled to ask for a $3 million loan. Clive, the Conquistador of India, took his own life. There then followed from the modest Regulating Act of 1773 and the India Act of 1774 a steady process whereby the British government took more and more responsibility for company affairs in India until in the wake of the Indian Mutiny of 1857 the Company was finally dissolved and its Indian possessions became legally as well as *de facto* British India.

Of the measures taken by the British to restore the solvency of Bengal and the Company, the most important was the Permanent Settlement, a new legal framework for agrarian property introduced in 1793, which proved disastrous. The revolution—it can hardly be called a reform—was based on the beliefs of the French Physiocrats and in implementation of the English Utilitarians. Bengal's prosperity and stability was to be ensured by the introduction of private property in land to create a capitalist landowning class on the model of the English squirearchy and to fix a land taxation requirement in perpetuity—the permanent aspect of the settlement. The landowner for these purposes was taken to be the *zamindar*, the erstwhile collector of tax on land. The argument was that if the landowner knew the state would not raise its demand on the agricultural surplus then he would have every incentive to increase productivity by reorganizing cultivation on more profitable capitalist lines. The perpetual demand was, however, initially set too high and it was also more efficiently collected than by the Mughal tax man before the British 'collectors'. Arrears of payment were put up for auction. The old Mughal estate owners found themselves forced to sell and subinfeudate their patrimony. A revolution followed in land holding with a net transfer of property from Muslim to Hindu landlords. The Hindu upper castes, already established in the service of the Mughals, had turned to service the European commercial interests and, post-Plassey, the European administration. After 1793 the big Muslim estates progressively passed into high-caste Hindu ownership.

Somewhat paradoxically in seeking to develop capitalist farming in Bengal, the British sought also to maintain the existing small peasant economy reliant on family labour. How small-scale the system was, is indicated by figures for the 1870s which show that 65 per cent of operational holdings had a rental value of less than Rs 5. Of these holdings, 42 per cent were located in east Bengal compared with 24, 17 and 16 per cent respectively in central, west and north Bengal (Sen, 1982, p. 106). Under the Mughal system the *ryots* or cultivators enjoyed a permanent right of occupancy and handed their holding on to the next generation, subject only to the payment of tax and actual cultivation of the land. The tax wiped out the peasant's surplus but, if he did not live in arcadia, the demand was fairly constant over time. The new system differed in depriving the cultivator of his customary title to the ancestral land and in introducing a tax which was much more nearly rent because the landlord could vary its level according to his needs and preconceptions. In practice, however, the system proved unworkable. The *zamindars* were frequently not equipped to become British-style landowners; and in the early part of the nineteenth century the main problem of agricultural production was finding labour to cultivate the available land. Where land was not sold, it was frequently sub-let to more commercially orientated (and usually smaller) landlords who undertook to organize cultivators to extend cultivation into new and waste lands. On the whole till the latter part of the nineteenth century, the peasantry cultivated according to existing customary practices rather than the new notions of contractual property.

As traditional textile production was destroyed by British protection of Lancashire mill cotton, deindustrialization in Bengal led after 1850 to assertive landlordism. Faced with the difficulty of containing the social consequences of large-scale evictions and the disruption of agricultural production, the British intervened on the side of the cultivators (Rent Act, 1859; Tenancy Act, 1885) to buttress the existing system of small peasant agriculture. Various groups of tenants, including the more prosperous ones and some who were really rentiers, were guaranteed occupancy rights and limits were set to the enhancement of rent. Full-blooded pursuit of agricultural capitalism was abandoned.

The agrarian economy was, however, increasingly subject to commercialization. After an abortive attempt to establish indigo as an export crop, jute became the principal cash crop. It required no major change in production since it was cultivated on small family plots—mainly in the east and the north. Through a chain of intermediaries, jute reached the British-owned manufacturing firms in Calcutta. Neither they nor the merchants in the chain passed on the benefits of higher prices when demand was buoyant and they were quick to depress prices when demand fell. By 1914 about 5 per cent of the net cropped area of Bengal was under jute, rising to 12 per cent in the east and the north. The trade in rice was very largely local, feeding city dwellers and agricultural labourers. Although the price of rice rose steadily until the Great Depression, there was again little benefit to the small peasant cultivator who rarely had any choice but to sell as soon as the harvest was complete.

As the market economy intruded further into the Bengal countryside and the population rose, more peasants fell into debt. Steadily throughout the nineteenth century, sales and mortgages of smallholdings increased, rising dramatically in the wake of the Great Depression of the 1930s. The erstwhile cultivator would normally still work what had once been his land but now as a sharecropper or labourer. In Bengal the percentage of the agricultural work-force classified as owner-cultivators in 1921 was 84 per cent. Ten years later it was 53 per cent. Conversely, the percentage of agricultural labourers rose from 12 per cent in 1921 to 31 per cent in 1931. Depeasantization occurred throughout Bengal but earlier in the west and south-west. The east (present-day Bangladesh) resisted the trend till the 1930s because of the importance of jute to the small cultivator but the collapse of demand with the depression affected the region catastrophically. The collection of rents halved between 1928 and 1941 and there was not even the money to purchase the defaulters' holdings. One must not romanticize the pre-British past, nor underestimate the impact of demographic pressures on the Bengali economy, themselves products of the new technologies in public health and medicine. Nevertheless the Permanent Settlement stands condemned at the bar of history. In 1943 at least one million Bengalis died in the famine which was a terrible epitaph on British rule in Bengal, the more so as enough food was available in India.

The overall effects of agrarian change under the British can be summarized as follows: the decline of the traditional *zamindari* class; the emergence of a quasi-kulak class of rich peasants, moneylenders and merchants; the growth of the rural poor—sharecroppers, labourers and dwarf landholders; and the creation of a powerful urban ruling elite, the *bhadralok*, unique to Bengal in India.

Literally the Bengali term, *bhadralok*, means 'gentlemen' but its connotations might better be grasped by equating it with the British notion of 'the establishment'. Yet, while that indicates something of its reach in the life of Bengal in general and Calcutta in particular, it conveys nothing of the peculiar social origins of the group. Perhaps the nearest characterization is that of a mischievous and anonymous administrator who defined it in 1915 as a 'despotism of caste, tempered by matriculation' (Bengal District Administration Committee, 1915, p. 176). A century earlier, in 1829, *Bangadoot*, a leading Bengali newspaper, had distinguished a newly emerging social grouping, *grihastha bhadralok*, made up of middle-income shopkeepers, small *zamindars*, merchants and white-collar workers, who fell in between petty wage earners below and *abhijata bhadralok* (aristocrats) above. This petty bourgeoisie were also identified as *madhyabitta sreni* or middle class. Their origin clearly lies in the service which the three Hindu upper castes— Brahmins, Vaidyas (doctors) and Kayasthas (writers) had provided to the Mughals and then the British by their knowledge of Persian and English. In principle a Muslim could be *bhadralok* but even in the twentieth century they were remarkably few. Likewise it was possible to be accepted as *bhadralok* though a Hindu from another caste. To that extent it was an open status group, but as those who belonged to the traditionally literate Hindu upper castes ensured at least that their eldest child secured the necessary education, the competition for places in educational institutions was fierce enough to prevent all but the most talented and ambitious of the lower castes breaking in to the circle.

The rapidly expanding British colonial state provided many new jobs in the nineteenth century and, after the adoption in 1835 of English as the administrative language and the foundation of the University of Calcutta in 1857, English education became *sine qua non*; and the best of the *bhadralok* became as fine exponents of their second culture as their first. At its weakest, the product was the maligned babu, unfairly so because the British were reluctant to open the higher ranks of administration to Indians.

The *bhadralok* took to urban ways of life but (and there is a faint parallel in the Kerala Nairs) they retained (or constructed) a rural connection. Many were rent-receivers, rarely, of course, with any direct link to the means of production in the countryside except as suppliers of credit. They had, an official report of 1940 concluded, 'built themselves up on the basis of [English] education financed by their income from their tenures or fields in the shape of rents since the mid-nineteenth century' (Bengal Land Revenue (Floud) Commission, 1940, vol. 1, p. 335). By 1901, 80 per cent of senior government appointments were held by the three Hindu writer castes who made up just 5 per cent of the population.

However, with inflation and declining income from landed property in the wake of the Great Depression and continued subdivision of family properties, the *bhadralok* became more and more dependent on English education as a passport to the official and professional posts in the city, which could support the urban gentility they had come to covet. The only difference Independence made to the position of the *bhadralok* was to widen opportunities still further at the top of the official and commercial hierarchies and to provide a new career, politics. Unsurprisingly, the *bhadralok* are prominent in all the major parties of West Bengal, perhaps more so in the CPI(M) and the CPI than in Congress by reason of the programmatic character of Marxism. In 1969, 72 per cent of the CPI(M) State Committee were from the three highest Hindu castes and all but two had been to college for at least a year, most were sons or relatives of landholders and professionals, while eight out of the nine members of the CPI State Secretariat were from high-caste families, all had been to college, and all came from respectable and fairly wealthy families (Franda, 1971, p. 14). A recent unpublished study suggests that both Congress and communist leaderships are still mainly from *bhadralok* backgrounds.

Some writers dispute the *bhadralok* thesis. Sumit Sarkar and Leonard Gordon, from very different standpoints, have both condemned the term as a far too sweeping and devoid of any real explanatory power, 'ranging presumably from the Maharaja of Mymensingh to the East Indian Railway clerk' (Sarkar, 1973, pp. 509–10). For Gordon it explains nothing because it seeks to explain everything (1974, p. 7). Certainly the British from Macaulay onwards held a low opinion of the Bengali babu (clerk) and attributed every political trend they disliked—nationalism, terrorism, communism—to the hapless *bhadralok*. The leading modern Western authority on Bengali communism is also inclined to look for babus under the bed. The 'most distinctive regional aspect of the Bengali communist movement', Franda believes, 'is its continued recruitment of leadership from ... the *bhadralok*'; the *bhadralok* were, he argues, attracted to Marxism by the late 1930s because they suffered a more rapid social decline in the twentieth century than any comparable social group in India; yet the group's attachment to communism is fragile as a result of the 'inner contradictions of the *bhadralok*-Marxist marriage' (Franda, 1971, pp. 12, 244–5).

The excesses of bhadralokian explanations of Bengali politics should not however lead us to dismiss a social category which Bengali commentators hold has provided the bulk of political leadership in Bengal, outside the Muslim community, from the 1920s onwards. Although as late as the 1930s the *bhadralok* had some rentier and family connections with land, post-independence material interest in land had diminished to the point of a dacha in the country. The city has during the last century come to dominate Bengal. Its upper-caste professional leadership has held virtually unchallenged sway politically and although this group has not differed in its partisan affiliations from the population at large, it has tended to judge agrarian issues, which are the stuff of state politics in India, 'not as insiders in a struggle between contending agrarian parties', sharing centuries' old modes and categories of thought but as urban consumers of food and agro-industrial commodities (Chatterjee in Omvedt, 1982, pp. 93–4). The three upper castes of Bengali society may, in a limited sense, still rule in West Bengal but they do not do so as a rurally dominant class.

After 1912 Bengal was redrawn to correspond closely to the natural region of the Lower Ganges Valley or Deltas and to the linguistic boundaries of the Bengali tongue. This vast alluvial plain was the hinterland of Calcutta as well as the focus of Eastern India. In the east—present-day Bangladesh—the delta was living; and amidst the network of rivers bringing down fertile silt from the Himalayas and the Tibetan Plateau rice was grown to feed the population of Calcutta and jute to feed its mills. During the rainy season in eastern Bengal, only the river banks and the artificial mounds on which the houses rested, appeared above water; and the countryside, unlike the Indo-Gangetic Plain, was verdant even during the hot season. Western Bengal was, and is, the old delta, a land of dead and dying rivers. Again much of it lies below 50 feet elevation. Rainfall is not so heavy and Western Bengal is prone to famine when the monsoon fails as well as to periodic catastrophic flooding. On the westernmost edge of Bengal, laterite appears and the land is undulating, rocky and infertile. North Bengal, at higher elevations rising into the foothills of the Himalayas, enjoys a cooler climate, especially in winter and has been largely devoted to commercial crops such as jute and, further north, tea.

What bound Bengal was language and ethnicity: 95 per cent of the population spoke Bengali. What divided Bengal was ostensibly religion. About half the inhabitants were Muslim by faith and slightly less than half Hindu. The small remainder were Christians or Buddhists. Broadly speaking the east was Muslim and the west Hindu and it was on this basis Lord Curzon, then Viceroy of India, decreed the partition of Bengal in 1905. At this time Bengal included Bihar and Orissa and the Presidency contained 78 million people. The adjustment of administrative boundaries, as Curzon called it, doubly affronted Bengali nationalists: the Bengali-speaking area was bisected; and the division of the homeland was along communal lines with the Hindu Bengalis a minority to Biharis and Oriyas in their portion. Despite massive protests which spread beyond Bengal, Curzon persisted but in 1911 at the Delhi Durbar, attended by the new King-Emperor George V, partition was revoked and Bihar and Orissa detached.

Curzon had, however, put forward the nationalist clock by at least ten years. Congress had thereby become a party with national aspirations rather than a disparate collection of individuals. The middle classes were mobilized as a powerful force in Indian politics. Previously Congress had been somewhat of an aristocratic body given to remonstrance rather than action. In Bengal (and in Punjab and western India), a terrorist movement emerged linked to the cult of Kali, the goddess of destruction, and in 1907 at its Surat session Congress split into Moderate and Extremist wings. It was from the terrorist groups, Anushilan and Jugantor, that in the inter-war years many socialists and communists were to be recruited.

For the British, the policy of 'divide and rule' rested on more than *realpolitik*. It reflected the imperial belief that Hindus and Muslims were different and that communal antagonism tapped primordial sentiment, which Hindus vehemently denied. Socially, however, there is no denying that 'Muslims were in most respects untouchables to Hindus'. 'If ... a Muslim somehow happened to enter the cook-shed of a Hindu, even if he did not touch food or utensils, all cooked food in the house stored in the house along with the earthern pots were considered polluted and thrown away' (Chakrabarty 1985, p. 90). Although there was a Muslim aristocracy in the east of Bengal, the bulk of Muslims were cultivating tenants and Hindus were disproportionately represented among the landlord class. In all probability the conversion to Islam from the thirteenth century onwards was of low-caste Hindus seeking to escape the stigma to which they were subject under Brahminism. Subtle distinctions were still observable in the twentieth century: Muslim tenants visiting their landlords' offices squatted on the floor or sat on low stools an inch or two off the floor while Hindus of equivalent status were permitted to sit on knee high platforms covered with sheets. The Hindu *zamindars* also patronized the Muslim elders with the colloquial *tui* instead of the respectfully polite *apné*. (Tamijuddin Khan, *Memoirs*, quoted in Chakrabarty, 1985, p. 90–1).

The Muslims themselves, however, often consisted of mutually exclusive social groups whose membership was defined by heredity in much the same way as Hindu castes. Muslims were not as caste-bound or priest-ridden as Hindus but in India generally Islam was affected by divisive attitudes based on pride of birth probably because the majority of Muslims were converted to Islam from the intermediate and lower rungs of society and the rules guiding their behaviour before conversion, though softened, persisted in their expectations and those of their new social masters (Ahmad, 1973, p. 29). The upper castes, the *ashraf* (honourable)—in Bengal normally Pathan and Saiyad—were of the order of 1.5 per cent of the Muslim population.

Demographically the Hindus were declining steadily as a proportion of the population of Bengal. The first fairly reliable census in 1881 showed Muslims as 1.7 per cent more numerous than Hindus. By 1931 the gap was 11.9 per cent with the Muslims constituting 55 per cent and the Hindus 43 per cent of the population. Although the growth of Muslims was greatest in the prosperous eastern delta, it was also evident in the decadent western region. The Muslims were, however, insignificantly represented in the urban areas, which in effect meant Calcutta and Howrah, and almost by definition therefore in the new middle class. In turn this was associated with lower levels of literacy in the vernacular and in English. In 1931 the Muslim literacy rate was 5.7 per cent and Hindu 14 per cent and the comparable figures for English literacy 1 and 3.4 per cent.

Muslim educational backwardness in Western education was not, however, as was generally supposed, a cultural phenomenon, the product of an inward-looking and conservative attitude. Of the Saiyads, 45 per cent were literate in English by 1921, which strongly suggests that the reason why the bulk of the Muslim community was illiterate was that they could not afford education, especially college education in Calcutta. Like the Hindu lower castes, they were not culturally subnormal, just deprived of the opportunity to secure education.

As in Kerala, the caste structure of Hindu society in Bengal deviated considerably from the norm. Two of the four *varnas*, Kshatriyas and Vaisyas, considered integral to the traditional caste hierarchy, were missing. And by the early twentieth century the ascriptive character of occupation by caste was beginning to crumble from the top downwards. The upper castes, who found it increasingly difficult to sustain their life styles under demographic pressures, were exposed to alternative life styles, and presented through the development of Calcutta with new opportunities to maintain and increase their income. In the 1900s, when a Namboodiri Brahmin was socially ostracized in Kerala for daring to travel by train and Kerala Brahmins thought their community degraded by taking tea, 'the middle and lower castes [of Bengal] saw the names of brahmans and pandits in the list of shareholders of Great Eastern Hotel Company [and] saw that even well-known brahmans took active part in tanneries, wine shops and other business'. 'When they [brahmans] intruded on the trades and occupation of lower castes, they had no moral right to protest against their coming up to them and shaking hands with them' (Mencher, 1966, pp. 183–96; *Census of India*, 1911, pp. 450–1). In fact, by 1911 only one-fifth of Bengali Brahmins were priests, scholars or teachers. Over two-fifths were in the professions, another fifth in agriculture and 3 per cent in industry. At the other end of the traditional scale, approaching half of the dhobis (washermen) had abandoned their trade for agriculture (41 per cent), industry (4 per cent) and even the professions (1 per cent).

As in the north generally, there were large numbers of castes but unlike the Hindi belt there has been much less of a tendency for one middle or lower caste to preponderate in a large geographical area. There was certainly nothing equivalent to the Nairs or Ezhavas of Kerala. Presumably the ecology of Bengal inhibited such a development while the conversion of many peasants to Islam may also have played a part. In the absence of large middle castes, political outcomes in modern electoral conditions were likely to be different than in, say, Uttar Pradesh. At the last count (1931), the biggest single caste in Bengal was the *mahisyas* (cultivators) at 11 per cent and no other caste exceeded 10 per cent of the total Hindu population. That said, there were regional variations of caste strength; the *mahisyas*, rising to a third of the total population in parts of south-west Bengal; the *rajbangshi* (now listed as scheduled caste), forming anything between one-fifth and a half in areas of north Bengal; and the *namasudras*, officially a depressed caste, were concentrated in east Bengal. These local concentrations do not however appear to have been of great political moment. The *mahisyas* had mobilized effectively as a caste during the late nineteenth and early twentieth centuries through caste associations and programmes of educational and social uplift and in the 1920s Congress drew its support in the Midnapore district in part from the caste authority of many of its leaders among the *mahisyas* but there was little evidence of caste conflict within the district Congress organization, although the Calcutta *bhadralok* Congressmen were inclined to treat the local leaders as if they were country bumpkins. The *namasudras* were organized under the Scheduled Caste Federation but as a depressed caste played a limited role in politics.

The contrast with Kerala is stark. There, caste and community was, and is, if not everything, certainly a great deal of the context of politics. In undivided Bengal, and, subsequently, in West Bengal, caste has rarely been a significant axis of conflict. Before Independence, the provincial leadership of Bengal was notoriously faction-ridden but caste was not at all important in these shifting alignments. Since 1947, to the extent that politics has had social dimensions, it has been class not caste—or community—which has articulated social conflict. West Bengal is quite simply the least caste-ridden major state in India.

10 Modern History of West Bengal

1905-47

The first generation of Indian nationalists had emerged in the 1880s and 1890s. Many had been educated in the University of Calcutta and some in Britain. As professional men working in what was still the administrative capital of India, they aspired to full participation in a liberal democratic government modelled on British parliamentarism. As yet, they perceived no inherent conflict between being a British subject and simultaneously an Indian citizen. Since Calcutta was the capital of British India, they saw no contradiction either between the interests of Bengal, and especially its urban elite, and India, overwhelmingly rural as it was. 'As Europe is unthinkable without France', wrote one; 'so India would be unthinkable without Bengal ... the fountainhead of ideas and the centre of patriotic inspiration ... [W]here can you find a land so fertile and a people so sharp in intellect, so subtle in perception so persuasive in eloquence, so cosmopolitan in ideas and so sanguine in patriotic fervour' (Gordon, 1974, p. 33).

The partition of Bengal in 1905—as much politically as administratively motivated—was a climacteric in Bengali politics, and a profound shock to the Moderates whose naïve faith in British motives was shaken to the roots. By the time the decision was reversed in 1912, Congress nationally, as well as in Bengal, had divided into Moderate and Extremist factions. Violent agitation had become an established form, appealing particularly to younger *bhadralok* who were facing diminished opportunities, and it produced a counter-elite among East Bengali Muslims, most of whom had favoured partition as a chance to escape from Hindu *bhadralok* dominance.

A fresh start appeared to be made in 1913 by the shrewd new Governor of Bengal, Lord Carmichael. In the wake of, and in the spirit of the Morley-Minto reforms, which seriously aimed to develop representative institutions in India, Carmichael established a Legislative Council which would satisfy the political ambitions of the *bhadralok* and at the same time force them to bargain with Muslim as well as British commercial and official interests. In fact, matters worked out otherwise. An attempt to assassinate the Viceroy in 1912 confirmed the fears of many in the British community that Indians could not be trusted which conveniently matched their reluctance to see their privileged status eroded by democracy. The nationalists, including the

Moderates, could hardly be seen to be unduly cooperative, even had they so wished; and the Muslim aristocracy was increasingly pressured to redress past grievances by their own young 'extremists', led by Fazlul Haq. His spontaneous outburst in Council in 1913 really did speak volumes:

> To me it seems that the Government has arrived at a parting of the ways, and has got to decide, once for all, its future policy regarding... the Muslim community... [I]n spite of their aversion to agitation, Muhammadans are drifting, owing to sheer force of circumstances, into the arena of political warfare... We require something more than a mere concession to our sentiments, something tangible which can be reasonably set off against our loss by the annulment of the Partition. [Broomfield, 1968, p. 64]

The final blow to Carmichael's efforts came with the beginning of the First World War which provided the Government with the excuse to turn from reform to repression with the Defence of India Act (1915).

During the war, slow and painful progress towards a new deal for India was made, culminating in the Montague–Chelmsford Reforms and the Government of India Act of 1919. Meanwhile, in Bengal, one event had shaken the confidence of all propertied parties in the stability of the evolving political system: the Calcutta communal riot of September 1918. A trio of non-Bengalis who were influential among the Urdu-speaking Muslim traders, small manufacturers and factory workers of the capital, backed by an irresponsible Muslim press, whipped up communal feeling, particularly against the successful small minority of Jain money-lenders, whose quarter of the city was adjacent to the Muslims. Fearing trouble, the Marwaris had brought in armed guards. Fazlul Haq, who had proved more prescient than he had intended, bravely tried to defuse the situation, the Government was slow in responding, and the inevitable occurred. After shots from the Marwaris, looting and arson ensued; and it was three days before order was restored by troops.

The riot gave added significance to the negotiations over the shape of the Bengali electorate for the new Legislative Council arising from the 1919 reforms. The twenty-eight-member Council had an electorate of a mere 9,000 educated and propertied voters. The new, and quasi-parliamentary not consultative body, was to have a mass electorate. One hundred and thirteen members were now to be elected by one million potential voters, the majority of whom were peasants. The key question was: would the allocation of territorial seats reflect Muslim demographic preponderance? The answer was that Muslim pressure reduced the imbalance but ultimately left them with only 45 per cent of the territorial seats. From the standpoint of the Raj, the

British had upset the Hindu leadership by giving ground to the Muslims without on the other hand satisfying the Muslims either. None the less, elites had to live with greater problems: politics could no longer be confined to parlours, coffee houses and the town hall. The fuse of democracy—or was it communalism?—was of unknown length.

A further complication was the rise in 1920 of Gandhi as India's premier nationalist leader. His first challenge was simply that Congress was no longer to be quasi-federal in character. Provincial leaders must be subservient to the larger purpose. Bengali politicians had, of course, not only a distinctive arena but a long tradition of providing a national input. Gandhi's second challenge was the doctrine of non-violence. Vivekananda was more in tune with Bengali thinking when he had said (1897) that 'What we want is strength', or, as Broomfield puts it, self-assertion not self-denial (Broomfield, 1968, p. 148). Third, much of the platform of Gandhianism seemed absurd—spinning wheels in Calcutta—or philistine—Indianization to the exclusion of the Western values in which so many of the Bengali elite were immersed. Rabindranath Tagore denounced Gandhi's alleged 'attempt to alienate our heart and mind from the West as an attempt at spiritual suicide' (Broomfield, 1968, p. 149) and the discussions between the two were said to have revealed a difference of temperament so wide that it was extremely difficult to arrive at a common intellectual understanding' (Broomfield, 1968, p. 150). It might also be noted that the *bhadralok* were in no hurry to renounce the good life for asceticism.

If Gandhi was less than lauded among the *bhadralok* elite, he had a real following among the masses, including the Muslim peasantry by reason of his support for the Khilafat movement. No less significantly, he had backing among the lesser *bhadralok*, the bulk of what the Bengali press really meant when referring to 'the people'. In the aftermath of the Amritsar Massacre and the repressive Rowlatt Act, not to mention the Russian Revolution, the Gandhian policy of non-cooperation had far more support than Council Entry. C. R. Das, the most prominent Bengali Congress politician, aware of the mood of the Bengal Provinicial Congress (BPC), bent with the wind and the BPC voted for non-cooperation, leaving the Moderates a virtually clear run in the inaugural elections to the new Council in 1920. By the time the British had become sufficiently alarmed to crack down on the non-cooperation movement in 1922 and were secure enough to arrest Gandhi himself, the Moderate Ministers in the diarchical administration were so compromised as to be politically finished. Agitation and violence had caused unease among the elites, who feared that the people might become a revolutionary mob sweeping away not only the British propertied classes but the Indian as well. It was the opportunity for C. R. Das, the leading Bengali Congressman, skilfully to argue that the British were not yet weak enough to be ousted by direct confrontation and that the next step should be to work to discredit the British from within by entering those very councils Congress had opposed for three years. Thirty years later the communists came to a similar conclusion in Independent India. Initially, Das failed to carry Congress nationally and (with Motilal Nehru, Jawaharlal Nehru's father) formed the breakaway Swaraj Party which was soon recognized in Bengal by the All India Congress Committee as the true BPC. Das's major problem was not the Gandhian minority in Bengal but the Muslims and in September 1923 he initiated negotiations with the community which led to the Bengal Pact (1923). In exchange for Muslim support in the elections the Swarajists promised to deliver 55 per cent of government jobs and 60 per cent membership of local bodies in Muslim majority districts. Whether Das's manœuvre to deliver Bengal from community and class, from Muslim and mob, would have been successful had he lived beyond 1925 is an open question, but an elite deal seems unlikely to have assuaged the grievances of the Muslims for long. The Pact was rejected by the BPC at its Krishnagar session in 1927 and so was lost all chance of a common secular mobilization of the Hindu and Muslim masses.

Central to the Congress decision was the opposition of the ex-terrorists, notably the Karmi Sangh, whom Das had brought into Congress in the early 1920s to increase the party's ability to organize at the grassroots and to strengthen his hand against the Gandhians in Bengal. However, not only were the terrorists bitterly anti-British, they were equally fiercely anti-Muslim. Karmi Sangh, and the Anusheelan Group with which they were aligned, further influenced the pro-landlord, and so anti-Muslim stance adopted by Congress on the 1928 Bengal Tenancy (Amendment) Act.

The net effect was to precipitate the formation of a new, and mass-political movement among the Muslims, the Praja Samiti, which in 1936 became the Krishak Praja Party, which received more votes than the Muslim League in the 1937 provincial Bengal elections. Muslim numerical superiority had been recognized by the 1932 Communal Award but the division within the Muslim community meant that no party could govern alone. Fazlul Haq, KPP leader, turned to Congress but Congress nationally had decided against accepting office and Congress locally was totally unwilling to participate in a government whose objective was to erode Hindu privileges. There was no alternative ally but the League although the price was to dilute the peasant-oriented programme. In 1937 Haq joined the Muslim League; in 1939 he announced that he was 'a Muslim first and a

Bengali afterwards' (B. Chakrabarty, 1985, p. 94) and in 1940 it was he who moved the famous Lahore Resolution, which demanded the establishment of Pakistan. Community had triumphed over caste; and, whatever part British 'divide and rule' tactics had played initially, Hindu chauvinist sentiments and the *bhadralok* and landlord refusal to see their privileged status reduced can hardly be ignored.

The partition of 1947 was a disaster for the economies of West and East Bengal alike. The Bengalis of the east exchanged a lesser servitude for a greater one; and the political equation of West Bengal was radically altered. Without partition and its economic and demographic consequences, it is entirely possible that the communist movement would not have achieved its present position in West Bengal.

The communist movement in Bengal dates back at least to 1921. M. N. Roy, famous for his debate with Lenin on the Colonial question, and Muzzafer Ahmed had by then well-established links with the Comintern. At one point Roy had great hopes of converting C. R. Das to Marxism (Overstreet & Windmiller, 1960, p. 47); but despite the ferment of ideas in Calcutta, the communist party did not really begin to develop until the late 1930s.

Three groups are of importance: firstly, the neglected young Muslim Khilafatists, who had direct and indirect contacts with the Soviet Union from 1919, and were the real communist activists in Bengal in the 1920s. The second group were the ex-terrorists, whose total number would have exceeded 10,000. Only a small portion espoused Marxism, and more may well have been attracted to the Das–Bose wing of Bengal Congress. Nevertheless, a significant number of the West Bengal Jugantor and the East Bengal Anushilan groups realized that terrorism was adventurist and that a mass-based socialist movement was the only credible way forward. The third source of recruitment was from among the young intellectuals who had been educated in Britain in the 1930s: Jyoti Basu, Chief Minister of West Bengal, is a prime example.

It is important, however, not to predate the rise of the communist party or—for there were other communist organizations—of Marxism as a serious political force. The CPI's membership in 1934 was thirty-seven, rising to 1,000 in 1942, and—the real growth—to 20,000 in 1947 (Franda, 1971, p. 13). It is also unwise to explain too much by reference to some assumed *bhadralok* outlook or socio-economic problems. Even among the young and volatile, far more of the *bhadralok* were unattracted to Marxism than were in the 1930s and early 1940s.

The dominant figure in Bengali left-wing politics—and in Congress politics—in the 1930s was the complex and controversial figure of Subhas Chandra Bose. From a very well-heeled family, Bose sampled a number of ideologies—Spiritualism, Vivekandandan philosophy and student radicalism; he had been to Cambridge to take the ICS examinations, and joined the University Officer Training Corps before becoming Das's lieutenant in 1923. Compared with many nationalist leaders, the impulsive Bose had a limited active political life because between 1921 and 1940 he spent more than six years in jail as well as a year in Europe where he met Hitler and Mussolini. Whether fairly or not the British soon regarded him as a very dangerous man, far more so than Gandhi. In the Calcutta Police Commissioner's view he had no scruple about political means. Bose's success in achieving dominance in the Bengal Congress Party and an all-India stature may be attributed to his ability to bridge old and new forms of politics both organizationally and ideologically. He was skilled in the arena of institutional politics—the Calcutta Corporation, the Legislative Council, and the Congress Committee, but more than most he quickly recognized the need for mass organization. Linked to this was his awareness that the old imperatives of high-caste Hindu interests must be overlain with the new socialist discourse as well. His true views are controversial but in 1940, standing on a radical platform, he defeated Gandhi's nominee in the election for the All-India Congress Presidency, overwhelmingly in Bengal (74 per cent) and by a margin of 7 per cent nationally. In the other radical strongholds of Kerala, Punjab and Uttar Pradesh, Bose's victory was also substantial. By dint of devious manœuvring Subhas Chandra Bose was prevented from taking control. He then founded the Forward Bloc and was promptly placed under house arrest by the British. After escaping first to Germany and then to Japan, he was to found the Indian National Army before dying (?) in a plane crash in 1944.

The legend of Netaji, as he became known, should not obscure the reality that Subhas Chandra Bose spoke what the majority of Bengalis wished to hear: the Depression had hit Bengal harder than most provinces; politically and economically Bengal was in decline, and in relative terms the Hindus the more so. At least at the level of political rhetoric Bose's genius was to package socialism within Hindu Bengali nationalism.

1947–67

The communists' appeal in the early 1940s was circumscribed by their opposition to Bose and the Forward Bloc, even more by the adoption of the People's War line and their refusal to participate in the massively popular

Quit India Movement of 1942. However, ground was recovered when, following the terrible Bengal famine of 1943 in which about a million people died, the communist-led Bengal Pradeshik Krishak Sabha launched the Tebhaga (Three-fourths) movement. Centred on the southern part of 25 Parganas district—the delta south of Calcutta—it fought for a new deal for the impoverished sharecroppers of three-quarters of the crop. (The Congress government later conceded a 60:40 division under the Bargadar Act of 1948.) Similar movements were also launched in several parts of North Bengal.

In contrast to the ambivalence of comrades elsewhere in India to India's Independence, the West Bengal unit was certain it was a sham and truly believed that a revolutionary situation existed in Bengal, if not the country as a whole. As far as Bengal was concerned, it was not entirely a ludicrous idea. There had been the Famine. Partition had been accompanied by a vast influx of refugees from East Pakistan, many of them high status and educated. Food shortage was chronic and communalism endemic. Rioting and the operation of vigilante groups placed the civil and police administration under severe strain at a time when the transfer of power and the division of Bengal made it more difficult to cope. British mishandling of the treatment of the captured Indian National Army personnel was also likely to have more impact on army loyalty in Bengal.

After the CPI's Central Executive Committee showed an inclination to ally with progressive elements in Congress and go soft on Nehru, the West Bengal party opposed the line. Party headquarters were moved to Calcutta, and in March 1948 the party adopted its variant of the Zhdanov line, the Calcutta or Ranadive Theses of insurrections. For eighteen months—from October 1948 to March 1950 the CPI and the Revolutionary Communist Party of India generated mayhem in West Bengal: sabotage, arson, murder, riot, strikes and demonstration. In the middle of 1949 proof that violence paid dividends in popular support appeared to be afforded by the sweeping electoral victory of Sarat Bose (Subhas's brother) and his left electoral alliance. The CPI then turned from city to countryside, notably to 24 Parganas. Ideologically it was a bridge too far; and, with information supplied, the police were now able to arrest the leadership and cow the rank and file. By early 1951 the West Bengal unit accepted the inevitable. With remarkable discipline, the party now turned to fight elections. The 1952 poll was something of an electoral jungle but essentially the fight was a three-cornered one between Congress, which took 150 (63 per cent) of the 238 seats and 39 per cent of the vote; and two leftist alliances, the communist-dominated United Socialist Organization of India (USOI) and, part Marxist part not, the People's United Socialist Front (PUSF). In percentage vote, the

PUSF (20 per cent) outperformed the USOI (11 per cent), but the USOI won forty-three seats to the PUSF's twenty-eight because the communist alliance was more cohesive. Most of the CPI's own twenty-eight victories were from the areas—such as Howrah, Burdwan, 24 Parganas, Hooghly and Midnapore—where there had been mass agitation. The exception was Calcutta—although the CPI did well among middle-class unionized employees. Congress's strength lay in non-caste Hindu Bengali areas, Muslim majority districts, immigrant industrial labour; scheduled caste and tribal seats; and the far north. The meaning for the communists was unclear: was the insurrectionist line correct after all? Should the party focus on Calcutta or the countryside? Was electoralism the real road forward?

On one thing most of the West Bengal unit could, however, agree: they would have nothing to do with the Soviet-led emergent national line of a more positive assessment of Nehru and Congress. Congress, for a variety of reasons—the treacherous acquiescence in the partition of Bengal at Independence, the central neglect of the state's problems, and the unsavoury character of provincial Congress politics—was deeply unpopular with the West Bengal communists.

Mass movements against Congress should be sustained. To an unusual degree these were masterminded and coordinated by a relatively few leaders, and especially Promode Das Gupta. In partnership with Jyoti Basu, who was nominally state party secretary during the 1950s though primarily active on the parliamentary front, the West Bengal unit maintained a degree of cohesion and purpose that was unusual among the communists at the time and was in stark contrast to almost all its political rivals, and especially the West Bengal Congress. Anti-Congressism made it nearly inevitable that the party members would overwhelmingly opt for the CPI(M), when the party split in 1964.

The 1957 to 1962 elections confirmed the growing polarization of West Bengal politics: Congress versus CPI-led alliances of smaller leftist parties. In 1962, despite allegations that the CPI was soft on the Chinese, the CPI vote had risen from 18 per cent in 1957 to 25 per cent. With its allies the share of the poll was 36 per cent to Congress's 47 per cent.

By the elections of 1967, the political situation had changed dramatically. Nehru was dead, as was his successor Lalbahadur Shastri. Mrs Gandhi was Prime Minister but not yet in command. Locally as well as nationally Congress was riven with dissent. Prior to 1966 the West Bengal unit of Congress was one of the most cohesive in the country (Franda, 1971, p. 141). The different interests had achieved accommodation and been careful not to interfere with each other's networks of patronage. In 1965, however, two of the big bosses, Atulya Ghosh and Ajoy Mukherjee fell out over the control of the Midnapore district party. Against the background of deep dissatisfaction with food supplies in West Bengal, culminating in an opposition-led strike in early 1966, the rules of the game broke down. Mukherjee, Congress state president, first lost a vote of confidence, then joined the agitation, and in June was expelled from the party. In reply Mukherjee formed a new party, Bangla Congress. Its constituency was—and there are echoes of Kerala Congress here—disenchanted rice growers and mill owners aggrieved by the imposition of a levy. Bangla Congress, like Kerala Congress, was to be critical in the outcome of the 1967 elections, and the state politics of the late 1960s. In view of the polarization of West Bengal politics, the only viable way to punish Mukherjee's long-time associates in Congress was to ally with the communists.

The communists had, however, split in 1964, and it was perfectly clear that the wing that mattered was the CPI(M). Given all that has been said so far, it is scarcely necessary to explain the ascendancy of the Left. The united CPI had a record of disciplined militancy. Congress in West Bengal was by no stretch of the dialectical imagination a progressive aspect of the national bourgeoisie. And the key figures, Jyoti Basu, Promode Das Gupta, Harekrishna Konar, Saroj Mukherjee and so on, were CPI(M), at a point when anti-Congressism was the minimum definition of who was Left and who was Right.

It proved easier for the Kautilyan (India's Machiavelli) capitalists of Bangla Congress to persuade their supporters to seek a deal than the Leninist Left to persuade theirs. The Bangla Congress leadership had to be content with an electoral front with the Right Communists, the CPI, together with the (Bose) Forward Bloc, the Bolshevik Party, the PSP, Lok Sevak Sangh and the Gorkha League, collectively known as the People's United Left Front, and notionally led by the CPI. In a three-way contest, the CPI(M) organized the United Left Front made up of the Forward Bloc (Marxist), the RSP, the Revolutionary Communist Party of India, the SSP, the Socialist Unity Centre and the Workers' Party of India, all small Marxist sects. In an election where sixteen parties won at least one seat, the intervention of Bangla Congress in a first-past-the-post system, handicapped by caste, community and patronage, was critical: Congress's share of the seats fell from 62 per cent in 1962 to 45 per cent in 1967 but its share of the vote was down only from 47 per cent to 41. Bangla Congress, on the other hand, took 10 per cent of the vote and 12 per cent of the seats. Of its allies only the Forward Bloc and the PSP counted. Summing the parent Congress and the breakaway Bangla Congress vote, the Congress forces had actually in one sense improved their position from 1962 to 1967 while in another exposed themselves to long-term divide and rule tactics by the CPI(M).

The communists—CPI, 6.5 per cent of votes; CPI(M), 18 per cent—together secured much the same share of the vote as in 1962, and also the same proportion of seats—20 per cent in 1962 and 21 per cent in 1967. In so far as splits in ideological parties might be thought to be more damaging than those in parties of interest (Congress), and the complication that the CPI(M) had been tarred with the Chinese brush to some degree, the communists has acquitted themselves tolerably well; but the fact remained that the logic of the situation was that the dominant wing of the movement, the CPI(M), either dealt with Bangla Congress and its PULF, or risked ending up as a footnote in the history of lost opportunities. Out of a total of 280 seats in the West Bengal Assembly, the PULF held 77, of which Bangla Congress had 34, and the ULF 74, of which the CPI(M) had 43. The opposition to Congress therefore commanded 151 seats to Congress's 127; and a ministry of the PULF and ULF—in effect Bangla Congress and the CPI(M)—was just possible. In the words of the Personal Assistant to the resigning Congress Chief Minister, Prafulla Chandra Sen, 23 February, polling day, 'was . . . a turning point in the political history of India'. Quoting the Congress Chief Minister he reported 'The Communists are coming' (S. Chakrabarty, 1978, p. 194).

The one obstacle was the divisions within the CPI(M) as to the acceptability of an alliance to take office with Bangla Congress, more strongly felt at state level than nationally. The argument is often presented in terms of battles between Centrist and Leftist factions (Franda, 1971, p. 150-1), where the former were closet electoralists and ministerialists. Such a view does not do justice to the degree of agreement on fundamentals. For Jyoti Basu, cast as leader of the 'Centrists', and Promode Das Gupta, as leader of the 'Leftists', the issue was tactical. The split in the party had turned on the attitude the communist movement should adopt towards Congress. Was Bangla Congress for these purposes 'Congress' or not? Would participation in such a Front ministry advance the cause in the long run by eroding the 'real' Congress's hegemony? And what was the balance of advantage organizationally? Would more cadres be offended by a species of political adultery than supporters pleasured by some small fruits of office?

After much heart-searching and inner-party manœuvring (*People's Democracy*, 5 March 1967; *Link*, 26 February 1967), the State Secretariat voted in favour of entering into a United Front government. Das Gupta, who had voted against, but had a long-standing relationship with Basu, obeyed party discipline and, in the face of a revolt from some of his followers, sought to deliver the organization.

Ajoy Mukherjee, the Bangla Congress leader, became Chief Minister and Jyoti Basu Deputy Chief Minister with two further ministries to their parties, two each to the CPI and Forward Bloc and one each to the other participants and one Independent. Coordination was to be achieved through a UF Committee as well as the Cabinet, particularly important when the ministry's majority was slender and the state's problems, especially food, were no less desperate before than after the election.

The government survived just over eight months before being dismissed by the new—and notoriously anti-communist—Governor, Dharma Vira. Following the defection of P. C. Ghosh and other BC MLAs to become the PDF (Progressive Democratic Front), and after consultations with Mrs Gandhi, Vira rejected it on the grounds that it no longer enjoyed a majority in the Assembly, a fact which had not actually been tested. That the UF was in a mess is incontrovertible but even the Chief Minister's personal assistant 'was certain that the Governor and the Chief Secretary had acted in a partisan manner' (S. Chakrabarty, 1978, p. 266). They knew Mrs Gandhi's mind.

The UF's eighteen-point programme was only in one respect not an uncontentious commitment to improvements in food, jobs, health, housing and welfare: an undertaking was given not to suppress the democratic and legitimate struggles of the people. The Labour Minister (Subodh Banerjee of the Socialist Unity Centre) among many otherwise commendable initiatives, supported by the cabinet, legitimized the industrial dispute tactic of *gherao* by which the manager was encircled by protesters and not permitted food, water or toilets until the demands were conceded. Its indiscriminate use was matched by a doubling between 1966 and 1967 in the numbers of strikes and in man days lost through strikes.

Still more problematic for the front, and especially the CPI(M) was the emergence of the Naxalbari agitation in the early summer of 1967. In the far north of the state around Darjeeling tribal people began to take direct action against landowners accused of *benami* (fraudulent) land acquisition, seize uncultivated tea estate land and storm grain stores. Matters escalated until after a policeman was killed on 23 May, the police opened fire. The cry of despair was increasingly organized by the local unit of the CPI(M) Krishak Samiti (Peasants' Organization) whose leader was Kanu Sanyal. Most of the leaders were comparatively young and usually themselves from tribal, low-caste or Muslim backgrounds but Sanyal was from the landed classes himself and had relinquished his rights to inherit family property. Claiming to have been inspired by Subhas Chandra Bose, and, in his idealism, a man of '68', Sanyal was to appeal to the youth of the state as the true revolutionary in contrast to the 'compromisers' of the CPI(M) and the 'revisionists' of the CPI. By July, as the wave of arson, murder and disorder grew, the cabinet, supported by the CPI(M) leadership, authorized the unequivocal quelling of the Naxalbari agitation. In three weeks the police had done their job.

The Naxalites had generated an incipient split in the CPI(M). Links with similar movements, especially among college students, elsewere led to the formation of the All-India Coordination Committee of Communist Revolutionaries and after disagreements between Sanyal and 'Naxalites' in southern India to the creation of the CPI(ML) in April 1969. Up to that point the CPI(M) had been reluctant to take firm disciplinary action against 'dual' membership, correctly perceiving that such a split would be far more damaging than that of 1964; but the efforts to persuade young hotheads of their erroneous understanding were then abandoned and party discipline invoked. The 'hotpotch of extremely irresponsible adventurism and sectarianism', not to be confused with the 'heroism and militancy of peasants' (Konar, 1977, p. 38) had become dangerous to the future of the CPI(M). May Day 1969 was marred by violent clashes between CPI(M) and CPI(ML). Over the next two years hundreds on both sides died in fratricidal affrays (S. Chakrabarty, 1978 p. 410). The CPI(ML) was finally effectively eliminated as a serious force in state politics by the growth of police intelligence and the use of the Central Reserve Police force in 1971–2.

After the dismissal of the first United Front, there was a brief period of near chaos before Presidential Rule was imposed in February 1968. Dr P. C. Ghosh had been appointed Chief Minister of a Progressive Democratic-Congress coalition on 21 November but the game of musical chairs continued among the non-left MLAs, the Speaker refused to preside over the Assembly, and civil disorder was so great that some 30,000 people were arrested.

When mid-term elections took place in February 1969, despite talk of the emergence of a 'third force' in Bengali politics, the contest demonstrated the increasingly bi-polar character of state politics: UF versus Congress, who between them took 96 per cent of the seats—214 to the Front and 55 to Congress—and 90 per cent of the votes. The UF's share was 49.7 per cent and Congress's 40.4 per cent. Although margins of victory were in some places small, 90 per cent of the seats won by the UF were by a margin of 10 per cent or more. The CPI(M) was the largest party in the Assembly with eighty seats, far ahead of Bangla Congress, its stable mate. On any assessment the CPI(M)'s tactics had been vindicated.

If the business of a ministry is to govern, the second UF Ministry can hardly be said to be any more successful than its predecessor. A thirty-strong cabinet with twelve parties represented was no recipe for harmony. Bangla Congress's Ajoy Mukherjee was again Chief Minister with Jyoti Basu as

Deputy and—in contrast to 1967—Minister for Home. This time there was little honeymoon between the two men or their parties. The other CPI(M) portfolios were valuable in building up the party's social constituency: Transport, Labour, Education, Land and Land Revenue, Relief and Rehabilitation, the latter in the wake of serious flooding. The CPI's important ministry was Planning and Development; and Bangla Congress's, Finance.

The second UF ministry lasted thirteen months to March 1970 when the Chief Minister resigned and Presidential Rule was again imposed. In many ways the administration was a replay of the first: bitter disagreement between the major constituents, Bangla Congress and the CPI(M); widespread disorder; clashes between the rank-and-file of any and all parties; industrial agitation including the 'gheraoing' of the erstwhile Labour Minister of 1967 and the CPI(M)'s Land Minister, Harekrishna Konar; and the steady progress of the CPI(M) in recruiting support among the organized working and middle class and in the countryside. Of the 32-point programme, the one area of real progress was in land redistribution. Harekrishna Konar continued his efforts during the first UF Ministry to reallocate land. How much land was redistributed and how far it benefited the real landless is almost impossible to tell. The CPI(M) claimed some 300,000 acres had been transferred. The actual amount, however, was not as significant as Konar's encouragement of mass action to seize it, supported by an acquiescent police force. The rural underclass now had evidence that the CPI(M) meant business. Conversely, the privileged took fright and their allegiance to Congress was confirmed.

By the next mid-term elections in 1971, further shifts in the political landscape had occurred. Congress nationally was now split. In November 1969 the CPI, even while in the UF Ministry, had declared that Mrs Gandhi's new Congress was 'progressive'; and, as noted above, the CPI(M) and CPI(ML) were engaged in a murderous war on the streets. The UF of 1969–70 was now defunct. In its place was a six-party combination of the Workers' Party, Biplabi Bangla Congress, RCPI, FB(M) and Bolshevik Party, led by the CPI(M), an eight-party combination, led by the CPI, which took the rest of the parties other than the Bangla Congress which stood aloof from both. On a very high turnout (81 per cent), particularly in light of the widespread violence during the campaign as well as before, the result was remarkably clear-cut: the CPI(M)-led Front won 123—of which the CPI(M) alone took 111—and Congress (R) 105. The CPI-front managed only twenty-five and Bangla Congress a derisory five seats. The CPI(M)'s share of the poll had risen from the 20 per cent of 1969 to 32 per cent. Congress (R) took 28 per cent, Congress (O) 5.6 per cent and Bangla Congress, 5 per cent. The CPI at 8 per cent still showed no signs of breaking through. Three points are clear from more detailed analysis: the CPI(M) had still further penetrated the countryside; it had lost some ground in Calcutta, presumably as a consequence of the concentration of violent political agitation in the state capital and its environs; and the Congress (R)'s success owed much to its Youth Congress wing and to Mrs Gandhi's appeal to the youth constituency.

No party had a majority in the Assembly but Jyoti Basu on behalf of the ULF formally claimed the right to be invited to attempt to form a government as head of the largest bloc. Shanti Dhawan, who had replaced Dharma Vira as Governor refused the offer and, after much manœuvring, a 25-member six-party Democratic Coalition ministry, took office on 2 April 1971, led yet again by Ajoy Mukherjee of Bangla Congress but dominated by eighteen Congress (R) ministers.

The ministry lasted only until 28 June when Mukherjee tendered his resignation. The government had been overwhelmed by the inrush of some 1.2 million refugees from the Bangladesh conflict, failed almost entirely to improve the law and order situation—nearly 500 were reported killed in just two and a half months—and was then faced, after the murder of a Youth Congress worker (by an alleged Naxalite) with a 72-hour ultimatum to stop the killings or be toppled in the Assembly.

Again under Presidential Rule, the Prime Minister appointed a 'West Bengal Affairs Minister' Siddhartha Sankar, who was already Minister of Education, in the Central Cabinet to deal with the refugee and other state problems. An *ad hoc* Congress party committee was appointed, at least half of whom were from the youth wing, to advise. Inevitably such arrangements gave Congress a boost in West Bengal. Still more important was the tide of popularity for Mrs Gandhi with the Indian victory over Pakistan in the Bangladesh Liberation Struggle, hardly diminished by the CPI(M)'s likening of Indira Gandhi to Yahya Khan, Pakistan's leader (Ghosh, 1981, p. 137). The CPI, following the Indo-Soviet Treaty and Mrs Gandhi's socialistic nationalization of the domestic banks and abolition of the princely privy purses, were now in alliance with Mrs Gandhi. On the crest of the Indira Wave with the Congress slogan *Garibi Hatao* (Eradicate Poverty) ringing out, the State went to the polls. The result was a foregone conclusion—and it remains puzzling why Congress should unusually have resorted to intimidation and, allegedly, ballot rigging. Of 280 seats Congress won 216 and the CPI 35 and the Congress-led Progressive Democratic Alliance 254 in all. The CPI(M) was reduced to fourteen and the six other members of the Left Front a total of five. As, however, the following table shows the CPI(M)'s loss in terms of share of the vote—down from 32 to 28 per cent—was modest; and although there was a swing towards Congress, taking account of malpractices and the CPI's net transfer of votes the CPI(M)'s base was little affected.

Table 10.1 Number of seats and percentage of votes won by Congress, CPI(M) and CPI in Assembly elections, West Bengal, 1967-72 (total seats = 280)

	1967		1969		1971		1972	
	Seats	% Vote	Seats	% Vote	Seats	% Vote	Seats	% Vote
Congress	127	41.1	55	40.4	105	28.2	216	49.0
CPI(M)	43	18.1	80	19.6	111	32.0	14	27.6
CPI	16	6.5	30	6.2	13	8.1	35	8.4

Source: Ghosh, 1981, p. 144

The new Ministry was the first since the mid-1960s to be a single party one with all that this implies for the electoral allocation of responsibility. Siddhartha Sankar Ray became Chief Minister on the basis of the Congress (R)-CPI PDA programme with the CPI's Biswanath Mukherjee as Deputy Leader of the alliance; but the CPI declined (and was not encouraged) to join the ministry. Since the Congress had no need of CPI votes to support it in the Assembly, and Mrs Gandhi's policies fell away from the 1972 slogans, Relations between the parties deteriorated until in June 1974 the CPI formally ended the alliance. Nationally, however, the CPI did not help the West Bengal unit by supporting the Emergency. As if to emphasize the contrast in party lines, the CPI(M), initially in protest against the conduct of the 1972 elections, boycotted the Assembly altogether. The real opposition in the Assembly prior to the Emergency proved to be within Youth Congress, which demanded its cut from the ministry, behaved with an increasingly unpopular arrogance, and—in contrast to Kerala—exploited the Emergency as Sanjay Gandhi's shock troops.

11 The Hegemony of the CPI(M)

Congress may be said to have wasted its opportunity after 1972. Under the Maintenance of Internal Security Act by June 1977 over 18,000 people had been arrested in West Bengal, by no means all known communists. Journalists from the thoroughly anti-communist Ananda Bazar publishing group were among those taken away. Little was done to alleviate West Bengal conditions either before or during the Emergency. In particular, agrarian reform remained a dead letter. In 1976 factionalism reached feuding proportions. When the parliamentary elections were held in March 1977, the result was a catastrophe for Congress. Of forty-two seats it managed to gain three compared with the CPI(M)'s seventeen and Janata's eleven, the latter working in electoral alliance. In the ensuing state elections held in June, Janata overestimated its strength. It declined to concede more than a hundred seats to the CPI(M). Negotiations broke down and so the contest was three-cornered: Congress versus Janata versus CPI(M). The CPI(M)-led Left Front put up candidates in all 294 constituencies. The outcome—on a low turnout of 54 per cent—was clear cut: the Left Front as a whole won 47 per cent of the vote and 230 of the seats. The CPI(M) alone had an absolute majority in the Assembly with 178 seats from 36 per cent of the poll. Janata won twenty-nine seats from 21 per cent of the vote and Congress a humiliating twenty seats from 23 per cent of the poll. The CPI was nowhere with two seats, and forty of its sixty-three candidates lost their deposits.

The result was something of a surprise even to the CPI(M). It did, however, persist with a multi-party Left Front Ministry including four Forward Bloc, two RSP and one RCPI Ministers in the cabinet, not all in unimportant ministries. Just as in 1972 Congress had had its chance to show what it could accomplish as a one-party show—and been found wanting—so now the CPI(M) was on trial. Whatever reservations follow, the Left Front has an enviable record of electoral success since. In the *panchayat* elections of June 1978 the ministry's initial move on land reform met with a huge affirmation of rural support: from 54 per cent of the vote, the LF took 69 per cent of the seats. When, at the end of its first term of office in 1982, the ministry sought a renewed mandate, two years after Mrs Gandhi's sweeping national parliamentary victory of 1980, the result was triumphant: the Left won 81 per cent of the seats in the West Bengal Assembly on a resounding 52.6 per cent share of the vote. The CPI(M) alone took 174 of the 294 seats, 39 per cent of the total vote, and 54 per cent of the poll in the 209 constituencies it contested. A further vote of confidence came in the next *panchayat* elections in 1983 when the LF edged up to 53.4 per cent of the vote. Although the Left Front bent to the wave of nationalist sympathy after Mrs Gandhi's assassination in 1984 in the Lok Sabha elections to confirm Rajiv Gandhi's mandate, the setback was far better contained in the state than in Kerala. In West Bengal the Left Front lost twelve seats and its representation in Delhi came down from thirty-eight out of forty-one in 1980 to twenty-six out of forty-two in 1984. The CPI(M) lost ten seats to reduce its MPs from the state to eighteen. In terms of percentage vote, Congress achieved its best performance since 1957, indicating that it had now—post Janata—aggregated the entire non-Left vote but its 48 per cent was still only equal to the Left Front's share with the CPI(M) securing 35 per cent. The arbitrary nature of the British-style electoral system in a multi-party environment is reflected in the fact that a share of the vote in the parliamentary elections that had given Congress four-fifths of the seats nationally gave the Left Front less than two-fifths from West Bengal. That not all the setback could be attributed to national factors was indicated when in elections to the Calcutta Corporation in June 1985, the Left Front scraped home with a wafer-thin one-seat margin over Congress. Nevertheless in 1987 the Left Front won a third term of office with an enhanced majority, up from 238 seats in 1982 to 251 with Congress down from fifty-three to forty. The CPI(M) now has 187 seats from 39 per cent of the votes and the Left Front 53 per cent of the vote compared with 42 per cent for Congress. Despite slippage in Calcutta, Cooch Behar, 24 Parganas and Howrah, the Left Front's electoral achievement was, in a situation like West Bengal's—many problems and few powers—little short of miraculous.

Miracles do not however occur in the very mundane world of politics, even in the heroic world of people's struggle. The factors that may be adduced to explain how so few loaves and fishes could satisfy so many for so long are fairly clear. First, the CPI(M) and the Left Front have succeeded in identifying themselves with Bengali resentment at what is perceived to be chronic central neglect of the difficulties of the state. The state Congress has, if anything, heightened this impression by its unremitting factionalism and, when in office, corruption. Second, the Left Front, both from conviction and calculation, recognized on taking office in 1977 that elections in West Bengal are won or lost in the countryside. The red belt of Calcutta and its industrial neighbours has—relatively speaking—been economically better off than the sharecroppers and smallholders of the rural areas; and in terms of command of the assembly it is not the quarter who live in 'urban' areas but the three-quarters who live in rural areas who determine the occupants of Writers'

Building, as the Government Secretariat of the Raj is still mordantly called. Third, whatever deficiencies there have been in the performance of the Left Front, it is perceived as having a mission, discipline and leadership, which, by comparison with anything else on offer, is worthy of respect. The world has heard of Mr Jyoti Basu; it has not heard of his Congress rivals. If, and I believe it, Rajiv Gandhi, did say at his first meeting with Jyoti Basu after becoming Prime Minister that the Chief Minister was more fit for the role, the comment was not only a gracious courtesy but a proper tribute to Basu's standing. Last, the CPI(M) and its partners have shown a capacity to learn from past mistakes: their ambivalent stance on law and order issues in the first and second UF ministries and their collective reluctance to face up to the logic of the necessity of capitalism as well as its evil, in the short or medium term have been overcome.

The Record

Crucial to an assessment of the Left Front's performance is the comparatively greater opportunity state governments in India have to hasten rural and agrarian change than urban and industrial change. Ironically, several of the agrarian reforms implemented by the Left Front government since 1977 were initially introduced by previous Congress governments—in response partly, it should be said, to communist-led agitation. In 1971 Congress amended the 1955 West Bengal Reforms Act to provide for three-quarters share of the produce and greater security for customary sharecroppers; but the measure largely remained a token of concern for the poor.

The LF government swiftly stayed all evictions pending or prospective from agricultural land. Land revenue rates were cut and in the case of the smallest categories abolished. It became a criminal offence for landlords to fail to issue receipts to sharecroppers when the crop was divided. These steps culminated in the celebrated 'Operation Barga' in 1978, an effective campaign to register sharecroppers officially. Prior to 1977 only some 275,000 sharecroppers had bucked the rural power structure and registered. By December 1984 as many as 1.3 million of the estimated 2 million West Bengal sharecroppers—96 per cent of all 'tenants'—were recorded. Of crucial importance in the sudden increase in the pace of registration was the reinvigoration of the *panchayats*. With the passage of time, the campaign slowed down, and a variety of explanations have been offered for this; but it remains a major accomplishment to push through so much in seven years in an Indian context. A more serious charge is the contention that whereas in other states, governments—as, say, in Kerala—have abolished tenancy altogether, the LF in West Bengal has simply entrenched sharecropping. However, given the agrarian situation in West Bengal, this may smack of perfectionism in a highly imperfect world. What the ministry has sought to do in its second and third terms of office under Benoy Chowdhury, Land Reforms Minister, is to liberate the sharecropper from total dependence for credit and investment on the landowner.

The LF ministries' record on land redistribution is indubitably impressive, particularly when compared with other states in India. Some 4.5 million acres were 'vested' (expropriated and held) in government nationwide. Of this West Bengal accounted for 1.2 million acres of which 800,000 acres have been redistributed to the landless (*Election Manifesto of the LF*, 1987). By late 1984 1.6 million families had benefited. Although the International Labour Organisation passed a favourable verdict in 1979 on West Bengal's efforts (ILO, 1979), there were still many loopholes for the bigger landlords in collusion with corrupt or dependent civil servants; and in 1981 the government passed a second Agrarian Land Reform Act which was designed to vest another one million acres of land. The act, as modified by Central government, however, was considerably diluted. In practice, the land–man ratio of less than 30 cents in West Bengal ensures that even a model Weberian administration would not be able seriously to redress the 'inequalities' in land ownership. In contrast to the thrust of land reforms in Kerala, West Bengal's policy has been to help the landless or nearly so. Of the land redistributed by the end of 1982, 55 per cent had gone to scheduled castes or tribes people. Politically, the consequences are obvious but it would be churlish to see vote-banking as a primary motive. Amrita Basu (1986, pp. 21-2) criticises the ministry's reluctance to experiment with collective or cooperative farming; but on the evidence of Kerala, to be effective this needs far more dedicated and knowledgeable cadres than are available. The government has been less attentive to the agricultural labourers than to the sharecroppers. While it has damped down clashes at harvest time, it has not attempted rigorously to enforce minimum wage legislation.

The deficiencies in a still forceful programme of agrarian reform may plausibly be linked to the suddenness of the party's electoral success. The ministry placed relatively major local responsibilities on the *panchayats*. Yet for the 1978 elections the West Bengal unit was faced with the task of finding some 47,000 candidates for the *panchayat* elections (of whom 34,000 won seats) at a time when the party's membership was barely 30,000. It was thus forced to nominate candidates who had joined the party after the fighting was over and whose subsequent service left much to be desired—in short opportunists, and often from the more privileged rural strata. An analysis of Gram Panchayat members by the West Bengal government showed that just 7 per cent were sharecroppers or landless labourers, 43 per cent were not agriculturalists at all, and only 22 per cent were owner cultivators with holdings below two acres compared with 15 per cent with holdings above five acres (Basu, 1986, p. 24). Where the cadres are experienced and the local government officers committed, on the other hand, the results can offer a showpiece (Burdwan, 1984).

Agrarian reform has been implemented during a period of extremely adverse climatic conditions: the greatest floods in living memory were followed by severe droughts; and it is clear that—in contast to the lethargy of the 1960s—in many areas the promptness of governmental action and the dedication of party workers and local officials materially contributed not only to welfare but to the raising of popular consciousness with consequential benefits for the Left Front's prestige. Utilizing central assistance through the Food for Work programme, for instance, 200 million man-days of work was claimed to have been allocated by the end of 1981 and 17,000 tanks or canals repaired (CPI(M), 1983, pp. 49-50). Later schemes, on the National Rural Employment Programme and the Rural Landless Employment Generation Programme were reported however to be seriously under-utilised (Basu, 1986, p. 28). On the other hand the CPI(M) Minister for Land Reform bitterly criticised in a Lok Sabha election post mortem the arrogance, high-handedness and sectarianism of some party functionaries. This had 'alienated the bulk of the middle peasantry and even some marginal farmers and landless labourers.' 'Imposition of punitive measures and social boycott by party leaders and workers had wreaked havoc in the rural areas. Sectarianism and partisanship while providing relief jobs or recording the names of sharecroppers also led to the alienation of natural allies of the Left' (*The Statesman*, 9 January 1985). Allegations of corruption at *panchayat* level are widespread (Basu, 1986, p. 27). Without a full-scale research project, it would be impossible to give a properly documented verdict on the Left Front's work in the countryside but the balance of probabilities is that the ministry has stumbled, not more. Its years in office have taken a toll of the energy of the core cadre but even so far more has been achieved than by any of the LF's predecessors in West Bengal.

In the first phase of the ministry priority was given to land reforms rather than improving agricultural productivity *per se*. Recently, however, more effort has been put into raising agricultural output. The State Planning Advisory Board's responsibilities for supervising development have been enhanced. Minor irrigation works in particular have burgeoned; and the index of agricultural production rose by almost half between 1982-3 and 1983-4 (West Bengal, *Economic Review*, 1985, p. 12).

The Left Front's record in the urban and industrial sector has been far less satisfactory. In part this arises from a simple political choice—there is neither the money nor the human resources to deal adequately with city and country simultaneously. The political power base of West Bengal is rural; and, whatever the current urban decay of Culcutta and its environs, historically the state capital has been a beneficial intermediary of the exploitation of Bengal in general and, until Independence, of East Bengal in particular. In part, the weakness of the Left Front now arises from the brute facts of the current economic relations in India. At partition in 1947 West Bengal was deprived of its eastern hinterland; its industries have, in key instances, been overtaken by technological innovation; communications are poor; and from the point of view of available investors, private, public or international, other areas of India have seemed more attractive, in some measure because of the uncertainty of the political situation at least prior to 1977 and because of industrial agitation.

West Bengal has undoubtedly suffered central neglect although to what degree is controversial. In evidence to the Eighth Finance Commission, the West Bengal Government spelt out its case in detail (Memorandum to the Eighth Finance Commission, 1983). Until the mid-1950s West Bengal had the advantage of proximity to industrial raw materials but coal freight costs were then equalized throughout India without compensating changes in materials West Bengal needed. Investment in thermal power generation has been neglected and the state government claims a central reluctance to invest in industry in the state and to grant industrial licences. Per capita central Plan assistance between 1980-1 and 1984-5 was only Rs 132 compared with an All-India average of Rs 214, and this despite West Bengal's continuing refugee problem. The Finance Commission did recommend an extra Rs 250 million, 15 per cent of the state's budget, but, according to Ashok Mitra, the state's Finance Minister and a reputed academic economist, the centre for dubious procedural reasons declined to accept the recommendation; and West Bengal was condemned to spend 40 per cent of its total capital expenditure in debt repayment (*Business Standard*, 28 March 1985).

At times central concern can be even worse, as with the foisting of a Calcutta Metro onto the city. The activities of the opposition—chiefly Congress—trades unions have also been unhelpful since 1977, just as the communist unions were earlier. The chronic problems of electricity supply and distribution are a leading example. However, industrial militancy has been curbed and West Bengal is now well down the list for days lost through strike action among Indian states. Investment has begun to pick up and the Chief Minister has been instrumental in attracting multinationals to West Bengal.

For the state to improve its industrial performance radically is beyond its capacity, but there can be little doubt that the running of state controlled or directed public utilities and services has not been up to the mark or even downright dismal. Power, transport and sanitation are notorious. Following the 1984 Lok Sabh electoral setback, the CPI(M) was very self-critical of the inefficient functioning of such portfolios (*The Statesman*, 9 January 1985). The reasons vary. In some cases the allocation of responsibilities within the Left Front results in ministers who lack the requisite ability, and in one instance of a minister (not CPI(M)) who was well known as corrupt, a blot on one of the few 'clean' governments in India. In other instances, conflict (or lack of coordination) between departments stems from the competing interests of rival members of the Front. The death of Promode Das Gupta, CPI(M) State Party Secretary, removed the one man other than the Chief Minister with the authority to impose solutions. Trade-union competition is merely an extension of the jostling for position between one party and another; and on occasion—the CPI(M) and transport is an instance—parties have been unable to force their own affiliates into line. Having found experts willing and able to render the Calcutta bus service efficient and profitable the CPI(M) leadership backed down in the face of union intransigence. Probably more critical than any resistance as such however is the failure of the government to motivate its own civil servants. Writers' Building is in its way as depressing as the tragedy of the street dwellers. Precious little bustle of CPI(M) headquarters is transmitted or the commitment of many ministers to the middle-rank and junior officials, the wheels of the Left Front's experimental design. Lassitude pervades the corridors, and time-keeping is conspicuous by its absence. 'Come back tomorrow' has Kafkaesque overtones of a journey on a bureaucratic time-scale somewhere near eternity. Ashok Mitra is quoted: 'Each minister says "reform, streamlining, yes—but not in my ministry"' (Basu, 1986, p. 38).

The CPI(M) in West Bengal has come far, but over a decade in *office*, like non-Marxist parties in the West, it has difficulty in sustaining a head of steam and perhaps because, like the parties of the communist bloc, the organizational principle of democratic centralism prevents renewal of personnel and ideas. That said, the unattractiveness of the provincial Congress unit makes it unlikely the CPI(M) will not win a fourth term in due course.

12 Communism in a Micro State: Tripura and the Nationalities Question

*Harihar Bhattacharyya and T. J. Nossiter**

Tripura, third of India's Marxist-led states, is tiny compared with West Bengal and Kerala but this micro state, scarcely better known within India than outside, is of an interest out of all proportion to its size because here the communist movement faced the Nationalities Question in acute form. Its record in managing ethnic–communal tensions bears favourable comparison not just with 'local states' in the rest of India but sovereign states anywhere.

With an area of only 10,486 sq. km. and a population (1981) of just over two millions, it could well be a district in one of the largest Indian states. Its remoteness and micro-state character are two factors in its quite undeserved political neglect. 'Backwardness' and ethnic tensions are others. Although literacy (42 per cent, 1981) is now above the Indian average, and under the communist-led governments developing rapidly, it is only now that a university has just been founded in the state capital of Agartala. Ten per cent of Tripuris live in the Indian census's generously defined 'urban area' and the only town of note is the state capital itself. Rural poverty and the linguistic babel of Bengali, the main tribal language, Kok Borok, and the subsidiary tribal tongues further delayed the development of book and newspaper publishing. The Journalists' Association of Tripura did not hold its first conference until 1954 and found no need for another until 1960; the first significant newspaper in Kok Borok did not begin until 1960 nor the first *daily* paper. As in Kerala the communist workers' commitment to mass literacy and their facility in pamphleteering in local as well as more abstract idioms should never be underestimated in the advance of the movement. The ethnic tensions, which have meant that Tripura is a 'disturbed area', dangerous to travellers in the interior and prohibited to foreigners without a central government permit, are such that while communism is the dominant ideology, it is not truly hegemonic. In a country where ethnicity, religion and caste, suppurating with inequality and poisoned by politicians, have required

* Mr Harihar Bhattacharyya is at present a West Bengal Government State Student working on his doctoral thesis, 'Communism in Tripura', at the London School of Economics with Dr Nossiter.

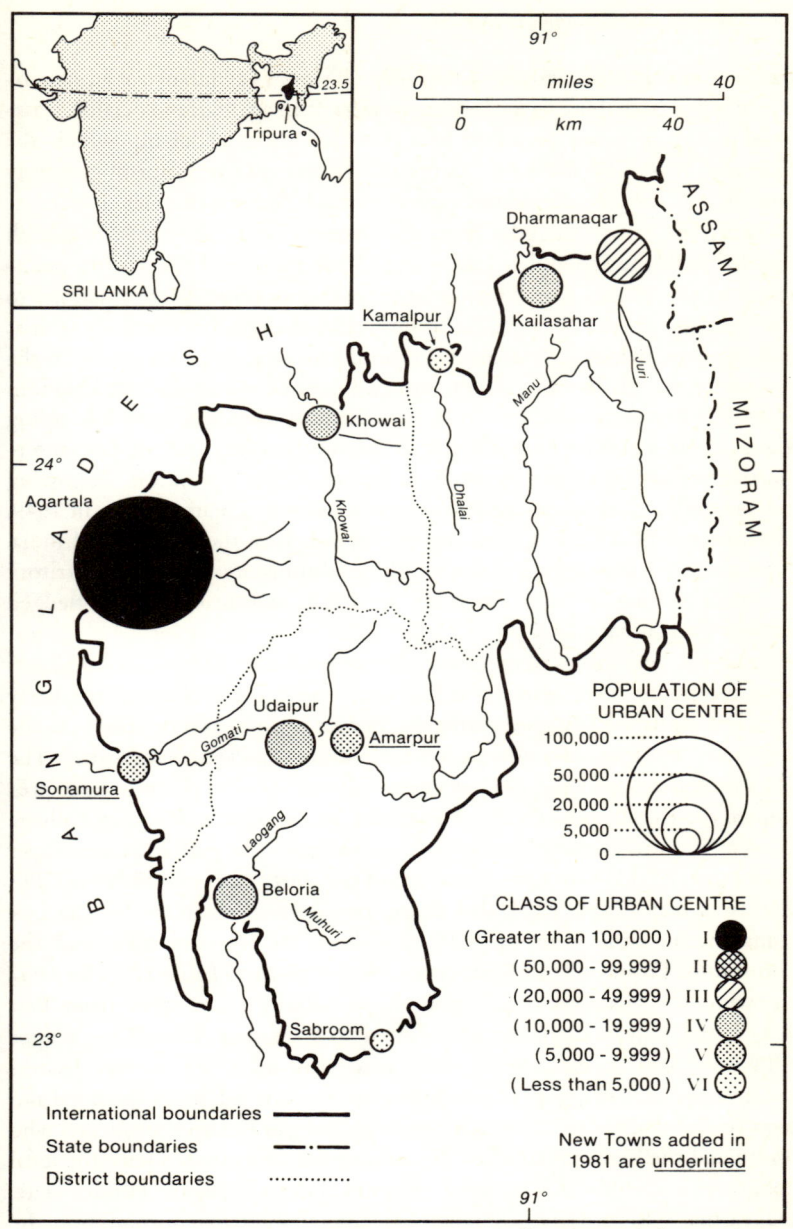

Map 3: Tripura

the lance of the *jawan* and the paramilitary, Tripura's avoidance of an Assam-type tragedy is a tribute to the healing powers of an egalitarian, socialist, class-based ideology when preached and practised by a leadership which the *Illustrated Weekly of India*—no particular friend of communism—recently described as frugally ascetic and quintessentially Marxist (Kumar, 1987).

The term 'tribal' in India normally denotes very low status. Although coupled with the Scheduled Castes and Other Backward Classes (untouchables) in the Indian Constitution as requiring positive discriminations to eradicate the impact of centuries of servitude, the tribal is routinely seen as ranking even below the outcaste. Tripura, however, is an exception to the rule. Here the tribals were Hindu and had maintained an ancient kingdom which the British recognised in 1765 as a princely state. The erstwhile ruling tribes are of a similar physical stature to the Bengalis and, of late, inter-marriages have become the rule rather than the exception. Following Independence, Tripura became what was known as a 'Part C' state in 1949, administered by a Chief Commissioner on behalf of the President of India. Subsequently it was upgraded to a centrally-administered or Union Territory in 1957, gaining a State Assembly in 1963, and reaching full-fledged statehood in January 1972.

From the beginnings of modern politics in the late 1930s the communists were the major force but it was not until the late 1940s when the party launched an armed struggle against the 'Nehru regime', as it defined it, in the state that communist ascendancy in local politics was clearly established. The CPI's performance in the 1952 elections entitles them to claim to have pre-empted the Kerala unit's 1957 achievement; in a poll for an Electoral College to select Tripura's representative to the Rajya Sabha (the parliamentary upper house) the CPI-led Front won nineteen of the thirty seats of which the CPI's share was fifty (Table 12.1); and in the first general elections for the Lok Sabha in the same year, the CPI took both the Tripura seats, and the Communist Front polled 61 per cent of the votes cast (Table 12.2). By 1957 following the electoral registration of post-Partition refugees from East Bengal, the political balance had shifted to Congress. That 'The refugee influx ... was a blessing to Congress' was admitted by its leaders (J. Chakrabarty, 1983, p. 77). Communist sources alleged 'a well-planned and deep-rooted conspiracy' in which 'minority Bengali Hindu bureaucrats who dominated the higher reaches of the administration colluded with the local Congress leadership to 'remake Tripura [as] a Bengali Hindu state' (Debvarma, 1981, p. 1). On a smaller scale than this 200,000 immigration, the 1967 exchange of population with (East) Pakistan (and refugees in 1971) also increased the pool of potential Congress voters. The communists ruefully

Table 12.1 Electoral College, Territorial Council and Legislative Assembly election results, Tripura, 1952–88

	1952		1957		1962		1967		1972		1977		1983		1988	
	Seats won	Per cent vote	Seats won	Per cent vote	Seats won	Per cent vote	Seats won	Per cent vote	Seats won	Per cent vote	Seats won	Per cent vote	Seats won	Per cent vote	Seats won	Per cent vote
CPI	15	48.3	13	38.4	13	44.9	1	9.3	1	2.8	0	1.1	0	0.8	—	
CPI(M)	—	—	—	—	—	—	2	21.7	17.3	8.6	53	49.2	37	46.8	26	50.27†
INC	11	29.5	15	40.3	17	43.1	27	58.2	41	44.9	0	17.5	12	30.5	24	
Neutral	2	16.4	1	8.3	0	7.5	0	4.0	0	12.3	0	2.1	2	2.9	—	2.13
TGS	2	3.6	1	4.4	—	—	—	—	—	—	—	—	—	—	—	
TUJS	—	—	—	—	—	—	—	—	0	0.4	4	7.9	6	10.5	7	
Other	0	2.2	0	8.7	0	4.3	0	6.8	0	1.1	3	12.0	3	8.5	2*	
Turnout	47.1		64.6		66.1		71.2		65.6		78.4		81.7		82.0	
Votes cast	127,961		279,894		317,867		432,019		500,866		753,062		926,928		1,114,687	

Source: Adapted from Ganchaudhury, 1985. * RSP † Left Front

Table 12.2 Lok Sabha Elections, Tripura, 1952–84

	1952		1957		1962		1967		1971		1977		1980		1984	
	Seats won	Per cent vote	Seats won	Per cent vote	Seats won	Per cent vote	Seats won	Per cent vote	Seats won	Per cent vote	Seats won	Per cent vote	Seats won	Per cent vote	Seats won	Per cent vote
CPI	2	61.3	1	45.1	2	51.3	–	–	0	6.8	0	2.2	–	–	–	–
CPI(M)	–	–	–	–	–	–	0	41.8	2	43.5	0	34.1	2	47.5	2	50.5
INC	0	25.6	1	46.0	0	42.8	2	58.2	0	36.3	1	39.7	0	22.9	0	45.6
Other	0	13.1	0	8.9	0	5.9	–	–	0	13.4	1	23.9	0	29.9	0	3.9

claimed that for every sixty Hindus who arrived in 1967 only one Muslim left. In the long run, however, Congress dissipated its opportunity to undermine the communist appeal beyond the tribals and the Muslim minority through a combination of personal rivalries between the two most prominent Tripura Congress leaders, Sacindralal Singha and Sukhumay Sengupta, and the local reverberations of national-level Congress factionalism (1966, 1969). The left's mobilization of discontent with the 1972 Congress Ministry's ill-conceived attempts to amend land reform legislation revived tribal support for the communists.

After Janata's victory in the post-Emergency general elections of 1977, any remaining party discipline in Congress(I) evaporated. The law of the surrounding jungle encroached on politics. It was every man for himself, and in March 1977 both Sengupta and Singha asked the CPI(M) to name the price of collaboration. Amid defections from Congress, the Sengupta Congress ministry finally fell. It was a situation which the CPI(M) exploited with great skill. In advance of state elections in December, the CPI(M) participated in two coalition ministries (with Congress for Democracy and then with Janata) which, though short-lived, played a valuable part in the left's advance. From a governmental base which included the Finance and Home portfolios, the CPI(M) was able to publicize the failures in the rival parties, exercise some patronage on behalf of its supporters and sympathizers, and win a platform with the more a-political sections of the electorate and bureaucracy.

The result of the December 1977 elections was a foregone conclusion. The communists' mass base among tribal and Bengali peasants alike was mobilized and the CPI(M) won an overwhelming fifty of the sixty assembly seats with 49 per cent of the votes cast on a turnout which had risen from 66 per cent in 1972 to an impressive 78 per cent. Congress's vote collapsed from 45 per cent to 17 per cent (Table 12.1). It could of course be argued that the electorate had voted against Congress rather than for the communists; but the result of the next elections in 1983, notwithstanding the bloody communal riots of 1980 when at least 1,000 people were killed, was striking confirmation of communist strength in the state. Although the CPI(M)'s seats fell to thirty-seven, its vote at 47 per cent on an 82 per cent turnout held up very well (Table 12.1).

In the most recent assembly elections (2 February 1988), the Left Front representation fell to twenty-eight (CPI(M) twenty-six and RSP two) despite a 50.27 per cent share of the poll on an 82 per cent turnout; and Congress (twenty-four) and the tribal Tripura Upjati Juba Samiti (TUJS, seven) in alliance have been able to form a ministry, irrespective of the outcome in one—CPI(M)-held—constituency where the death of the candidate prevented the ballot taking place. The Congress (I) leader, Sudhir Ranjan Majumdar, heads a ministry whose fragility is reflected in the fact that sixteen of the thirty-one government MLAs have been given portfolios so as, according to the Chief Minister, to represent 'all sections of the people of the state' (*The Sunday Observer*, Bombay, 7 February 1988). *India Today* sees it as a 'fissile coalition' of a Bengali-dominated Congress (I) and a purely tribal TUJS (29 February 1988).

Full details of the results are not yet available but it is clear that while there was a swing against the Left Front it was far from a landslide. 'So close was the result that the Congress-TUJS victory rests on the irregular and dubious recount which took place in the constituency of Majlispur. The CPI(M) candidate, Manik Dey, was first declared elected by 204 votes and the result announced. After a Congress (I) mob had invaded the building and manhandled the returning officer, the CPI(M) victor was summoned and a recount ordered. For his own safety the CPI(M) man had to leave and the result was reversed (*People's Democracy* 14 February 1988) allegedly by double stamping, and so invalidating, a bunch of CPI(M) votes. Elections were held in crisis. A 250-strong guerrilla force known as the Tripura National Volunteers, said to be the armed wing of the TUJS, and perhaps aided by fringe elements in Congress, was responsible for the killing of 105 people, including children. All appear to have been tribals and most, if not all, communist supporters. According to the (non-communist) well-informed correspondent of *The Sunday Observer* (7 February 1988): 'Reports reveal that the Congress (I) leaders ... hired the TNV gangs to kill and create terror' and an intelligence official 'had information that a Congress (I) MLA has given Rs 100,000' to the TNV for this purpose. Villagers noted non-tribals among the killers.

On the eve of the campaign, the Congress Central Government declared the entire state a disturbed area, not just parts as before, so introducing a large-scale military force, and in effect rule from Delhi. Besides the army, some 18,000 paramilitary forces were deployed; and it is in fact the first time that an election has been held in an Indian state totally designated as 'disturbed'. The TNV's reign of terror has to be seen in the context of the LF government's refusal to implement the (Federal) Anti-Terrorist Act on the grounds that it was undemocratic. As the Congress poll manager said 'introducing the armed forces ... had helped Congress' (*The Guardian*, London, 5 February 1988) by making Congress the party of law and order, and presumably in other ways as well. Polling at 82 per cent, at least, was peaceful and high. If the induction of the army into Tripura during the campaign was a politically motivated ploy, it would be wrong simply to argue that this determined the outcome of the election. The CPI(M) had become over-confident in the wake of their recent successes in West Bengal and Kerala, grossly underestimated the Congress (I)'s commitment, and, in any case, had lost the support of the floating vote in Tripura not just on law and order issues, but through an evident loss of direction and performance after a decade in government.

On the face of it, Tripura was one of the most unlikely parts of India to have become a communist stronghold. Its tribal character was matched by a shifting method of cultivation, locally known as *jum*, or slash and burn. It was in the 'development' stages of classical Marxism a primitive mode of production. Any Arcadian idyll was, however, ruptured first by intermittent tribal risings and rebellions against the ruling tribe (1850, 1860–1, 1863, 1877, 1939–44), and second by the royal family's encouragement of Bengali settlement in their domain. This love affair with Bengal had begun as early as the fifteenth century. Bengali was adopted as the court language; and by 1872 when the first (inexact) census was held, the tribal proportion of the population had fallen to 64 per cent. By the turn of the century, tribals were down to 52 per cent; but it was between 1941 (50 per cent) and 1951 (35 per cent) as a consequence of the turmoil of Partition that the indigenous people became a minority in their country. By 1981 according to the official census the tribal percentage was as low as 28 per cent while the Bengalis had risen to 70 per cent. A press report in early 1987 gave a figure for Tripura's eighteen tribes as low as 15 per cent (Associated Press, *The Guardian*, 1 February 1987).

Clearly Tripura communism is not Bengali communism in exile. It is the Congress party in the state which is the profoundly pro-Bengali party, to the degree that it is not seriously disputed that some of its leaders had an active role in collusion with the Bengali communal party, Amra Bengali ('We the Bengalis') in the 1980 anti-tribal riots. The CPI(M) can fairly claim to be the one party which draws support from majority and minority communities. The evidence of the exclusively tribal elections to District Councils in the 1980s confirms that the communists enjoy significant support among the tribals. In 1982 and 1985 the CPI(M) and CPI combined won 59 and 44 per cent respectively of the votes for these Left Front-created bodies (Table 12.3).

Given that the tribals now, however, form about one quarter of the state's population, it follows that the Left has support among the Bengalis, otherwise the Front's performance in recent assembly elections is inexplicable. The secular character of CPI(M) support is reflected in the communal composition of the party's own hierarchy: Nripen Chakraborty, Chief Minister from 1977 to 1988, is Bengali; his Deputy, Dasarath Deb, is tribal; of the 35-member state committee, twelve are tribals and three of the

Table 12.3 Tripura: Tribal Area Autonomous District Council Results, 1982 and 1985

	1982		1985	
	Seats won	Per cent vote	Seats won	Per cent vote
CPI	1	3.3	0	1.4
CPI(M)	19	56.0	15	42.3
INC	—	—	3	14.3
RSP	0	1.2	—	—
FB	1	1.3	—	—
TUJS	7	37.5	10	33.5
Neutral	0	0.1	0	1.8
THPP	—	—	0	7.2

nine-member state secretariat, proportions which are roughly in line with the communal balance of the state as a whole (Kumar, 1987, p. 27).

Social Roots of Tripura Radicalism

To understand the complex interplay of class, ethnicity and religion three groups of Bengali migrants should be distinguished: the earlier waves of land-hungry peasants; the far smaller number of Bengali middle classes in search of professional opportunity; and post-Independence refugees from Pakistan and then Bangladesh. The first were pushed by the pressure of population on land, high rent levels and eviction in Bengal and Assam, and pulled by the liberal land-grant and low rent policies of the Tripuri kings who were anxious to introduce settled agriculture and so raise the country's income. The net result of the interaction over time between the peasant-hungry land (Tripura) and the land-hungry peasants (Bengal) was the development of rural social stratification. Of the nearly half a million agrarian population in 1951 (Census Reports, India, 1951) 2.5 per cent were rent receivers, 79.5 per cent owner-cultivators, 11.6 per cent tenant-cultivators and 6.4 per cent agricultural labourers. By 1981 labourers were 29 per cent of the rural work-force. Plough cultivation had extended to

13.6 per cent of the tribal population in 1931 and by 1961 the formation of rural classes among the tribals was paralleling that among the Bengalis and other non-tribals settled in Tripura. Of the rural tribals 69 per cent held some kind of tenure (100 per cent of the non-tribals): 17 per cent as *ryotwari* (29 per cent non-tribals); 30 per cent as sharecroppers (52 per cent non-tribal); and 11 per cent (5 per cent non-tribal) as sub-tenants. Although much more research needs to be done, it seems probable that the common experience of tribal and non-tribal people in a new rural economy has until relatively recently minimized communal tensions and maximized possibilities for class-based political mobilization. Latterly, however, the scale of demographic upheaval and the exhaustion of any remaining opportunities for agricultural expansion have threatened the historic accommodation of Bengali and tribal.

Tripura also received members of the Bengali middle classes who constituted a significant part of migration to Tripura. Unlike Bengal, Tripura did not witness the growth of an indigenous middle class. Men of liberal profession, though small in number, were mostly immigrants. Trade, commerce and services were in the hands of the outsiders. Under the impact of the Bengal Renaissance of the nineteenth century, Tripura experienced its 'own' Renaissance which ran from the late nineteenth century through the reign of King Birendra Kishore Manilkya (1909-23). But this so-called Tripura Renaissance was mainly brought about by 'surplus *bhadralok*' from Bengal who enjoyed royal patronage. As a movement it did not go beyond the charmed circles of retainers. For obvious reasons, the Tripura Renaissance did not give rise to political contradictions between the middle classes and the political rule of monarchy.

The third, and post-1947 element in Bengali migration is the most problematic. Arriving in three surges—1947, 1967 and 1971—they are poor, frightened, and the most directly in competition with the tribals for a bare subsistence. Disproportionately, they have turned to Congress (I) for protection and their most extreme fringe is the core of the Amra Bengali movement, which engineered the anti-tribal riots of 1980. Conversely, it is they who are the first targets of the TUJS's platform of land recovery and the TNV guerrilla attacks, which resulted in the loss of 105 lives in the month-long election campaign of early 1987.

In conventional terms Tripura was regarded as 'backward' even in the early twentieth century but by 1951 nearly a quarter of the male population was literate (6 per cent of the female population). To a limited degree by the 1940s this expansion of educational opportunity had created a new group of educated tribal youth discontented by their denial of posts in senior administration. Educated Bengalis had been and were employed in the modernization of government as a matter of royal policy. The senior echelons were typically filled by retired civil servants from Bengal. In so far as there were real avenues of employment in public service for native Tripuris, they were in the King's Bodyguard Force or, more often, in the First Tripura Rifles, who in 1948 were to attempt a *coup d'état* against the unpopular Regency.

It was this group of educated but under-employed tribal young men who took the initiative in forming the Tripura Rajya Jan Sikha Samity (Organization for Eradication of Mass Illiteracy) in 1945, which was to be important both as a vehicle for the development of Tripuri nationalism and for communist proselytization. There is a striking analogy with equivalent campaigning in Kerala in the late 1940s. Members of the disaffected tribal elites, many of them self-professed Marxists, turned in the late 1940s to the development of a radicalized doctrine of Tripuri nationalism. The process was, in several respects, akin to that of nationality formation in northern India analysed by Paul Brass (1974). An elite group takes up the leadership, attaches symbolic values to certain objective characteristics of a group, creates a myth of group history and destiny, and attempts to communicate that myth to the target population (p. 44). As symbols of language, religion, history and cultural traits are added, a full-blown and coherent myth may develop (p. 413). In the adumbration of Tripuri nationalism at this time three themes are notable: the self-consciously Marxist approach; the central concern for political power; and the deployment of Tripuri language as a major symbol of group identity and an argument for self-determination within the Indian Union. Realistically it was known that the only alternative could have been incorporation within Bengal or Assam, neither of which was tolerable.

History, for this Tripuri counter-elite, was that of the common man long subjected to a tribal-feudal socio-economic order: 'these people by their valour and heroism, struggle, hard labour and sacrifice, had laid the foundations of the history of Tripura; by clearing up the jungle full of wild animals, they had transformed this barren land into a resourceful and wealthy one' (*Chiniha*, edited by Prabhat Roy and Bansi Thakur, No. 1, p. 1). The real Tripuris had been alienated from their heritage by the malign influence of the 'surplus *bhadralok*' from Bengal who had brought with them the Bengali renaissance and given rise to the pseudo-Tripura Renaissance so subordinating Tripura language and culture. The vitality of Tripuri culture however was so strong that, although compelled to speak Bengali in trade, business and exchange, their own language survived. 'Language was organically connected with the mode of production. The existence of class divisions within the mode of production was anathema to the development of language. Economic discriminations were at the root of linguistic discrimination and domination' (*Chiniha*, No. 2, p. 94). Passages from the *Rajmala*, the chronicle of the Tripura dynasty, were cited: 'In order to conquer Bangladesh [Bengal], the great king Bijoy Manikya mobilised 24,000 infantrymen. He easily conquered the nearby Bengal areas and seized enormous amounts of wealth'. 'What we see today in the demand for Tripura language is a demand of the struggling people of a backward nation. Exploited and oppressed by the Bengalis, the Nationalist movement of the Tripurs is basically manifesting itself in the demand of language. This demand is as natural as the natural laws of history' (*Chiniha*, No. 37, p. 246). (Religion was not used as a symbol since Hinduism was common to most Tripuris and Bengali migrants.) For Marxists the contradictions should have been obvious. Despite the awareness of the tribal-feudal order, the writers were emphasizing the political unity of Tripuri ruler and ruled at the expense of the class unity of peasants and labourers of tribal and non-tribal origin. With the reduction of the monarchical power first to constitutional status and later its extinction, the contradiction diminished and a more doctrinally pure Marxism came to prevail but the cleavage between tribal and Bengali remains only just below the level of acceptable communist discourse in the 1980s.

As in Kerala, communism had arrived late in Tripura—towards the end of the 1930s. It was brought there by a group of ex-terrorist nationalists from Tripura who had been converted in jail.

In 1939 the local Police Commissioner complacently reported that 'the only disturbing element was a batch of the ex détenus, numbering 22 who were sitting idle in the State. Each', he continued patronizingly, 'considered himself a martyr to the cause of the country and thought it was up to him to redress the grievances of the dumb millions of the land' (Chakravarti, 1985, p. 363) The ex-détenus mainly worked through the Janamangal Samity (Anusilan terrorists by origin) founded in 1938, although Gana Parishad (Jugantar) was a further vehicle of propaganda as well as, somewhat improbably, the Tripura Automobile Association.

The initial communist cell (?1937) concentrated on ideological work among the students at the Umakanta Academy in Agartala itself and the Students' Federation presented an address to M. N. Roy when he passed through neighbouring British India. The difficulties of organizing among the tribals, as yet rarely literate, still primarily practising shifting cultivation and generally in thrall to their tribal chiefs and to the king, were all too real. From 1938 onwards, however, the communists began to operate through a succession of emergent mass organizations dedicated to popular uplift; Jana

Mangal Samity (1938-42); Jana Shikha Samity (1945-8); and Praja Mandal (1946-8). Their aims were, variously, welfare, literacy, responsible government, (tribal) national liberation, and agrarian reform; and all provided a fertile ground for recruitment to the communist cause. The intelligence forces were well informed in the late 1930s, quickly noting the formation of a student library and the real function of the Tea Stall party 'office', which was 'purely a political institution in disguise . . . financed by the Anusilan Group' (p. 366); but they failed to forestall the distribution in Agartala of leaflets in Bengali headed 'Impending Revolution' on the night of 3 August 1940, which marked the point at which the communists went public.

The legalization of the communist party after the entry of the Soviet Union into the Second World War on the Allied side enabled the members to operate more freely but the local unit was still too small to capitalize on the possibilities of war-time economic deprivation in Tripura in the remote north-east. The one social protest movement of the People's War era, 1942-5, was the (tribal) Reang Revolt of 1943, which was unconnected with communist activity. Information is scanty on the use to which the small party unit put the new-found legality but a revealing illustration is the formation of a Boy's (which included girls) Association (Kishore Sangha) in Agartala. Besides distributing food, this communist-led club founded rural libraries and sought to build 'ideal character' (T. C. Sen, 1970, p. 83). The anti-illiteracy movement (Tripura Rajya Janashiksa Samity) formed by a few educated tribal young men in 1945 and opposed by the Maharaja developed a close relationship with the communists and when the CPI was banned by the new Indian Government in 1948 the Samity was also suppressed, though not formally outlawed. After the war it became clear the party had laid the groundwork in 1939-42 for the successful identification of the liberation struggle of the Tripura tribespeople with the communist cause. At the CPI's 2nd (Calcutta) Congress in February-March 1948, the party nationally had adopted an all-out insurrectionary line. In Tripura this reinforced an existing readiness to engage in armed struggle but the Tripura unit's analysis of its local conditions led to a strategy not dissimilar to that of the Andhra unit, which circulated their dissenting *Letter* three months after the Calcutta gathering. Whereas the Calcutta line presumed, on the Soviet model, an urban-based attempt to destabilize the government through politicized strikes leading to a general rising in the countryside, the Andhra line envisaged a quasi-Maoist tactic whereby a prolonged civil war would be fought from liberated villages by a united front of the entire peasantry. Clearly this model was far more relevant to an area where the only town was Agartala and there were neither factories nor trades unions.

Following the close of the Calcutta Congress, the Tripura delegates, Aghore Devbarma and (the Bengali) Biren Datta, who has most claim to be the father of Tripura communism, returned to Agartala. Together with Sudhanwa Devbarman and Dasrath Dev(barman), the future Deputy Chief Minister, then a postgraduate at Calcutta University, they took to the hills to form the Tripura Rajya Mukti (Liberation) Parishad (TRMP/GMP) and consider tactics. The GMP rapidly became the political platform for the tribals. The outcome was a distinctive synthesis of Tripura experience with the Calcutta and Andhra lines.

The economic situation in Tripura had not begun to recover from the war-time privations when the dire effects of Partition were visited on the state: a massive influx of refugees from East Pakistan; and an economic blockade by the new Pakistani government. To the dislocation of the market for forest products was added an outbreak of disease among the cattle population, while at a political level there were rumours that Pakistan would invade and an unpopular and insecure Regency in the Palace.

The party leadership watched and waited. Tripura was gripped by an acute food crisis in 1948. A mass tribal rally organized in Agartala in September focused on the shortages, agrarian exploitation, and above all on the practice of *dadan*, the advance purchase of tribal crops by moneylenders at a massive discount on what they would have fetched later in the open market. On 9 October 1948 the anticipated spontaneous combustion took place, which later became known as the Golghati Incident. One of the most notorious of the moneylenders, Hari Charan Saha, a Bengali merchant, had recently extended his operations to the tribal hamlet of Golghati, near Agartala. News came that he was preparing to take a large quantity of foodgrains to the distant Bishalgarh market, so aggravating the local shortage. Negotiations opened between tribal and Muslim peasantry and Saha to secure local sale on reasonable credit terms but, despite the offer of written documentation, Saha resiled on the agreement. On the basis of a secret understanding with (Bengali) police, an ambush was set up at the site for the final talks; and seven tribals and two Bengali Muslims were killed. The incident, Dasarath Deb, one of the leaders of the GMP later wrote, convinced them that 'the Congress regime was on a war path, and the time was ripe to launch a powerful armed resistance ... thus the decision to acquire arms, if necessary by force, and to form guerrilla squads was taken' (Deb(varma), 1987, pp. 40-1).

Meanwhile the GMP conspired with the state's 'army', the First Tripura Rifles, some of whose officers as well as many other ranks had become disabused with the government's policies, to seize power. The plot inevitably failed, several leaders were arrested and, in 1949, the regiment was disbanded.

None the less, the sum of these and related incidents ensured the GMP, and so the CPI, a mass base. Cashiered soldiers took to the hills; several of the GMP key figures evaded capture; and tribals, Bengali Muslims and non-Bengali Hindus provided safe houses. A four-man team, which included Nripen Chakrabarty, the future Chief Minister, was despatched from Calcutta to assist in the organization of the underground and within months a liberated area had been established on sufficient scale to merit the epithet, Parallel Government. For over a year, the legal authorities writ was largely confined to the vicinity of Agartala itself.

In contrast to other areas of communist penetration, where the cadres were decimated during the 1948–51 attempt at insurrection, in Tripura it was the communists' class enemies who bore the brunt of the violence. But since the majority of the privileged were Bengali, the class enemy quickly became conflated in the tribal consciousness with the communal enemy; and relations between the Bengalis and the tribals deteriorated. Trade was at an absolute standstill. When in 1950–1, the CPI nationally changed its line to constitutionality and acceptance of the new Indian state's legitimacy, the Tripura comrades moved rapidly to set up a Peace Committee (1951). The government had, however, meanwhile begun to reassert its position; a Gurkha regiment and harsh repression were eroding the rebels' military position at the same time as the influx of (pro-Congress) refugees from East Pakistan was laying an anti-communist support base. Nevertheless, when the insurrectionary line was abandoned there were some 800 dedicated and proven party members and a remarkable 300,000 members of the GMP, when the total population was only 700,000. With nearly half the people opposed to the regime, it was a moot point where legitimate authority lay.

The difficulties of adjustment however were real despite the remarkable party discipline. Of importance in bringing about the transition was the establishment of the 50,000-strong Santi Sena, at once committed to reconstruction and election campaigning. The party needed, as elsewhere in India, to persuade its cadres to commit themselves to the ballot box but they had also to subordinate themselves to the aims and line of the all-India party. When the Tripuri movement entered the arena of Indian communism in the early 1950s, it already had a distinctive tradition of its own: a decade-long proto-nationalism; a communist and tribal armed struggle; and what state-communist leaders later described self-critically as the bourgeois-led traits of a peasant movement—localism, sectarianism, opportunism, terrorism and 'tailism' (following on behind). The validity of the charges is less relevant than the fact that their very assertion reflected serious inner-party conflicts centring on the relations between the party and its mass organizations, in particular between the Gani Mukti Parishad and the Kisan Sabha, the CPI-led orthodox peasant association.

At the first general elections of January 1952 the Tripura communists followed united front tactics, utilizing the political platform of the Gana Tantrik Sangha (Democratic Association). In a semi-legal situation, this paid dividends and showed the support that the communists enjoyed among earlier Bengali immigrants particularly Muslims and among the tribals. The recent pro-Congress and entirely Hindu refugees were not, of course, yet generally registered to vote. Congress was routed in those areas which had been the base of the GMP and secured only 26 per cent of the parliamentary vote overall. As the official report on the elections stated: 'The communist party is the most active party in Tripura. [It] emerged as the largest single party in the state, the only state where the CPI has been able to attain that position' (Kogelkar & Park, 1956, pp. 312-15).

Since 1952 the electoral contest in Tripura has been essentially bi-polar: communists versus Congress. Splits in the two major parties have tended to weaken Congress(I) rather than the communists. In 1964 virtually the entire CPI switched over to the CPI(M) and although there have been minor defections (or expulsions) since, the CPI(M) has remained publicly at least more or less united. Interventions by third forces of national origin, such as Jana Sangh or the Praja Socialists, have only briefly disturbed the pattern. Local communal parties have in recent years created something of a two-and-a-half party system. The All Tripura People's Liberation Organization was won over to the CPI(M) ranks but significantly it is the TUJS, a tribal youth association formed under the combined auspices of the CPI(M) and CPI in 1967, which has latterly complicated the electoral equation. The influx of Bengalis in 1967 and 1971 led to its capture by tribal separatist elements and its current platform is the disenfranchisement of those not eligible to vote in 1952. In 1977 TUJS won four seats and 8 per cent of the poll in the assembly elections and in alliance with Congress(I) in 1983 six seats and 7 per cent of the poll. Again allied to Congress, TUJS won seven out of twenty-eight seats (38 per cent of the poll) in the 1982 Tribal District Elections and ten out of twenty-five seats (34 per cent) in the 1985 District elections. As this book goes to press TUJS has done much to deny the CPI(M)-led Left Front a third term of office through its blocking and opportunistic alliance with the almost exclusively Bengali Congress unit in Tripura. If the CPI(M) managed with great difficulty to reconcile tribal and Bengali interests within one party, it is hard to see TUJS and Congress(I) working harmoniously in government together, especially when Congress nationally controls the deployment of troops and paramilitary forces in a 'disturbed area'. The Bengali communal party, Amra Bengali, won one seat with 6 per cent of the vote in the 1983 assembly elections.

The TUJS is a legitimate political party but it is alleged to encourage the small but effective guerrilla grouping, the Tripura National Volunteers (TNV), said to be not more than 200 strong but enjoying sufficient sympathy among some sections of the tribal people to require thirteen battalions of paramilitary forces to maintain something approaching law and order in Tripura. On the eve of the February 1988 elections, they were responsible for the massacre of thirty-one people in one incident. The TNV leader, Bijoy Hrangkhwal, had unsuccessful talks with Nripen Chakraborty in 1982, and the TNV has written to the Indian Prime Minister.

The Nationality Question and Tripura Communism

In handling the differing degrees of tribal resentment, the Marxist-led government has combined political solutions, such as the 1979 Tribal Autonomous District Councils Act, which, however, was clumsily handled and provoked a bloody Bengali backlash, with periodic all-out offensives against communal outrage, but the future is increasingly uncertain. On the one hand, the local Congress(I) unit is less than scrupulous in its attitude towards communalism—the mobilizing of one caste or community against another—the more so because it has precious little stable organization and even less 'ideology'; on the other hand the CPI(M) has had a hard fight to maintain secularism in Tripura politics. Chakraborty, the 'Bengali', was selected as Chief Minister and Deb, the 'tribal' as his Deputy in 1977 by Promode Das Gupta, the West Bengal party secretary, on expedient rather than dispassionate grounds. The party has struggled continually to dampen down incipient Bengali/ministerial-tribal/mass front factionalism within the movement, up to and including the state committee itself. Deb, in particular, is subject to cross pressures: within his 'community' he can be a 'traitor' by virtue of his loyalty to his 'class', the peasantry. Writing recently on the GMP's history, Deb ended an historical account of the Tripura peasant front with a clear warning which re-emphasized the fact that ethnicity vies with class in the consciousness of many in Tripura: 'there is no way we can avoid finding a solution to the nationality question' in Tripura (Deb, 1986, p. 16).

The crucial moment will undoubtedly be the point at which the veteran Chief Minister finally steps down. For all his charm, asceticism and integrity, Chakraborty has been an authoritarian as well as an authoritative figure in

Tripura communism since the early 1950s. While as a Bengali it may be that he has been more capable of making concessions to tribal interest than his heir apparent, Deb, there are critics within the party who feel that his Napoleonic style of political leadership has at least latterly been at odds with the party political accommodation implicit in efficacious democratic centralism. The Deputy Chief Minister, twenty years younger than Nripen Chakraborty, is the only candidate with the weight and experience to succeed him. If his tribal origin will be a gloss on his every action, the fact that the transition is likely to take place out of government may facilitate that reintegration of the communist movement which may well be a necessary condition of success in future elections.

The nationality question has been central to left politics in Tripura and the interplay of class and ethnicity has posed, and continues to pose, the greatest challenge to communism in the state. Paradoxically, the Tripura communists whose original support base lay with the tribes have only recently focused on the tribal nationality problem as a distinct issue of urgent concern. The movement has, historically, confined itself to the specific economic demands of the tribes. As Aghore Devbarma, a veteran communist tribal leader—now with the CPI—self-critically observes:

the question of the national self-determination of the tribes was (in the past) avoided on the grounds that it was alone in socialism that a solution to the nationality problem was to be found. Therefore whatever was done for the tribes, was only partially so done. The communist party never launched any determined struggle for the national self-determination of the tribals of the state [Devbarma, 1981, p. 12]

The 1986 Conference Report of the Tripura Agricultural Workers' Association, while noting the emergence of a homogeneous class of landless agricultural labour, 'admitted that this class, economically the weakest but politically the progressive, have apart from their economic demands, demands for their overall development as a nationality'. In order, the report went on, to 'fight back the forces of ultra nationalism, we need to develop class consciousness among them' (Tripura Agricultural Workers' Association, 1986, pp. 12–13).

The Left Front's reconciliation of the conflict of class and ethnicity takes the form of the creation of autonomous tribal self-government which 'is an organic part of the democratic movement in the state' and designed to lift the tribes who are lagging behind in development 'to the level of the other advanced nationalities' (ibid., p. 12). In 1979 the Assembly passed the Tripura Tribal Areas Autonomous District Council Act. This set up—following elections in January 1982—an Autonomous District Council (ADC) over

68 per cent of the state with a population of 31 per cent, which was 76 per cent tribal. The council is made up of twenty-eight elected members (twenty-one of whom are reserved for the Scheduled Tribes) and two nominated members, and has a seven-member Executive (one non-tribal) with portfolios and staff covering land, education, industries, tribal welfare and so on. Initially, the ADC's freedom of action was constrained by its constitution under the Indian Constitution's Schedule VII but its inclusion in the VIth Schedule in 1985 gave it much more freedom of action by conferring powers to frame by-laws, especially in agrarian related matters, and a range of important executive powers to match. There are also powers to levy taxes (professional, land revenue and agricultural income), market and other fees, and to receive a share of forest and mining royalties (Tripura Tribal Areas Autonomous District Council, n.d. ?1986). Although the cash available is obviously limited and the powers finite, there is no doubt that the ADC has worked well and begun to reduce the gap between advanced and backward sections of society. What has been more difficult is to persuade the majority Bengali community to accept the claim of the tribals for the return of lands alienated in dubious circumstances; and it is this failure which has, more than anything else, contributed to the support for the TUJS and the TNV. None the less the ADC is a sign that the communist movement has increasingly recognized tribal nationalism as a distinct force in the state and not as merely a second-order derivation of capitalism reducible in the last analysis to the economic distortions of true class consciousness.

The Left Front's Record in Government

In general how effective was the CPI(M)-led Front in government over the ten years to 1988? The limited character of provincial administrations to bring about change in India applies with special force in a state of Tripura's size. With two MPs Tripura counts for next to nothing in the all-India power equation even if Rajiv Gandhi visited it during the 1988 election campaign. The north-eastern zone as a whole claims neglect but Tripura's plan assistance is miserly by this regional standard: in the 6th Plan period (1980-5) Tripura's estimated receipts of Rs495 per capita compares badly with Nagaland's Rs 1624 and Sikkim's Rs 2316, other 'special category' states. Until 1972 when Tripura became a full state, there was little scope for formulating any development plans independently of central government. Natural resources are meagre and communications poor, both internally and externally. There is no rail link with the rest of India and Tripura's isolation is conveyed in the fact that the border with Bangladesh is five times as long as that with the adjacent provinces of Assam and Mizoram. The tiny population (estimated 2.5 million in 1988) means that the quantum of cash, whether generated domestically or through central aid, is far too small for major investment programmes. Plan contributions at current prices were only Rs 51 per capita in 1972-3 and Rs 222 per capita ten years later, well below the national average despite the special factors of refugees, tribals and near total dependency on agriculture. In 1982-3 less than £40 million was available to the state in sum. Worse, what funds were approved were far from fully utilized: 82 per cent of state plan outlays and an utterly unsatisfactory 56 per cent of central schemes in 1977-8 (M. Dasgupta, n.d., p. 7). Two-thirds of the State Domestic Product is generated in the primary sector and the latest (1977-8) estimates of poverty on official all-India criteria are that as many as 86 per cent of the rural population (44 per cent of the small—11 per cent— urban) and 82 per cent of the total survive rather than live. One-third of the rural population (1977-8) spends less than Rs 40 per capita per month and 92 per cent less than Rs 80 (Government of Tripura, 1983, p. 35) Literacy is only 42 per cent overall and down to 12 per cent among tribal women.

Understandably, before and after 1972 planning in the state has emphasized social services, agriculture, and irrigation and power. Less defensibly, until 1977-8 and the Left Front, it was the western part of Tripura—the plains and the urban areas—which benefited most from modern education, communication and health care. The largely hilly and tribal east was neglected as were the scheduled castes (15 per cent) and tribes (28 per cent) generally.

When the Left Front took over in 1978 it was pledged to redirect planning to the relief of the poor and to involve the people in the process of planning while at the same time ensuring that the limited growth potential in the economy was fully utilized. The Chief Minister's initial statement to the State Planning Board was cautious: the short term goals of planning must be 'very moderate' as 'in the present frame of things' it was impossible to 'radically change the conditions of the people' (p. 10). Among the proposals were more attention to small-scale agricultural and forest-based industry, the protection of the sharecroppers from eviction, free land to the *jhumias* and landless, improved rural credit especially through cooperatives, and education and health for the hitherto neglected areas. For some within and without the Front the approach was seen as anti-growth while an ultra-left group attacked it as welfarism, the giving of trivial concessions which would tend to maintain, not undermine, the status quo. The shift in objectives—and popular involvement through *panchayats*, blocks and ADC was given concrete shape in the Sixth Plan (1980-5): a distinct improvement in standards of living and a more equitable distribution of assets and income. Both the Sixth and Seventh (1985-90) Plans embody the overarching importance attached to social and community services on the one hand and agricultural and rural development on the other (pp. 12-13).

The delays in the publication of data in India make it difficult to offer a properly documented assessment of the achievement of the Front between 1978 and 1988, but nevertheless progress has clearly been made. The average annual growth rate has risen from 3.6 per cent in 1978-80 to an estimated 4.2 per cent in 1980/1 to 1984/5 although this is still below the all-India figure for the early 1980s of 5.2 per cent. It is presumed that the poverty alleviation programmes have had some impact also. Various sectors are showing some growth, notably fisheries, forestry and animal husbandry, the health services, irrigation and roads. Some 60 per cent of all households in the state are now members of reconstructed cooperatives and the decentralization of plan execution, especially through the ADC, has been effective. The funds that have been allocated are much more fully utilized and some additional funds for particular projects have been obtained from the centre.

The shortcomings and failures of planning under the Front are itemized in a recent semi-official Tripura commentary as: the growth rate of the agricultural sector; the discovery and distribution of surplus land; the negligible progress on industrialization; villages still without primary schools; the continuing imbalance between health care in the urban and rural areas; the appearance of a new class of vested interests who have benefited from the welfare measures; and the absence of any real popular involvement in plan formulation as opposed to plan execution.

'The critics of the Left Front Government'—and we can safely take that to mean those who are friendlily disposed—

> blame it for not being able to distribute surplus land and for not decentralising planning to the desired extent. They also find fault with the Government for not educating the people politically so that they expect too much ... [but] the state Government would do well to take heed of the legitimate criticism ... It should cut down administrative and bureaucratic delays, introduce a system of monitoring the performance of plans, lay stress on identifying, acquiring and alloting surplus land and ensure that popular participation becomes effective in plan formulation and execution. It should consider the possibility of laying down the perspectives for the long run development of the State as till now the short run approach to planning has been clearly enunciated. In the final analysis, planning only can be successful if the level of consciousness of the people is raised ...

and that is what could provide a viable alternative to the conventional approach to planning in India as a whole.

The CPI(M)'s own report (CPI(M), 1982, p. 43) on the first four years of Left Front government is sparse. After reference to the Tribal District Councils, the recognition of the tribal language, Kok Borak, and 'to the extent possible' restoration of land alienated from the tribals, the brief account refers only to (i) the reduction in the burden of taxation and debt on the weaker sections; (ii) the introduction of free education at all stages; (iii) enhancement of agricultural and other labourers' wage rates; (iv) the (centre-funded) food-for-work programme; and (v) attacks on moneylenders and contractors through the development of co-operatives.

Agrarian reform is the principal sphere for state-level governmental action. In Tripura such efforts are, of course, caught up in the trammels of community, Bengali versus tribal. In princely Tripura no land reform measures were undertaken at all and the state's first such legislation was the 1960 Land Revenue and Land Reforms Act. Landlord-tenant relations had been governed by a law of 1886 and broadly speaking the land system resembled that of Bengal. Apart from general arguments from equality and efficiency, the particular grounds for reform in Tripura were the impact on rentals of the inflow of refugees, many of whom had been cultivators in East Pakistan before leaving, and the sale, forced or free, of tribal-held land to Bengalis. The 1960 Act dealt with a range of issues: the abolition of intermediary interests in land; the rights of the cultivating tenants; land ceilings and the acquisition of any excess; the proper maintenance of records; and, above all, the prevention of the alienation of tribal lands. All transfers of land by tribals to non-tribals were disallowed, except where prior permission had been given by the collector (district officer) in writing or as a mortgage to a cooperative society.

For reasons peculiar to Tripura as well as all the usual recourses of the privileged classes of agrarian society, the Act was of more symbolic than substantive import. In practice the ceiling for a family's personal cultivation turned out to be 150 acres, not counting the scope for circumvention given by the exclusion of land used for non-agricultural purposes. Very little land was recovered for redistribution. Much land in the 1950s had been allocated to refugees from East Pakistan, often in small parcels, which was then sub-let to sharecroppers or other sub-tenants mainly on verbal, not written, contracts. Both sharecroppers and tribals were at a grave disadvantage in securing their paper rights. In fact the alienation of land continued unabated after the Act. Since the official figures rest on the clearly incomplete and dubious field index of rights, it is certain that their analysis seriously underestimates inequalities. Eleven per cent of landholders ten years after the Act came into force operated 46 per cent of the total area of holdings and 46 per cent of poor tenants (with less than 0.5 hectares) operated only 11 per cent of the total area of operational holdings. Apart from the high ceiling and the holes in it, the growing pauperization of the rural population led to still more alienation of land from tenants to the big landowners and money lenders. The various plan schemes for raising agricultural production have, if anything, only served to strengthen the position of the bigger farmers, even better placed to lease land from refugees who could not afford to cultivate it. The failure of the parent act to make more than marginal inroads into rural inequality, insecurity and exploitation led to major amending acts in 1974 and 1976.

Two features of this last Congress government legislation stand out. The onus of proof that a sharecropper or under-tenant was the true tiller still lay with the *bargadar* not, as in Kerala (1969) or West Bengal (1977), the landlord farmer or lessor. In the absence of an adequate index of right, 'deemed tenancy' is a necessity for real land reform. The second frustration of a fundamental object of the legislation was the cut-off date for restoration of lands illegally alienated from the tribals by government action: 1 January 1969. The Amendment did not of course 'bar any aggrieved person from seeking redress in Civil Courts' in relation to alienations prior to that date but the chances of a tribal succeeding in such an enterprise were as great as him flying to Delhi. Last, the 1974 amendment repealed 1931 and 1943 Tribal Reserve Orders. Although modified in 1975 to give first right of purchase of land in 137 scheduled villages to non-tribals, the change was only cosmetic. In the words of an academic commentary 'the number of landless tribals has so swollen up that something is urgently needed to be done to provide lands to the needy tribal households to check the mounting tension in the countryside' (Ganguly, 1981, p. 68). Legislation implemented by a bureaucracy and adjudicated by courts close to the relatively privileged classes is no solution. What was required was a government with the will to support popular participation in land reform through an organized party movement. Did the Left Front offer it?

The short answer is no. The land question in Tripura is very different from that of West Bengal. The fundamental problem in Tripura is the restoration of illegally transferred land from Bengalis to tribals in the absence of any record of sharecropper rights and the presence of a politically powerful Bengali vested interest. The 1977 Left Front Manifesto recognized this but its performance was far from adequate. The government's own reports are scanty—two references in the 1985 CPI(M) Congress report the redistribution of land to 100,000 landless (p. 173)—or apologetic—restoration of alienated land to the tribals *'to the extent possible'* (p. 27, emphasis added). In fact the 1988 election manifesto records the Left Front's 'most remarkable achievement' as the formation of the Tribal ADC (p. 8). The CPI(M) Land Reforms Minister, Biren Datta, who resigned ostensibly on grounds of health in the middle of his second term of office is both publicly and privately disillusioned with governmental achievement of its agrarian aims. The 'record of rights of the [sharecroppers] is far below the expectations of the exploited'; in the first two years only 2,730 *bargas* were recorded and only 5,912 granted land (Datta, 1983, pp. 19 and 21). Datta complains that 'in my whole career as Land Reforms Minister I could not get the Agricultural Workers Act passed ... [because of] fear all round the party of losing the middle classes and absentee landlords' support'. 'In 99 per cent of cases we failed to record the sharecroppers' rights and we have by-passed the Agricultural Workers Act (interview, 21 November 1986). Usually reliable sources assert that only Datta and the Chief Minister did not themselves possess land.

The CPI(M)'s most recent report (CPI(M), 1986, pp. 171-6) concentrates almost exclusively on efforts to manage the continuing problem of tribal separatism and extremism. 'The Party is educating all its ranks on [the] lines, "Struggle for the conservation of tribal rights is a struggle of the whole Party"' (p. 174). If the continuing need for such education is poignant, the CPI(M) is right to claim, that 'Had it not been for the Party's front-ranking role in championing the tribal rights, language, culture and autonomy, the situation would have worsened as in other north-eastern States'. Class differentiation among the tribals creates 'fertile ground for the petty-bourgeois sections to be swayed by chauvinism' (p. 174). The party's local reviews of the 1983 Assembly, 1984 *panchayat* and 1985 Tribal District Council elections all underline loss of support among the middle class, especially in the urban areas (Table 12.4). 'Unrealistic expectations of relief from the government' were cited (p. 175) as causes, besides communalism and growing unemployment. The solution lay in more stress on ideological campaigning. An inner party 'Analysis of the Overall Situation' in the wake of the 1980 riots, warned of the dangers of 'self-complacency' and urged the party to re-establish leadership over the masses, shorthand for the failure to manage communal tension (Provincial Committee of the CPI(M), undated, p. 12). Some measure of corruption is also admitted but, perhaps, as in West Bengal, temporary setbacks in the urban areas may be a predictable response to the rural (and here pro-tribal) tilt of government initiatives.

Table 12.4 Tripura: Municipal election results, 1978 and 1983

	1978		1983	
	Seats won	Per cent vote	Seats won	Per cent vote
CPI	0	1.7	1	5.1
CPI(ML)	0	1.4	—	—
CPI(M)	7	49.9	9	40.2
RSP	1	9.1	1	6.6
INC(I)	0	9.9	0	40.0
Neutral	0	11.2	0	2.3
FB	2	6.3	2	5.8
INC(S)	0	2.0	—	—
Janata	0	1.8	—	—

However, more problematic for the CPI(M) in Tripura than the ebb and flow of electoral fortunes among the small middle class are the growing signs of tension within the party: between organization and government; between factions within the State Committee, whose alignments at times dangerously reflects the cleavages in the wider society; lack of coordination between the peasant movement and *panchayats* and cooperatives. 'Meetings of Party Secretariat and ministers are also held but these must be held more frequently. To make the ministry more effective in the second term (1983-88), important comrades had to be assigned ministerial tasks ... this step was required to instil confidence in the people about the Government' (p. 175).

The cart and horses problem—who is in charge, the movement or the ministry—is one which has equally affected Marxist-led governments in Kerala and West Bengal: it is the special paradox of communists who are in office but not in power. In Tripura the veteran communist, Biren Datta, who laid the foundations of Tripura communism more than anyone else, expresses the tension. A man with a deep emotional attachment to the 'movement', a sceptical view of election-oriented communism, and a distrust of the effects of ministerial office on comrades, Datta recently denounced 'the faction in power' in Tripura as Right Opportunists 'more concerned with official position than ideology, training and organisation' (interview,

25 November 1987). Although Datta might have reasons for personal resentment of Chakraborty's hijacking of the party leadership in the 1950s when he (and Deb) were MPs in Delhi, Datta served as Labour and Land Reforms Minister in the first ministry. Though demoted to Fishing and Local Government Minister in the second government, and resigning on 'health grounds' in 1985, he does remain a party member. Fair or not, the fact that such a respected figure should deliver such a bitter denunciation is redolent of the problems communists face in reconciling mass mobilization with the ministerial foothills of state power, most especially when, as the conclusion will argue, real theorization of the communists' experience in India has been in such short supply.

13 Conclusion

The two really important issues which a book on Marxist state governments in India should address are: has there in the world's second largest country with all its distinctive features developed something which could be called an Indian form of communism? And how far have the communist governments been successful in using their limited autonomy to change the conditions of the people in the states of Kerala, Tripura and West Bengal whether in liberal-democratic or Marxist terms? We will then be in a better position to answer the more speculative question which is inevitably asked on communism in India: what is its future?

An Indian Form of Communism?

The early debate on the nature of Indian communism turned on whether there was really an independent movement at all. Did the CPI simply take orders from the CPSU and the CPGB? Up to 1950-1 the answer was affirmative, qualified only by the development of semi-autonomous movements on the periphery and by the shock inflicted on cadres by the imposition of the People's War line in 1942. From the early 1950s until the end of the Emergency, the communists steadily emancipated themselves from Soviet direction: the CPI was slower than the CPSU wished to recognize the Prime Minister's domestic policies as significantly progressive; the 1964 split in the CPI; and the CPI(M)'s stance as independent of both Soviet and Chinese tutelage. By 1980-1 the process was complete. The CPI had aligned itself with the CPI(M), whose respectful autonomy from the Soviet party had been a long-standing irritant for the post-split CPI. When, in December 1980, on the occasion of Brezhnev's visit to Delhi, Mrs Gandhi hinted she would like him to induce more charity from the CPI towards her domestic policies, the Soviet leader passed on the message but apparently no more (Singh, 1986, p. 173). Soon afterwards the CPI National Council expelled S. A. Dange, a founder member and one of its most senior figures, and a long-time advocate of a special, not to say servile relationship with the CPSU. Indian communism had been totally repatriated.

The current debate is of a different kind. Are the Indian communists—and the question is applied to the CPI(M) as much as to the CPI—really communists at all in the sense of Marxist–Leninists committed to revolution and an irreversible transformation of society? One version claims the Indian communists as an Asian variant of Euro-communism; another that they are 'communist in name and organisation but "social democratic" in ideology and practice' (Kohli, 1987, p. 9); still more extreme versions are put forward by the CPI(ML) who see the CPI(M) as no less reformist and revisionist than the CPI. A remark by the CPI(M)'s general secretary E. M. S. Namboodiripad recently that 'Life was a compromise and since communism was life', it followed that 'communism was compromise' (Miller, 1988) is a statement of the obvious, not evidence of a sell out. The ultra-left view hardly deserves refutation but the Euro-communist and 'social democratic' interpretations are worth taking more seriously.

An assessment of the Euro-communist charge is difficult in so far as it is by no means clear that there is a coherent body of Marxist thought which could be elaborated under that label. If it means the acceptance of the ballot box as the only means of advancing the communist programme, then the CPI(M) has never officially, much less privately, forgone the alternatives. Likewise the Indian communists may not adumbrate the dictatorship of the proletariat but they have not formally abandoned the concept. The acid test is that leaders as different as E. M. S. Namboodiripad, the CPI(M)'s General Secretary and leading theoretician, and Jyoti Basu, the West Bengal Chief Minister, vehemently reject the label. Nor do the CPI(M) and CPI have particular contacts with Italian or Spanish comrades.

The 'social democratic' argument has several forms: *The Economist* (London)—tongue in cheek— can damn with faint praise by so reporting the willingness of Jyoti Basu to seek arrangements with international capital for investment in West Bengal and praising the largely strike-free industrial climate of the state in the 1980s. In the 1970s Achutha Menon, CPI Chief Minister of Kerala, was put about by senior Congress circles as 'the best Congress CM we've got'. More interesting is Atul Kohli's argument in an excellent study of how poverty has been tackled in three contrasted Indian states in the last decade: West Bengal, Karnataka—under the left Congress Dejraj Urs government—and Uttar Pradesh—under Janata. To the Marxists, Kohli gives an A−, to Urs a B, and to Janata a straight D, conclusions from which few scholars would dissent.

The pertinent parts of Kohli's argument are twofold: first, given India as a liberal democracy and a private-enterprise economy the introduction of redistribution into the developmental process would require the following: a coherent leadership; an ideological and organizational commitment to exclude property from direct participation in government; a pragmatic, non-threatening and predictable political atmosphere for the propertied classes; and an organizational arrangement that is simultaneously centralized and decentralized. Second, Kohli contends that the 'revolutionary perspective overemphasises class constraints at the expense of the role of the state in mediating and structuring class relations' (p. 38).

Class constraints [are] serious [but] not determining. The prospects for generating effective lower-class power in a stable democracy require exceptional political circumstances ... the emergence of disciplined left-of-centre parties as ruling parties. Such parties, and not merely the organisation of the poor, enable a degree of separation between social and political power. This degree of state autonomy can then be used to implement redistributive reforms. [p. 43]

Significant political power passing into the hands of the lower classes, he sees as a possible scenario, but a rare one that has to be consciously contrived. 'It requires rule by parties which are specifically designed to institutionalise—ideologically and organisationally—the power of the lower classes within the democratic political process' (p. 45).

As a specification of the criteria by which 'growth with redistribution' could—and has—occurred within the presently existing Indian political economy, Kohli can hardly be faulted. The relative failure of the CPI(M) in Kerala, in this writer's view, to achieve what the state unit has done in West Bengal, would add grist to Kohli's mill. On more than one occasion, however, Kohli refers to an 'ideal typical' method. Weber validated his approach in two ways: the type needed to be objectively possible but it also must be subjectively meaningful—to the historical actors. In this context then 'objectively possible', yes; but 'subjectively meaningful', invites a *very large* question mark.

There are two approaches to the problem. On the one hand, we can read the party documents: the carefully weighed Congress reports and resolutions and the less guarded pamphlets of lower organs; on the other, there are off and on the record statements made in interviews with party workers, high and low, and—more cautiously—with third parties: civil servants, journalists, academics and opposition politicians. Kohli, in fact, entirely ignores this data.

The printed record of communist thinking in no way supports the view that the CPI(M) or the CPI are some kind of Indian version of the British Labour Party whose Marxist fringe gives its political opponents a frisson or two but no real cause for alarm. Namboodiripad—Indian communism's leading theoretician—in *Indian Planning in Crisis, Conflicts and Crisis* and recently in *A History of Indian Freedom Struggle* rests his work on the creative application of historical materialism. He ends his *Reminiscences of an Indian Communist* with the reiteration that the 'effectiveness of Party leadership lies in keeping constant watch on the developments and working out the correct line in accordance with the universal and well-tested principles of Marxism-Leninism' (p. 224). B. T. Ranadive, author of the Calcutta Theses, and still a member of the CPI(M) Politburo as well as President of the Centre of India Trade Unions, concluded a review of 'Forty Years of Indian Independence' with a striking coda that is at once an expression of collective self-criticism, admonition not to lose sight of the ultimate objective, and a firm statement of that goal in unequivocally communist language.

The experience of the last four decades shows that the continuance of the capitalist path of the bourgeois-landlord regime means preparing for disastrous consequences for the country. The failure to complete the task of democratic revolution is threatening their country with repression, loss of independence, unity and even neo-colonial enslavement. It will be ruinous if the CPI(M) and the left parties confine their attention to the demand for Rajiv's resignation and forget that the movement must gradually move forward to demand basic changes. A basis must be created in the course of a gigantic movement for the immediate resignation of Rajiv Gandhi, for a new correlation of class forces, a correlation favourable to the basic masses. The planned struggle against immediate dangers and for ousting Rajiv must teach the masses to look beyond the present framework and create an urge for moving towards finishing the urgent task of the democratic revolution and towards a people's democratic revolution based on worker-peasant alliance. The failure to create this urge and mobilise the masses for this purpose has been the main weakness of the last four decades endangering the future of our country and our people. (*The Marxist*, 5, April–September 1987, p. 35).

Whatever else might be said, this is neither Euro-communism nor social democracy.

What then is it? Put in its plainest form—with reference to his state—Jyoti Basu has said that 'What we have been trying to do is to adapt Marxist-Leninist ideas on the formation of the united front government to the specific situation of West Bengal' without yet forgetting 'our long term objective' (1984, pp. 1–3). In similar vein Namboodiripad has commented on the fact that the problems the Party faces always change because the 'economic and political situation in the country and in the world as a whole' is 'ever in a state of flux' (1987, p. 224). In more formal terms, his introduction to *A History of Indian Freedom Struggle* underlines Marx and Engels' own absence of dogmatism and their emphasis on the interaction of non-economic with economic factors. The choice of quotations in a mere ten-page preface to 900 pages of modern Indian history is significant:

The economic situation is the basis, but the various elements of the superstructure—political forms of the class struggle and its results, such as constitutions established by the victorious class after a successful battle, etc., juridical forms, and especially the reflections of all these struggles in the brains of the participants... and their further development into systems of dogmas—also exercise their influence upon the course of the historical struggles and in many cases determine their *form* in particular. *There is an interaction of all these elements in which, amid all the endless host of accidents... the economic movement is finally bound to assert itself*. Otherwise the application of the theory of any period of history would be easier than the solution of a simple equation of the first degree... [Engels to Joseph Bloch, 21 (22) September 1890 with Namboodiripad's added emphasis, 1987, p. 7]

No less leading is the citation of Engels' introduction to the republication of Marx's *Class Struggle in France, 1848 to 1850*: 'we declared as early as Autumn 1850 that at least the *first* chapter of the revolutionary period was closed... The mode of struggle of 1848 is today obsolete in every respect' but 'it has also completely transformed the conditions under which the proletariat has to fight' (Namboodiripad, 1987, p. 9). Presumably if we move on a century, the mode of struggle of 1948 is equally obsolete. As a result of Indian independence and its bourgeois landlord-dominated political structures, the revolutionary struggle must necessarily take new forms.

Bearing in mind Bhabani Sen Gupta's cutting remark in *Communism in Indian Politics* (1972) that the Indian communists had made no creative contribution to the pool of applied communism, what new forms have been pioneered by the Indian movement? (p. 39). A summary answer would be that they have learned by trial and error to utilize the whole apparatus of liberal democracy—elections, parties, parliaments, levels of governance from *panchayat* and municipality to province and the federal structure itself—to advance popular mobilization in ways which were unavailable to Lenin and the Bolsheviks and only hinted at by Marx.

Little need be said on the subject of elections. The, at best, idealistic, and, at worst, downright naïve view of the CPI(ML) that participation in the bourgeois democratic electoral process is itself a compromise is eschewed not only by the CPI but by all sections of the CPI(M), even those whom Franda counterposes to the 'electoralists' in West Bengal (p. 77). The CPI(M) is, in fact, committed to the reform of the system by the introduction of proportional representation.

The communist parties have competed vigorously—and fairly—for electoral support since 1952, and even before. Namboodiripad's observation that 'every vote recorded in favour of the Communist Party [is] a vote of a soldier fighting for the proletarian revolution' is an optimistic gloss on the reality, particularly when the party takes careful account of the caste and communal composition of constituencies in its choice of candidates, but the share of the poll does reflect the broad character of the mass movement (*Hindu* 30 November 1970). Election results are, reasonably, understood as merely partial reflections of more deep-rooted changes (Karat, 1972, p. 72) but even published analyses in party journals show careful attention to the significance of movements of opinion for party tactics and strategy.

In a deeply stratified (and gender-ridden) society, the verdict of the electorate honestly interpreted can be a valuable corrective to the wishful thinking of the ideological missionaries or the defensive reports of *apparatchiks* and has frequently been heavy calibre ammunition in inner party debate. We can be sure that this will be the case in the wake of the 1988 'setback' in Tripura as it was after the parliamentary elections of 1984 in Kerala and West Bengal. One particular attraction of elections for the Indian communist movement is the opportunity it gives for the theatre of mass rallies, normally uncomplicated by the deterrent effect in agitational rallies that either the police may intervene or rival political gangs may disturb the event. The imponderable is how far growing access to television may affect face-to-face political communications either by the distraction of films or, if Doodarshan (Indian television) should be so directed by election campaigns fought on television.

The sophistication of the Indian communists' exploitation of parliamentary institutions is as far removed from Lenin's well-known use of the propagandist opportunities of the Russian Duma as Tsarist representative democracy is from today's Lok Sabha or state Assemblies. That said, there has been considerable variation in communist style and level of performance depending on the prevailing party line, the quality of legislators, the temper of their rivals and the traditions of the legislative body. A reading of the debates in the Lok Sabha before and after the switch to 'peaceful transition' in 1956-7 reveals more frequent interventions and a more 'constructive' tone. Men of the calibre of Jyoti Basu, Biren Datta or Achutha Menon proved formidable parliamentarians, well-prepared, quick on their feet and masters of the highways and byways of parliamentary procedure. If the rhetorical abilities of MPs and MLAs of all parties have declined over the forty years of Indian independence as the generation of the freedom struggle was gradually replaced by a new breed of professional politician, and as college and university education deteriorated, the contrast may have been more marked in the communist case than in Congress. On the one hand, in the early days the communists recruited more than their share of the outstanding talent of the time, whether the formally educated Basu and Menon, gold medallist from Madras, or the autodidact, Namboodiripad. On the other hand, student politics, even in the communist SFI and AISF, is a career which leaves little time for study and does not necessarily attract those from the top of their batch. Observers close to the Kerala Assembly certainly draw a sharp contrast between the communist MLAs of the late 1950s and early 1960s, more than a match for their Congress opponents in parliamentary warfare, and their 1980s successors.

Congress's own attitude to the legislative process and the scrutiny of executive action is undoubtedly a factor in the changed communist approach evident in the 1970s and 1980s. In both the West Bengal and Tripura Assemblies Congress has been increasingly reluctant to play by the rules of the game, while in Kerala the fragmentation of the party system in the 1960s and 1970s blurred the party battle of government and opposition and through extra-parliamentary liaison committees of governing parties diminished the stature of legislative institutions, and indeed the Council (cabinet) of Ministers. The traditions of the different assemblies, perhaps even the political subcultures of the elites from which the legislators are recruited, have also had their effect. Although West Bengal is popularly associated with a delight in ideas and argument, antagonisms between communist and non-communist, periodic outbreaks of bloody street politics, and the recourse of Congress in particular to electoral malpractice on an unacceptable scale have vitiated the work of the assembly. The printing of the Legislative proceedings, and especially of select committee reports is so far behind schedule that when published they are fit only for the archive. In contrast the Kerala Assembly is not only up to date but produces a swift English-language synopsis. Its Select Committee reports—published in English—bear comparison with those of the British parliament, and like the Mother of Parliaments, are almost always consensual. Scrutiny is taken sufficiently seriously for the Kerala Assembly to have taken up the Departmentalized select committee system adopted in the United Kingdom in 1979. Symbolically, in West Bengal, after the ballot-rigging of the 1972 elections, the CPI(M) declined to take up its seats in the new assembly, whereas in Kerala what was considered flagrant misuse of government control of procedures in 1974 only precipitated withdrawal from the house when it seemed that the elections were imminent. Even unparliamentary language is different. 'Thief' and 'scoundrel' have been permitted in West Bengal but not in Kerala. Ironically, since 1952, threats to parliamentary democracy have come from non-communist not Marxist quarters, if we discount the Naxalites. Saroj Mukherjee, Personal Assistant to West Bengal Chief Ministers for thirty years after Independence, cites an incident in 1969 when the police invaded the Assembly chamber, smashed the furniture and drove out the MLAs. They then set off in pursuit of Jyoti Basu in the Deputy Chief Minister's room. Basu rose from his chair to thunder 'It is a naked act of disorder. No one ever desecrated the sanctity of the Assembly even during the British Raj and Muslim League rule. Today ... you dared to do this. Now you go and face the people in the Assembly without arms. I will see how you do it' (S. Chakrabarty, 1978, p. 331). A year earlier, Harekrishna Konar, a prominent peasant leader of the West Bengal CPI(M), summed up the Indian communist movement's attitude:

> even the limited rights of parliamentary democracy, which itself is a form of bourgeois class rule, have become dangerous to the bourgeois-landlord ruling classes because [with] the deepening crisis the working class and the people are intensifying their class struggle by utilising these very limited rights. For that reason attempts are being made to establish police *raj* by butchering parliamentary democracy. In this situation, the struggle for [the] defence of parliamentary democracy has assumed particular significance ... [*People's Democracy*, 7 April 1968]

The trickiest aspect of operating within a competitive—or to be more exact a multi-party competitive—political system is how to handle relations with rival parties, especially since the unit of Marxist analysis is class. As early as 1952, K. Damodaran, then secretary of the Malabar (Kerala) District Committee, was opposing a tendency in the Kerala leadership to negotiate united fronts of parties not classes and so substitute party for class as the unit of revolutionary action. The 1953 Madurai Congress simply fudged the issue, since the purist North was at odds with the pragmatic South, and resolved that the current situation required united front committees made up of various parties and organizations representing the interests of all classes and elements opposed to imperialism and feudalism and concluded that these *ad hoc* committees varying 'from place to place and from issue to issue' could only strengthen the mass movement. (Nossiter, 1982, pp. 108-9). Even more bluntly the CPI Politburo endorsed the view at the time that:

> Communist Party's conception of united front is basically a front of classes... In our country today different democratic political parties or groups exist... *It will not help us to discuss here which party represents which class most or which ideology or practice is more correct. We have to take this reality of the existence of these parties and groups. Wishing them away will not do* ... [Nossiter, 1982, p. 135, n. 18, emphasis added]

It would be reasonable to infer that not only were the communists divided on the principle of the equivalence of class and party but were aware that the status of Congress itself in class terms was a potential challenge to an anti-Congress united front. In so far as there was one determinant of which side individual comrades took in the 1964 split, it was precisely on the question of whether the cause required uniting with or against Congress. Was it a basically progressive or reactionary manifestation of the bourgeoisie? Between 1969 and 1978 the CPI might be said to have fought the neo-imperial war—contingent alliance with Congress against international capitalism—while the CPI(M) fought the People's war of unremitting struggle against Congress even when on the principles of either 'my enemy's enemy is my friend' or dividing the bourgeoisie, this led them into temporary electoral arrangements with parties which were self-evidently communal (Muslim League) or capitalist (Kerala or Bangla Congress).

The late 1960s were critical to future strategy for both wings of the communist movement. Hitherto the membership of united fronts had extended no further than democratic socialist or peasant parties, and there had been no significant rightist anti-Congress parties to complicate the application of theory to reality. Now, the party systems of West Bengal and Kerala were fragmenting, and the question arose as to whether to persist with anti-Congressism based on coalitions confined to progressive and 'like-minded' parties or to include virtually any group opposed to a tottering INC. In Kerala, guided by Namboodiripad, the CPI(M) rejected the breakaway Kerala Congress but not the Muslim League, while in West Bengal—where there was no complicating League—the CPI(M) formed a strictly United *Left* Front of Marxist parties and sects. The CPI, which in Kerala, had suffered a humiliating defeat at CPI(M) hands in the 1965 elections, joined the United Front but in West Bengal went along with Bangla Congress and, incidentally, the communal Gorkha League, in the People's United Left Front.

After the elections and to avert Congress rule, the CPI(M)'s ULF joined forces with the Bangla Congress–CPI combine to form a United Front Ministry which was ousted after just eight months by the anti-Congress Governor. The ministerial UF contested mid-term elections in 1969 and defeated Congress but the apparent vindication of the tactics of chopping off bits of Congress was challenged when after little more than a year the twelve-party UF ministry collapsed from its own internal tensions. Yet further elections occurred in 1971 and 1972. The CPI was now on the side of Congress, pursuing a United *Democratic* Front line while the CPI(M) was the one real force in a United *Left* Front. Although in 1972 the outcome was vitiated by Congress ballot rigging, the CPI(M)'s share of the vote held up well. The situation in West Bengal was now clarified: Congress ruled as a single-party government while the CPI(M), the principal opposition party, boycotted the Assembly altogether. In 1977, after the Emergency, the West Bengal CPI(M) firmed up its commitment to Left Fronts that deserved the label. 'United' was dropped since all parties were at least programmatically socialist, if not Marxist. Despite an absolute majority in the assembly the

CPI(M) gave not unimportant portfolios to its allies, Forward Bloc, the Revolutionary Socialist Party and the Revolutionary CPI; and in 1982 the formula was repeated, this time including the CPI which had at last abandoned Congress(I).

The continued Left Front success in the 1987 elections in one of India's most intractable states can be fairly taken to justify Jyoti Basu's reiterated claim that '(W)hat we have been trying to do is to adapt the Marxist-Leninist ideas about the formation of the united front government to the specific situations of West Bengal'. A similar claim might be made by the Tripura party which has also pursued straightforwardly Left Front tactics and abjured the temptation to monopolize office on the basis of its absolute majority in the assembly.

In contrast the Kerala unit of the CPI(M) has a more chequered record. Kerala's party system has been much more fragmented than West Bengal's. With the exceptions of the CPI(M), the CPI, and more debatably the RSP, no party has recognizable ideological principles. Caste and community are the geology of the party structure and factionalism and personalism the shifting sands which blind the observer. Although the CPI(M) and the Congress(I) are the poles of party competition, their magnetism is less than in West Bengal. After the UF of 1967-9 had quarrelled its way to collapse, the CPI, led by two exceptionally talented figures, Achutha Menon and Govindan Nair, and moved by a mixture of conviction and calculation, skilfully exploited the situation to pursue a National Democratic alliance with Congress(I). For the CPI(M) the alternative front strategies were equally unpalatable: on the one hand to sweat it out in the wilderness with only minor socialistic sects for company; or to build anti-Congress coalitions necessarily involving some unsavoury political partners and try to explain the necessity to its members and sympathizers in terms of long-run objectives.

Guided by Namboodiripad, it was the latter course that was adopted, influenced as the 1970s developed by his view—and the Emergency supported it—that authoritarianism was the immediate threat to popular advance. In the 1980 Assembly elections the CPI(M) therefore led not a United *Left* Front but a Left *Democratic* Front, which included two components of the planters' party, Kerala Congress, and one of the Muslim League, as well as a chastened CPI and a progressive wing of Congress. The viability of the approach was challenged as Kerala Congress and Congress (S) turned against the LDF ministry, bringing it down after eighteen months and in 1982 the CPI(M) turned its back on communal entanglements not without dissent. In the 1987 Assembly elections the Kerala CPI(M) eschewed the communal embrace of Kerala Congress and Muslim League to lead a Left

Democratic Front—and, whether coincidentally or not—won. The contribution of the 'democratic' elements—Congress (S), Janata and Lok Dal—amounted to 9 per cent of the poll and eleven of the 140 seats. The significance of the LDF/Kerala–LF/West Bengal contrast is encapsulated in the 1987 results: in Kerala the CPI(M) won 22 per cent of the poll and the entire front 45 per cent while in West Bengal the CPI(M) took 39 per cent of the poll and the LF overall 53 per cent. In the former the CPI(M) won 26 per cent of the seats and in the latter 64 per cent. Kerala may well be a far more taxing political environment for a Marxist party than West Bengal but it is a sobering reflection on the relative efficacy of the differing approaches to front politics that twenty years earlier in 1967 the CPI(M) share of the vote was 24 per cent (of seats, 39 per cent) in Kerala but only 18 per cent (of seats, 21 per cent) in West Bengal.

The Communists' Use of Government

The utilization of elective posts, and particularly ministerial posts in state government, has been through three phases. In the first communist government in Kerala of 1957-9, though the party was cautious in its public statements, there is little doubt that the CPI believed that significant change could be brought about in agrarian relations, in education, in law and order, and generally in honest and efficient administration. The experience, compounded by the split in the party and the influence of the ultra left, led the CPI(M) to revert to a position which was more consistent with what a Leninist perspective might have been: the simultaneous pursuit of administration and agitation. All that could be expected was some minor immediate relief to the poor since provincially and nationally the bourgeois-landlord regime would not permit any real change. The aim then was to highlight the essential nature of the system through popular agitation.

Demonstrations against central government policy however were one thing; militant protest against the action or inaction of ministers of other parties in a United Front was another. Further, the line could, and did, lead to a counter-productive breakdown of the rule of law as understood within a liberal democratic framework though the CPI(M)'s understanding was that it was as yet unchallengable by revolutionary action. From the party's own point of view, agitation which lacked direction by class-conscious cadres could easily succumb to left-wing adventurism and be taken over by anti-social elements masquerading as 'true believers'. The original peasants of Naxalbari in northern Bengal represented a genuine grassroots upwelling but the privileged students of Calcutta University who appropriated the Naxalite name, albeit brave, were, for communists simply misguided. On the industrial front, the acceptance of *gherao* (encirclement) as a legitimate alternative to strikes by otherwise judicious as well as talented Labour Ministers in the West Bengal and Kerala UFs was another instance of the difficulty in reconciling administration and agitation. Ironically, both ended up being subjected to *gherao* themselves.

There was one area in which administration was the more effective when combined with agitation, the sphere of land reform. Both in Kerala in the early 1970s and in West Bengal in the late 1970s the mobilization of peasants, labourers and sharecroppers forcibly to assert the rights conferred on them by legislation did much to explain the relative success of land reform. In contrast, in Tripura the communists' inability—or unwillingness—to mobilize the tribals to assist in the recovery of alienated land helps to explain the comparative failure of land reform in the state.

The third and current use to which communists put ministerial position is something of a *via media* between the bright eyed, bushy tailed optimism of the late 1950s and the over-subtle dialectic of the late 1960s. Communists are in office not in power. At one level this is an accurate assessment of provincial government in the present Indian situation but at another the proposition affords a convenient if not always electorally convincing explanation of the failure of LF and LDF ministries to achieve that quality of efficient and honest discharge of everyday business that distinguished municipalities in Kerala in the 1950s, at least some *panchayats* and *zilla parishads* in West Bengal after 1977 and the Tribal ADC in Tripura from 1982-8.

Where the communists have tended to lose ground is among what passes for the floating vote in the three states: the urban middle class. 'Law and order', as in Kerala in 1982 or Tripura in 1988, is a potent platform for the enemies of communism; and, although the West Bengal LF has lost some support in the metropolitan and industrial areas, Jyoti Basu cannot be criticized on that score in town or countryside. Calcutta, under the LF, is despite its poverty one of the safest, if not the safest, metropolis in the world. In West Bengal, as in Kerala and Tripura, however, the petit bourgeoisie, themselves disproportionately in government service of one kind or another, and expecting standards from the Left they daily ignore, perceive too little difference between the workings of government offices under communist authority and Congress. Their experience is confirmed—fairly or not—by the reportage of a daily press which is less than sympathetic to a radical transformation of society. For an anti-communist newspaper, a little corruption goes a long way.

The CPI(M) and the Left generally would be less than human and far from politically astute if, given the patronage dispensed by their rivals, and in particular Congress, they did not look after their friends and followers when in government. Personal corruption is by no means unknown but, by Indian norms, surprisingly rare. What the CPI(M) and CPI justifiably do, is recompense those who have worked in hard times for the cause. Members of course contribute a proportion of their income to party funds. The declaration of income by delegates to party Congresses is in the author's experience consistent with the very basic standard of living of the communist movement as he has known it but quite out of line with that of the generality of Indian politicians. Both in Kerala and West Bengal the embarrassments to LF ministries have been from ministers belonging to parties other than CPI(M) and CPI. An altogether more searching criticism of Marxist-led state governments in India is that communist ministers still largely fail to accept the force of the dictum that communism equals 'electricity plus socialism'. The post-split CPI, always closer to the Soviet Union, has more frequently taken the implications to heart. Economic modernization, industrialization and power, and growth in production and non-confrontational industrial relations have, until the mid-1980s generally been more determinedly pursued by CPI ministers. 'New' industrial policy tended to be a bone of contention between the wings of the party in the first Kerala CPI government, and was certainly so in the Kerala UF ministry of 1967-9, as well as requiring Jyoti Basu's persuasive skills in West Bengal to reconstruct West Bengal's industry through domestic and foreign investment. The extraordinary remark of a CPI(M) Minister in 1968 that Kerala would not be washed into the sea if the giant Idikki hydroelectric project was not completed was matched only by the totally cynical attitude of the responsible RSP minister for its progress in the early 1970s that he did not expect to see it completed in his lifetime (Nossiter, 1982, p. 246). (It was not.)

A contrast appears to have emerged between West Bengal (and Tripura) on the one hand, where industrial relations have improved dramatically under the LF governments and the importance of production as well as redistribution is increasingly recognized, and Kerala, where the LDF ministry of 1980-1 did little to curb the excesses of party-controlled unions and virtually nothing to control the inefficiencies of the public sector. Such evidence as is to hand on the new LDF government in Kerala of 1987 suggests that the machinery for improving the performance of nationalized industries in the state, largely attributable to the senior civil servant M. Ramachandran, is to be allowed to fall into disuse.

Ministers are of course heavily dependent on their civil servants for the implementation of policies and competent administration. The IAS is ultimately subordinate to the central government. Its failings—generalism, arrogance, conservatism, and so on—are well known but if the clashes between Ashok Mitra, CPI(M) Minister of Finance, and S. M. Murshed of the IAS are legendary in Writers' Building, there is little doubt that Marxist-led ministries have not made best use of either the stiff efficiency of the older school of officers nor the progressive aspirations of some of the younger ones. A senior CPI(M) figure in Tripura in 1987 commented that 'the young IAS officers are more progressive than our party. The real obstruction to the implementation of land law and land reform came from our party' (unattributable interview). Similar sentiments were expressed by the Kerala Land Reforms Commissioner in 1974, and by various civil servants in West Bengal in 1983.

Clearly linked to the below par performance of Left governments also is the inability to motivate the great mass of executive and clerical staff in public service. To the extent that they are predominantly unionized by the communists in the three states, the parties face very real difficulty in persuading or coercing supporters to abandon their customary inertia and petty corruption. Half-educated, underpaid, short on commitment at work and long on transport to work, it is hardly surprising that they perform their tedious tasks with little enthusiasm. Politicians who need their votes are inclined to back employees against disciplinary officers. In a despairing effort to rationalize the situation, the LF now permits government employees to arrive at their offices in central Calcutta at 11 rather than 10 a.m. but it is well known that 'bureaucrats often arrive at noon and, after frequent tea breaks and a leisurely lunch, begin their exodus at 3 p.m.' (Basu, 1985, p. 35).

In West Bengal, if not so obviously in recent years in Kerala, the ministry is entirely seized of the problem. In September 1982 an Administrative Reforms Committee was set up under the chairmanship of Dr Ashok Mitra. By April 1983 the report had been published. As a blueprint, the document is outstanding, underlining that reform at state level was very dependent on the wider constraints of the all-India administrative system. The Committee ended by denying any illusions that even if its ninety-one recommendations were implemented in full, there would be a major qualitative improvement without a sense of commitment on the part of those involved. 'The Committee' professed 'to have every confidence that State Government employees at all levels will offer their fullest co-operation to the political leadership ...' (p. 28). Annexure V, 'The Movement of A File', is a droll commentary on that pious hope as it charts the progress of a file involving the complaint of defalcation of funds against two employees of the Land Reforms

Department, commencing with a letter from the Additional District Magistrate (Land Reforms), Murshidabad, to the Commissioner (Presidency Division) across 104 leisured desks until in November 1982 the Public Service Commission returns the file and asks for the opinion of the Legal Remembrancer: 'No further action is taken'. In any case the employees had long since retired. Mitra who brought similar drive and talent to all that he did was suddenly to resign from the ministry in 1986 in part on grounds of ill health but one may also presume because of sheer frustration. No progress had been made with administrative reform yet.

In terms of performance, the three unequivocal successes of some or all of the Marxist-led governments have been: land reform; rural local government; and minimum needs programmes in food, health and education. Significantly, each area is, more or less, within the state governments' competence under the Indian Constitution and each closely echoes the demands of the developing mass movement. To a considerable extent, formal and informal popular participation—land grabs, *panchayats* and *zilla parishads*, and local party committees and locally recruited officials—has done much to energize the implementation of legislation and executive orders. The record varies as between the states. In land reform Kerala was the pioneer but, for reasons beyond the control of the CPI and UF ministries, by the time adequate land reform was on the statute book (1970), propertied interests had made their getaway. A similar situation obtained in Tripura, complicated by the political implications of restoring land from the majority Bengali community to minority tribals. In West Bengal, whatever criticisms and reservations may be offered in academic commentary, the new deal for the sharecroppers was a truly remarkable accomplishment. In each case, however, the communist-led governments pursued land reforms more geared to the emancipation of tenants and the abolition of feudalism than to the problem of the landless agricultural labourer. Only in West Bengal was much surplus land ever redistributed. The approach to the real tillers of the land has been to treat them as a kind of proletariat but to the extent that the policy succeeds— through higher wages, guaranteed employment and pensions—it can, as in Kerala, lead farmers to employ less labour, or even to migrate to other states. In any case farm labour has neither the credit lines nor the management skills to run the land even if the opportunity is available.

Rural local government has been a relative success in West Bengal and, in the special form of the Tribal Autonomous District Council, in Tripura but despite legislation in Kerala has been disappointing there. How far this can be attributed to communist failures is unclear but commentators hold that the Kerala CPI(M) has been unenthusiastic about the reality as opposed to the rhetoric of decentralization perhaps because of the extreme politicization and communalization of decision-making in the state.

In the most 'immediate forms of relief' to the people, the Marxist-led ministries have excelled, although in Kerala basic welfare has been something of an all-party affair. In West Bengal and in Tripura food distribution, village dispensaries and village primary schools grew rapidly after the arrival of the Left Front ministries in 1977-8 and the imbalance between urban and rural facilities, and caste and outcaste inequalities of access has been somewhat redressed. In the medium to long term such social investment should lead—as it has in Kerala already—to reductions in the birth rate and a near universally literate work-force.

Higher education is, like primary and secondary education, provided either by the private sector or by the provincial state. Sadly here, Marxist-led ministries have surrendered to partisan interest (in West Bengal) or communal interest (in Kerala). In both cases some of the worst scandals have involved universities, as indeed is true throughout India. Calcutta, until the late 1960s, a great institution of higher learning, is quite devalued though only in part through the LF's sins of omission and commission, while the University of Kerala's reputation is far from what one should expect in such a literate state.

As must by now be very clear, any dispassionate assessment of the performance of Marxist-led governments in India, and so any projection of what a Marxist-led Central government might be like, is confounded by the difficulty of apportioning responsibility between state and federal governments. It is incontestable that while provincial ministries are naturally tempted to shuffle off the blame on to Delhi the constitutional arrangements positively encourage this. India is federal in form and unitary in character but the fiction is maintained that there is a real division of political, administrative, and financial labour. Three points only need be made: the allocation of legislative responsibility places ninety-six subjects on the Union (Federal) list, sixty-six on the States list and forty-seven on the Concurrent one. Second, for all practical purposes, funds are distributed by the centre; and third, the Governors of the states, appointed—and politically so—by Delhi, have powers in consultation (*sic*) with the centre to dismiss state governments, impose Presidential Rule, and call new elections as and when they see fit. Governor—in other words, Prime Ministerial—interference, with due political process, began as early as 1952 when the formation of non-Congress governments was prevented in Travancore-Cochin (Kerala) and Madras, and aborted in PEPSU (Punjab). The ouster of the Kerala CPI Ministry in 1959 confirmed a pattern which, under Mrs Gandhi, was to become almost a routine and, under Rajiv Gandhi, has continued unabashed. The West Bengal UF has learned to tread warily for fear of providing an excuse for its dismissal. Just one gloss is required on the demarcation of legislative responsibilities: virtually everything on the States list as well as obviously on the Concurrent list of any substance is likely to require central advice or approval, which, at best, betokens delay. Nowhere more clearly seen is the adage that, in parliamentary democracy, the opposition's best weapon—and Congress is that opposition in Marxist-led states—is the sands of time. Land reform so well exemplified this in Kerala.

On funding, it is unnecessary to accept every charge by Marxist-led ministries of politically-motivated neglect, to assent to the proposition that Congress (and between 1977 and 1980 Janata) would be an unnatural political animal if it went out of its way to feed the rivals for its territory. Even so, Marxist governments can be fairly criticized for the degree to which they have underspent allocated funds in all three states and, in Kerala, at least, in the casual political attitude evident in draft state plans to Delhi. At the margin the allocation of resources between states is competitive, and in effect decided by (technically equipped) civil servants in the Planning Commission. On all but the biggest scale it is apolitical.

Centre-State Relations from a Marxist Perspective

How do the communists themselves see centre-state relations under a People's Democratic Government? Namboodiripad, General Secretary of the CPI(M), has for long made federalism a part of Indian communist theory. His 'Centre-State Relations Over the Years' (*The Marxist*, 1987) is a succinct summary of his influential views. Not in question is 'the preservation and promotion of the unity of the Indian Union' because (?) it will be then 'the basis of real equality and autonomy for the different nationalities' of the country and will have a proper democratic State structure (p. 14). The key features of Namboodiripad's outline are as follows (my italics):

1. The Indian Union shall be a federation *based on democratic centralism*.
2. The people are sovereign. *All organs of State power shall be answerable to the people. The supreme authority in exercising State power shall be the people's representatives elected on the basis of adult franchise and the principle of proportional representation, and subject to recall.*
3. At the all-India centre, there shall be two houses, the House of the People and the House of States. *Both shall have equal powers* and equal numbers... The *President shall act in accordance with the decisions of both the houses and shall have no other powers.*
4. *All states... shall have real autonomy and equal powers.*

5. ... Nor shall there be Governors for the states. All administrative services shall be under the direct control of the respective states or local authorities ...
6. Equality of all national languages in Parliament and central administration shall be recognised ... The use of English ... shall be discarded.
7. *The People's Democratic Government will take measure(s) to consolidate the unity of India by fostering ... mutual cooperation between the constituent states.* It will pay special attention ... to economically backward and weaker states ...
8. The People's Democratic State, in the field of local administration, shall ensure a wide network of local bodies ... provided with adequate finances.

State autonomy, Namboodiripad argues, is an essential element of real and full democracy. 'Hand in hand with this conflict on the question of centralisation and state autonomy between the bourgeoisie and the proletariat is the conflict between the two sections of the bourgeoisie—those ruling at the centre and the states respectively.' Secession is ruled out: in 1964 when the CPI(M) adopted its Programme, differences among the delegates led to the decision being held over till the 1972 Congress when self-determination for the various Indian nationalities was definitively rejected.

How far such a framework could be viable is a moot point. Democratic centralism, answerability to the people, proportional representation, real autonomy and powers to the states governments seem contradictory. As to the preclusion of self-determination, it would seem more than likely that such a People's Democratic Government would—with or without outside aid—find it difficult, if not impossible, to prevent secessionism unless the army was wholeheartedly on the new regime's side.

An interesting gloss, however, on centre–state relations from the CPI(M) perspective is its own problem with the federalist deviation. Although this Conclusion began by asking whether there was a distinctive form of *Indian* communism, it can be argued quite reasonably that the question is equally well put as 'Are there Keralite, Bengali and Tripuri forms of communism?'. On the evidence of this book there appear to be dual communist nationalities among Indian Marxists, as indeed there are among India's citizens generally. Explicit recognition of this occurs in official party documents.

The left's support base is *regional* and effectively confined to West Bengal, Kerala and Tripura. The CPI(M)'s membership exceeds 10,000 in only five states with Kerala (38 per cent) and West Bengal (30 per cent) accounting for two-thirds of the total. In the last parliamentary elections the CPI(M) contested only fifty-nine of the 508 seats fought and all but sixteen were in the three core states. The CPI's fifty-four candidates were scattered somewhat more widely but three of its six victories were in West Bengal and two in adjacent Bihar. Apart from one seat each for the CPI(M) and CPI in

Andhra, all other left successes (or near misses) including the RSP and Forward Bloc, were within the citadels of communism.

However, the two communist parties have their headquarters in Delhi and adopt a national posture in their propaganda. The tensions between the nationally oriented CPI(M) Politburo and the powerful State Committees surfaced at the 1982 Congress. The Political Organizational Report censured those who had succumbed to 'federalism'. 'Comrades who are victims of this trend', the Report continued, 'do not realise that without a strong all-India centre and its intervention no strong state Parties... can continue for long in face of the onslaught... of the Central Government' (CPI(M), 1982, pp. 140-2). The implication is clear: the only *Indian* communists work in the Politburo. Perhaps centre-state relations are not simply reducible to the antagonisms of national and local bourgeoisies after all.

Future Prospects

What are the prospects for the Marxist left? In Tripura, where elections were held in February 1988, the Left Front experienced a setback and has been replaced by a Congress-TUJS ministry, although one seat is vacant and one result was very dubious. Margins of defeat were, however, narrow and of the eight CPI(M) seats lost to Congress, half were in urban constituencies. The urban middle class, including public sector employees has always been crucial to the outcome of Tripura elections; and, while some disenchantment with LF performance may be a factor, 'law and order' was clearly the Congress's trump card with the army brought in on the eve of the campaign. As was argued in the last chapter, the Left Front has lost some momentum, has paid a price for the effort to redress the balance of development expenditure in favour of the backward and tribal East, and is uncertain how to reconcile a tribal ethnicity, driven by agrarian resentments, with a class-based appeal which cuts across community. There are tensions between the movement and the ministry and the possibility of a succession 'crisis'. Nevertheless the Marxist-led LF in Tripura retains a solid support base. It secured as high as 50.3 per cent of the popular vote in the February 1988 State Assembly Elections overall, 52.29 per cent in the seven Scheduled Caste seats and 53.44 per cent in twelve out of sixteen Scheduled Tribal seats for which details are available (*India Today*, 29 February 1988; *People's Democracy*, 7 February 1988). The Bengali-dominated Congress and the tribal TUJS have no common programme. Given the near inevitable conflict of interest between Congress(I) and the TUJS, the Left Front can be expected soon to edge forward again.

In Kerala, paradoxically, though the ULF won the most recent elections in 1987 the communists appear to be stuck at a level of support little different from that of twenty years earlier: around a quarter of the voters for the CPI(M) and some 8 per cent for the CPI. Measured by the 1984 parliamentary elections, the hard core CPI(M) following may be as little as one-fifth of the voters. Detailed analysis suggests that the communists have been losing ground in old bases especially in Malabar with inadequate compensation in Travancore. Whatever the precise judgement—holding the position or slowly surrendering it—the fact that the CPI(M) in Kerala has not been able to progress from the ULF to LF stage is symptomatic of weakness relative to Tripura and, more relevantly, West Bengal.

The reader must have been struck—despite my efforts to simplify—just how complex Kerala politics have become. In 1987 twenty-six parties contested 140 seats and Congress(I) and the CPI(M) did not manage 50 per cent of the votes between them. No party is in a position to win an absolute majority on its own. The party system has become ever more fragmented and successful alliances have perforce been motley affairs, although in 1987 the communists have broken with the Muslim League and Kerala Congress. To point out that the communists must negotiate the spider's web of caste and community is not to suggest they are entangled in it. In many respects, notably their efforts to rebuff the RSS, they have fought hard. Nevertheless the resurgence of community as opposed to class as the basis of Kerala politics is both cause and consequence of a slow and long-term decline in communist support. In 1960 the united CPI won around 40 per cent of the vote against a formidable combination of vested interests, a determined Congress high command and injections of foreign finance. By 1982 the CPI(M), effectively the heir of the old CPI, could only manage 19 per cent; and in 1987 22 per cent. If this may state the contrast too starkly, the slow downward turn in communist support is incontrovertible. Of the three early citadels of communism in Kerala, only Cannanore remains secure. Palghat and Alleppey are now contingent supporters.

One way to look at the communists' assiduous involvement in electoral competition in India is to see it as a part of the 'war of position' which Gramsci regarded as the only way forward where capitalist society buttressed itself with mass suffrage. However in Kerala, that civil society which Gramsci, using a seventeenth-century military metaphor, saw as the other bulwark of the state, is profoundly different from that of twentieth-century Italy, advanced capitalism or liberal democracy. In 1939 the British Agent in

Travancore and Cochin wrote that 'Not only is communalism rampant, but discipline, *civic* sense ... and genuine respect for authority are notably lacking in public life' (Nossiter, 1982, p. 38). Ironically, though he was defending the Dewan's efforts to frustrate the development of responsible government in Travancore, it is a view which still has wide support. *Mathrubhoomi*, one of Kerala's most famous newspapers, has recently launched an editorial crusade against communalism. Fairly or not, the CPI(M) has failed to convince the Kerala electorate over the years that it will have no truck with anything other than a class-based approach to elections or government.

A sample of school pupils interviewed in the vicinity of the state capital in 1974 offered instructive evidence of how politics and government was and is perceived. Half thought communalism influenced government whether it was under the control of Congress (53 per cent) *or* the CPI(M) (48 per cent). Despite Marx on one side and Gandhi on the other, only 15 per cent approved of inter-caste marriage. The teenagers' party preferences were still highly correlated by caste and community. Irrespective of family, occupation or income, Christians, Nairs and Muslims were resistant to communism. Support for the communists was much greater than average among the low castes and actually rose with income levels until the family was quite prosperous by Kerala standards. Perhaps for this group, education raised consciousness but it is more likely the key factor was that the better-off Ezhavas were employed in white-collar public-sector occupations, which are heavily unionized by the CPI(M). The same enquiry showed that there was some difference in the political beliefs of CPI(M) and Congress supporters—around 15 percentage points—but open-ended as well as closed-ended questions elicited a common agenda among young people: jobs, food and prices. The issue of communalism was an also-ran. Nationalization was rarely mentioned; public servants were widely impugned as self-seeking; but despite this disenchantment, four-fifths of the sample, including the CPI(M)'s own followers, believed not only in the citizen's duty to vote but in democracy as the best form of government (Nossiter, 1982, pp. 356-7).

Those teenagers of 1974 are now electors. Indeed it is worth remembering how youthful the voter profile of India is—one source of Rajiv Gandhi's appeal. In the thirty years between Kerala's first assembly election in 1957 and its ninth in 1987, the total electorate has grown by nearly three-quarters. The survey suggested that two-thirds of young people might at least initially be expected to vote for the same party as their father—as many as four-fifths of those with CPI(M) fathers (and perhaps 55 per cent of those from CPI homes). Such a high level of transmission of party allegiance is a considerable achievement but the new generations experience the vibrant radicalism of the early communist movement at second or third hand.

Literacy, which in the past served Kerala socialism so well, is now a mixed blessing. The daily press disseminates a political awareness predicated on news values of conflict, personality and human frailty. The most popular leisure activity, cinema, is not only a south Indian Hollywood but in the 1980s has produced at least one highly popular film of great political cynicism and another of how youthful idealism might fight a wicked adult world. Neither owed anything to Marxism. In the schools and colleges, which provide the paper qualifications without which secure and salaried employment is virtually impossible, teaching is by rote; and textbooks are little affected by interpretations other than the dominant nationalist account of Indian history and society.

Caste and communal segmentation has been entrenched by the privately managed educational institutions, a process scarcely checked by communist-led governments. The elaborate system of job-reservation in the public service affects some 40 per cent of posts and, even where the criterion for appointment is solely merit, careful regard is had to preserving communal balance. In the Hindu community, the principal beneficiaries are the low castes and it is these, notably the Ezhavas, who have historically been the mainstay of the communist vote. In 1957 and 1960 at least four-fifths of all Ezhavas probably voted communist. By 1982 informed observers reckoned the figure was nearer 55 per cent, a measure of the impact of education in SNDP yogam colleges, land reform, job reservation, communal organization and government action.

One should not exaggerate the progress of the Ezhavas. Most still labour in poverty but a section of the community has risen socially and economically to the point at which they can challenge their former landlords, the Nairs. In 1973 Nair leaders responded with the formation of a National Democratic Party to act as a lobby for job reservation on an (individual) economic test of 'backwardness' instead of the existing (group) social criterion. Two years later the SNDP responded with a Socialist Republican Party to defend the interests of the socially backward classes. Both were represented in the 1982-7 UDF ministry. In myriad ways, caste and community, so much a part of Kerala traditions, have been transposed into a modern political and economic idiom to the detriment of the communist advance. The emergence of a 'third force' in the 1987 elections of the Hindu chauvinist Bharatya Janata party–Hindu Munnani combine (7 per cent of the vote) is a further sign of how social tensions run in communal 'backwaters' in Kerala.

The relatively high rate of unionization, high that is in an Indian context, has not accomplished as much as might have been expected to create class identity. With the exceptions of the Non-Gazetted Officers (civil servants), some field labour and farmers' associations, the typical union is small and localized. Many are transient and few have any well-developed organization. The quality of leadership is on the whole poor and the management of union finance leaves a great deal to be desired. Any political party with pretensions forms unions; and class consciousness has been a casualty of political divisions between the Marxists as much as between communist and Congress parties. A study of agrarian unions and associations in Alleppey district in 1971-2 showed that there were eight parties operating among peasants and labourers of whom the CPI(M), CPI, Indira Congress and Kerala Congress were the most active. At the top and bottom of rural society there is a clear congruence between caste, class and party. The scheduled caste field labourers are normally organized by the CPI(M) or the CPI; and the rich and middle-level farmers are organized by Kerala Congress or Indira Congress. But Nairs and Ezhavas are less predictable. They may be middle peasants, poor peasants or labourers and their political affiliation though more likely to be with the Marxist left, is also somewhat diffused (Oommen, 1985, p. 147). The left gains from unionization but not as much as it once did; and in the declining coir industry, Kerala's major cottage industry, employment is too precious to permit effective unionism. Over the last decade the resurgence of caste and community as channels of political action has undoubtedly been stimulated by the impact of Gulf employment and expatriate remittances. With a flow of funds almost certainly in excess of Rs 220 crores ($220 million) and quite probably nearer twice that amount, Kerala has rapidly gone from a deeply traditional society to a materialist one. The fact that the chief beneficiaries have been the formerly disadvantaged castes and communities, coupled with the soaring rise in the price of land, buildings and eligible husbands, has fuelled communal jealousy, resentment and rivalry. One of the most striking political consequences is the emergence of the RSS—which lies behind BJP—as a major socio-political movement in the state. The RSS articulates the animosity of Hindus—especially the young men of declining high caste families—towards the newly rich Moplahs (Muslims). Links are alleged with the (Nair) National Democratic Party but the RSS has enrolled low caste Hindus also. With its emphasis on religious observance, self discipline and physical training, the RSS appears to mobilize the idealism of a section of the young in the way that the communists, and later the Youth Congress, did in the past. The atavism of caste and community challenges the analysis of class; and RSS membership may well be as much as half of the CPI(M) itself.

Gulf money, some of it 'black', has also affected the implicit rules of political life in more direct ways. Corruption, as is well known, has been endemic in Indian politics; and Kerala is no exception. Nevertheless until the late 1970s it was within bounds. The Chief Ministers of Kerala, notably Achutha Menon of the CPI and A. K. Antony of Congress (S) were distinguished by their personal integrity; senior civil servants, with rare exceptions, were unimpeachable; and more politicians than the average in state governments were 'clean'. The injection of Gulf monies has however enlarged the scale and scope of corruption in Kerala to the point at which it would appear to be pandemic. While the communists have more or less maintained their individual standards of probity—the CPI and CPI(M) do, of course, accept donations—the monetization of politics presents acute difficulties for them.

Faced with such changes in the political economy of Kerala it would have taken a remarkable communist party to hold the line; and in fact the CPI(M) has achievements to its credit: the construction of the A. K. Gopalan centre, a new party headquarters in the capital, financed by contributions, large and small, from party sympathizers at home and overseas; a doubling of party membership in five years and a substantial increase in membership of mass front organizations; efforts to improve party education and training; and a courageous fight against the more extreme communal forces.

However, at present the CPI(M) does not capture the imagination of the young on whom its progress must be founded, nor excite the fear of its political opponents. If this is true, then a number of explanations may be offered. First the provincial party lacks interest in class analysis. The party has not responded to the invaluable input of Kerala's left-leaning social science research centres. *Deshabhimani*, the party's Malayalam organ, is not only dreary, it contains—according to the CPI(M)'s 1982 Congress report—'no political guidance worth mentioning from the state Party leadership' (CPI(M), 1982, p. 121). It is officially regarded as poorly managed and fails to reach even its modest target sales of 100,000 copies. Second, although the CPI(M) produces considerable quantities of material for party education, the leadership has no systematic programme for using it. The high dropout rate among new recruits reflects this. Third, despite their rich experience, the State Committee 'have yet to develop themselves into a collectively functioning unit. Meetings are not properly prepared; subcommittees exist on paper; and discussions are lengthy and un-business like' (CPI(M), 1982, pp. 184–5). Taking a longer view, the Kerala party had not been able adequately to replace two key organizational personnel, C. H. Kanaran and Azhikodan Raghavan, the latter assassinated in 1971.

The party's own assessment of the Kerala unit's deficiencies did not deal in detail with the working of the Left and Democratic Front (LDF) ministry of 1980-1, but similar conclusions might have been drawn. It was alleged (by those in a position to know) that the elderly Chief Minister dozed in cabinet; the CPI(M) ministers frequently appeared ill-prepared to the point where arguments sometimes broke out between them; while in the assembly CPI(M) MLAs failed to display that mastery of their brief and parliamentary skill which had earned so much respect in earlier administrations, especially in 1957-9. Of course, the management of a government of such disparate coalition partners was bound to be difficult, but the Chief Minister did not show the skills with which Achutha Menon has sustained a ministry from 1969 to 1977 against equal, if not greater odds.

The problems of the CPI(M) in Kerala are in the last resort more than the deficiencies of organization. Over time, the interaction of the state's traditional social structures, its complex political geography and party competition for the control of scarce governmental resources has brought about the total fragmentation of the political system. Ideologically, the CPI(M) is committed to a class analysis of society but that analysis had proved less and less susceptible to realization as the Marxists sought to sustain themselves as a political party in a competitive electoral system rather than as a social movement engaged primarily in class-based mobilization. The nine-party Left and Democratic Front which the CPI(M) led in 1982 has only residual ideological content. It was a coalition for winning power almost as much as the UDF it opposed. To the extent that the CPI(M) tactic of dividing progressive from reactionary wings of bourgeois parties has contributed to this denouement, the line has been counter-productive. It remains to be seen whether matters will be otherwise in the LDF Ministry of 1987.

Of the Congress(I)-UDF ministry which succeeded the LDF after the 1982 elections, even its political friends had little good to say. Corruption and communalism were rampant. It may then be inferred that, while the LDF did win in 1987, the fact that it did so by little more than 1 per cent of the poll, just as with a slightly different structure of electoral alliances it has lost by the same margin in 1982, does not augur well. The CPI(M) itself took only 22.34 per cent of the vote compared to Congress(I)'s 24.50.

In West Bengal, the Left Front has not only in 1987 entered on its third successive term of office but both the Front as a whole and the CPI(M) within it won a greater share of the poll and even more seats than in 1977 (or 1982). Considering the problems facing the government, it is quite an astonishing electoral accomplishment. The failure of Congress(I) more than to dent the LF's position in the 1984 parliamentary elections—when it swept the board in

Kerala—also indicates that mass consciousness is more than just 'provincial'. Analysis of the results shows that the LF increased its share of the poll in the rural areas from 42.46 per cent in 1982 to 44.03 per cent in 1987. Except in the metropolitan and some industrial areas, the LF vote also held up well in the urban areas, and registered a 7 percentage points increase in Darjeeling district, where the CPI(M) have strongholds among tribes and scheduled castes, and the tea garden workers generally.

Commenting on the result, the *Economic and Political Weekly* (Bombay, 4 April 1987) saw the result as a foregone conclusion. 'In spite of the administrative inefficiencies and creeping corruption among the party ranks, the CPI(M) is still regarded by the West Bengal electorates as head and shoulders above the Congress(I) hoodlums who dominate the various factions of Rajiv Gandhi's party in the state.' The factionalism of the Congress unit in West Bengal is proverbial and its party organization is 'a bit of a joke'. Das Munshi, Rajiv Gandhi's lieutenant in the state, later admitted that realizing they could never match the Marxists' organizational capacity, they had relied on the Prime Minister's flying visits to dazzle the voters but 'the people in the state more than any other state do not want anything from Delhi' (*India Today*, 31 March 1987, p. 43). The non-communist *India Today* magazine credits the LF claim that every one of the state's 41,000 villages has at least a unit of one of the left parties. The CPI(M)'s front organizations, whatever their deficiencies, can claim 9 million members. Against this Rajiv Gandhi's royal progress and offers of largesse—Rs10,007 crores of investment, 1 million jobs and rice at Rs2 per kg.—was a grave miscalculation, as Congress organizers admitted (*India Today*, 31 March 1987). Of the issues, Gorkhaland—a secessionist movement by Gurkhas in North Bengal—proved damaging not only in the north (the Gorkha National Liberation Front boycotted the election) but throughout West Bengal, a state particularly sensitive to partition after 1905 and 1947. Congress regionally had flirted with Subhas Ghisingh, the leader of the movement, and the Prime Minister's pronouncements were ambiguous. In contrast the Chief Minister and the CPI(M) had a long record of viewing regional autonomy favourably but secessionism with a heart of stone.

Except in the industrial and metropolitan areas where trade-union stagnation, industrial closures, bungling in health administration, transport, and municipal developmental works took their toll, the electorate of West Bengal clearly regards the LF as a success: land and wages in the countryside; salaries for government employees; the disappearance of communal and caste clashes; freedom from the gangsterism which had been a nightmare during Congress rule; diminished corruption in politics and government; and, not to be underestimated, in Jyoti Basu a man who represented Bengalis in a way no one on the Congress side could aspire to do.

The LF and, in particular, the CPI(M) is then very secure in the rural areas and most urban areas. In the countryside this is amply confirmed by the Panchayat Elections in March 1988. With four-fifths of the *gram* (village) results declared, the Left Front's share of the seats had risen from 61 per cent to 74 per cent in 1988. The CPI(M) alone held 66 per cent of *gram panchayat* seats in 1988. At the higher levels of Panchayat Samity and Zilla Parishads, the LF had done equally well. Already the CPI(M)-led Front is addressing the weakness in the industrial and metropolitan region. Despite opposition from delegates from Kerala, Andhra, Bihar and Assam, Jyoti Basu secured from the 1986 Congress approval for a new industrial policy that would encourage multinationals and Indian monopoly houses to set up industry in West Bengal; and contracts have already been signed for a major chemical plant. Another target of urban middle-class criticism, universities and the University of Calcutta especially, is being tackled. Basu himself has retained the higher education portfolio and measures have been taken to check corruption. Above all, perhaps, the West Bengal electorate has confirmed its belief in the fight for more powers and autonomy for the states. Congress(I) stands condemned for its centralizing tendency, and the provincial unit for its subservience to Delhi over many years.

The All-India Prospects

Has the communist movement any chance of participating in government at the all-India level in the foreseeable future? The honest answer must be that such a development is unlikely but it is not impossible. The unlikelihood rests on the failure of the communist movement to penetrate the Hindi heartland of India, and the channelling of anti-Congressism into provincially specific parties. There is a sense in which the communists are seen by the Indian public as the regional manifestations of anti-Congressism in West Bengal, Kerala and Tripura rather than truly national parties. To the extent that each is *sui generis*—Kerala with an extraordinary degree of institutionalized competition between communities as well as parties, West Bengal with low caste saliency, the imperial heritage, and the *bhadralok* establishment, and Tripura with indigenous tribals and immigrant Bengalis at both ends of the social scale—none offers any easy blueprint for India at large.

The remote possibility of Marxists in Delhi derives from the proven adaptability of communism in such unusual Indian states and the fact that the communist movement is the only 'party' with an ideology and programme, organizational capacity and collective discipline. In December 1987 the communists made the point in mounting a one million strong demonstration in the capital to demand the resignation of the Prime Minister. Rajiv Gandhi in a sense offers a far greater opportunity than his mother or Pandit Nehru not simply because he is the only adult representative of the Nehru 'dynasty' or because of his perceived failings as Prime Minister but because his vision is a sharp break with the past and a clear contrast to the communists: a commitment to capitalism, technology and the free market. In the event of his electoral defeat, the CPI(M), which has played the leading role in forming an all-India oppositon front, just might be able to begin the long haul from sharing 'power' in New Delhi in a united democratic front through, years down the road, a Left Front, and finally reaching via the ballot box a People's Democratic Government—provided that is the opponents of communism played by their own rules of liberal democracy. If we credit that on learning he was to become Prime Minister, Rajiv Gandhi said to Jyoti Basu that it was he who should be the nation's leader, we have to accept that the generation that Basu represents, which in their 70s and 80s controls the two communist parties, will soon be replaced. Of the values of their successors, we know very little but for all the charges that the CPI(M) hierarchy no less than the CPI's has surrendered to electoralism, there is no other path than the dialectic of mass movement and Marxist ministry.

Bibliography

Government of Bengal

Bengal District Administration Cttee, 1915.
Bengal Land Revenue (Floud) Cttee, 1940.

Government of India

Census of India
Ministry of Home Affairs. 1949. *Communist Violence in India.*

Government of Kerala

Administration Reports.
Administrative Reforms Cttee. 1961. vols. II and III.
Backward Classes Reservation Commn. 1970. 2 vols.
Bureau of Economics and Statistics. 1975. *Basic Statistics Relating to Kerala Economy 1956–7 to 1973–4.*
Economic Review (annual 1957–   )
State Planning Board and Bureau of Economics and Statistics. 1974. *Statistics for Planning.*
Survey on Housing. 1980.
Taxation Enquiry Cttee. 1969.

Government of Travancore

Economic Depression Enquiry Cttee. 1931.
Unemployment Enquiry Cttee. 1928.

Government of Tripura

Directorate of Statistics and Evaluation. 1983. *Some Basic Statistics of Tripura.*
Directorate of Statistics and Evaluation. 1979. *The National Sample Survey: Jhum Cultivation in Tripura 1976–77.*
Pledges and Performance. 1984. n.d.?

Tripura. Agartala. 1982. n.d.?
Tripura Tribal Areas Autonomous District Council: Structure and Function. 1986. n.d.?
Wave of Development in Tripura. Agartala. 1982. n.d.?

Government of West Bengal

Administrative Reforms Cttee. 1983.
Memorandum to the Eighth Finance Commission, 1983.

Communist Documents

Political Thesis of the Communist Party of India. Adopted at the Second Congress, held in Calcutta from February 2 to March 6, 1948. Bombay, M. V. Kaul for CPI, 1948.
Programme of the Communist Party of India. Adopted at the All-India Party Conference, held in October 1951. Bombay, People's Publishing House, 1951.
Political Resolution. Adopted by the Fourth Congress of the Communist Party of India, held in Palghat from April 19 to 29, 1956. New Delhi, CPI, 1956.
Constitution of the Communist Party of India. Adopted at the Extraordinary Party Congress, Amritsar, April 1958. New Delhi, CPI, 1958.
Resolutions of the Communist Party of India. Adopted at the Extraordinary Party Congress, held in Amritsar in April 1958. New Delhi, CPI, 1958.
Fight Against Revisionism. Political-Organisation Report adopted at the Seventh Congress of the Communist Party of India, Calcutta, October 31-November 7, 1964. Calcutta (CPI(M)), 1964.
Resolution Adopted at the Seventh Congress October 31 to November 7, 1964 [CPI(M)]. Calcutta, National Book Agency, n.d.
Constitution of the Communist Party of India. Adopted at the Seventh Congress, October 31 to November 7, 1964. Calcutta, Communist Party of India-Marxist, 1965.
Resolutions of the Central Committee of the Communist Party of India, Tenali, June 12-19, 1966. Calcutta, CPI(M), 1966.
Election Review and Party's Task. Adopted by the Central Committee of the Communist Party of India-Marxist, Calcutta, April 10-16, 1967. Calcutta, CPI(M), 1967.
Ideological Debate Summed Up by the Polit Bureau. Calcutta, CPI(M), 1968.
Our Tasks on Party Organisation. Adopted by the Central Committee of the Communist Party of India-Marxist, Calcutta, October 28-November 2, 1968. Calcutta, CPI(M), n.d.
Political Resolution Adopted by the Eighth Congress. Cochin, CPM, 1968.
Political-Organization Report of the Eighth Congress of the CPI(M). Calcutta, CPI(M), 1969.
Comintern, *Principles of Party Organization*. Calcutta, National Book Agency, 1973.
Political Review Report (Adopted by the Eleventh Congress), New Delhi CPI, 1978.
Naxalbari and After: a Frontier Anthology, 2 vols. Calcutta, 1978.

Documents of the Eleventh Congress of the CPI, 1978.
Political Organization Report of the 11th Congress of the CPI(M). Vijayawada, January 26–31, 1982.
CPI(M) 1982. *Documents of the Eleventh Congress of the CPI(M)*.
CPI 1982. *Documents of the Twelfth Congress of the CPI*.
Reports and Resolutions Adopted by the National Council of the CPI, New Delhi, September 17–20, 1983.
Communist Party of India, 1985. *On Certain Harmful Practices in Internal Party Life*. Resolution of the National Council of the CPI.
West Bengal State Committee CPI(M). *Marches On an Untravelled Path* (1977–85). Calcutta, 1985.
West Bengal State Committee *Reports of CPI(M) and its Various Frontal Activities* (1982–1985). Calcutta, 1985.
Resolutions Adopted by the National Council of the CPI, New Delhi, January 20–23, 1985.
CPI(M) 1986. *Documents of the Twelfth Congress of the CPI(M)*.
CPI 1986. *Documents of the Thirteenth Congress of the CPI*.

Books and Articles

Adhikari, G. & Sen, Mohit (eds.) 1970. *Lenin and India*. New Delhi, People's Publishing House.
Ahmed, Imtiaz (ed.) 1973. *Caste Among Indian Muslims*. Delhi.
Bandopadhay, Suprasanna 1982. *Tripurar Itihash (A History of Tripura)*. Calcutta, Firma KLM.
Bardhan, Pranab 1984. *Political Economy of Development in India*. Oxford, Basil Blackwell.
Basu, Amrita 1985. Dilemmas of radical reform: parliamentary communism in West Bengal (mimeo, n.d.).
Baxter, Craig 1969. comp. *District Voting Trends in India: a Research Tool*. New York, Southern Asian Institute, School of International Affairs, Columbia University Press.
Brass, Paul 1974. *Religion and Politics in North India*. Cambridge, Mass., MIT Press.
Brass, Paul & Franda, Marcus 1973. *Radical Politics in South Asia*. Cambridge, Mass., MIT Press.
Broomfield, J. H. 1968. *Elite Conflict in a Plural Society: Twentieth Century Bengal*. Berkeley, University of California Press.
Burdwan 1984. Annual Plan on Agriculture 1983–4: Burdwan Principal Agricultural Officer, Burdwan, mimeo.
Centre for Development Studies (Tvm, Kerala) 1977. *Poverty, Unemployment and Development Policy: a Case Study of Selected Issues with Reference to Kerala*. New York, United Nations Department of Economic and Social Affairs, 1975; Bombay, Orient Longman.

Chakrabarty, B. 1985. Middle Class Radicalism in Bengal: A Study of the Politics of Subhas Chandra Bose. (Unpublished Ph.D. University of London.)

Chakrabarty, Jiban 1983. *Tripura Between 1930 and 1980*. Agartala.

Chakrabarty, Saroj 1978. *With West Bengal Chief Ministers: Memoirs 1962 to 1977*. New Delhi, Orient Longman.

Chakravarti, Mahadev 1985. Communist Activities in Tripura 1939-42 in *Proceedings of the North East India History Association*. Agartala.

Chander, N. Jose 1986. *Dynamics of State Politics: Kerala*. New Delhi, Sterling Publishers.

Chatterji, Partha 1982. Caste and politics in West Bengal. In Gail Omvedt (ed.), *Land, Caste and Politics in Indian States*. Delhi, Authors' Guild.

Chatterji, Rakhahari 1985. *Politics in West Bengal*. Calcutta, World Press.

Chaube, S. K. 1985. *Electoral Politics in North East India*. Madras, Universities Press.

Chiriyakandath, James Lazar 1985. Social change and the development of 'modern' politics in Travancore: from the late nineteenth century to 1938. Doctoral dissertation, University of London.

Comintern 1973. *Principles of Party Organisation*. Calcutta, National Book Agency.

Crouch, Harold 1966. *Trade Unions and Politics in India*. Bombay, Manaktalas.

Damodaran, K. 1975. Memoir of an Indian Communist. *New Left Review* 93, Sept.-Oct.

Dasgupta, Biplab 1974. *The Naxalite Movement*. Bombay, Allied Publishers.

— 1987. Urbanisation and rural change in West Bengal, *Economic and Political Weekly*, 14 February.

Dasgupta, Malabika. *Then and Now: Planning and Plan Implementation in Tripura*, Agartala.

Datta, Biren 1983. *Tradition of Popular Movement in Tripura and Present Responsibility*, Agartala.

Debvarma, Desaratha 1986. *Gana Mukti Parishad in Building the Peasant Movement in Tripura*. All India Kisan Sabha and Golden Jubilee Publications, New Delhi.

— 1987. *Mukta Parishader Itikatha* (A History of the GMP). Calcutta, National Book Agency.

Democratic Research Service (Bombay) 1957. *Indian Communist Party Documents 1930-1956*. Bombay, Democratic Research Service and Institute of Pacific Relations.

Devbarma, Aghore 1981. *The (Tripura) Riots (1980): a Survey*.

Duyker, Edward 1987. *Tribal Guerrillas: the Santals of West Bengal and the Naxalite Movement*. Delhi, Oxford University Press.

Farmer, B. H. 1983. *An Introduction to South Asia*. London, Methuen.

Fic, Victor M. 1969. *Peaceful Transition to Communism in India: Strategy of the Communist Party*. Bombay, Nachiketa Publications.

— 1970. *Yenan of India*. Bombay, Nachiketa Publications.

Field, J. O. & Franda, M. F. 1974. *Electoral Politics in the Indian States and the Communist Parties of West Bengal*. Delhi, Manohar Book Service.

Franda, Marcus F. 1971. *Radical Politics in West Bengal*. Cambridge, Mass., MIT Press.

Frankel, Francine R. 1971. *India's Green Revolution: Economic Gains and Political Costs.* Princeton, N.J., Princeton University Press.
—— 1978. *India's Political Economy 1947–1977: the Gradual Revolution.* Princeton, N.J., Princeton University Press.
Ganchaudhury, Jagadish 1985. *A Political History of Tripura.* Delhi, Inter-India Publications.
Ganguly, J. B. (ed.) 1981. Progress of Land Reforms in Tripura in Manjula Bose in *Land Reforms in Eastern India.* Planning Forum Jadaypur University.
George, K. C. 1975. *Immortal Punnapra-Vayalar.* New Delhi, CPI.
Ghosh, Anjali 1981. *Peaceful Transition to Power: a Study of Marxist Political Strategies in West Bengal 1967–1977.* Calcutta, Firma KLM.
Ghosh, Ajoy 1954. *On the Work of the 3rd Congress of the CPI.* Delhi, CPI.
Gladstone, William Ewart 1851. *First Letter to the Earl of Aberdeen on the State Persecutions of the Neapolitan Government*, section 8, p. 9n.
Gopalan, A. K. 1959. *Kerala—Past and Present.* London, Lawrence and Wishart.
—— 1973. *In the Cause of the People.* New Delhi, Orient Longman.
Gordon, Leonard A. 1974. *Bengal: the Nationalist Movement, 1876–1940.* New York, Columbia University Press.
Gough, Kathleen 1968a. Communist rural councillors in Kerala. *Journal of Asian and African Studies*, vol. 3, nos. 3–4.
—— 1968b. Literacy in Kerala. In J. Goody (ed.), *Literacy in Traditional Societies.* Cambridge, Cambridge University Press.
—— & Sharma, Hari P. (eds.) 1973. *Imperialism and Revolution in South Asia.* New York, Monthly Review Press.
Griffith, W. E. 1964. *The Sino-Soviet Rift.* Cambridge, Mass., MIT Press.
Gupta, Bhabani Sen 1972. *Communism in Indian Politics.* New York, Columbia University Press.
—— 1973. India's Rival Communist Models. *Problems of Communism*, vol. 22, January–February.
Gupta, Bhupesh 1978. Communists in Parliament. *World Marxist Review*, vol. 21, no. 9, September.
Haqqi, S. A. M. 1967. *Union-State Relations in India.* Maarut.
Hardgrave, Robert L. 1970. The Marxist dilemma in Kerala: administration and/or struggle. *Asian Survey*, vol. 10, no. 11.
—— 1973. The Kerala communists: contradictions of power. In Paul Brass & Franda (eds.), q.v.
—— 1975a. The communist parties of Kerala: an electoral profile. In M. Weiner and J. O. Field (eds.), *Electoral Politics in the Indian States*, vol. IV. New Delhi, Monohar Book Service.
—— 1975b. *India: Government and Politics in a Developing Nation*, 2nd edn. New York, Harcourt, Brace.
Hart, Henry C. & Herring, Ronald J. 1976. Political Conditions of Land Reform: Kerala and Maharashtra. In R. E. Frykenberg (ed.), *Land Tenure and Peasant in South Asia.* New Delhi, Orient Longman.

Herring, Ronald J. 1980. Abolition of landlordism in Kerala: a redistribution of privilege. *Economic and Political Weekly*, 28 June.

Hunter, Thelma 1972. Indian communism and the Kerala experience of coalition government 1967–69. *Journal of Commonwealth Political Studies*, vol. 10, no. 1.

ILO 1979. *Overcoming Rural Underdevelopment*. Geneva, ILO.

International Yearbook of Communist Affairs.

Irani, C. R. 1971. *Bengal: the Communist Challenge*. Bombay, Lalvani Publishing House.

Jeffrey, Robin 1978a. Matriliny, Marxism, and the birth of the Communist Party in Kerala, 1930–1940. *Journal of Asian Studies*, vol. 38, no. 1.

— 1978b. Peasant movements and the Communist Party in Kerala 1937–57. In D. B. Miller (ed.), *Peasants and Politics: Grass Roots Reactions to Change in Asia*. Melbourne, Edward Arnold.

John, K. C. 1975. *The Melting Pot: Kerala 1950s–1970s*. Tvm, Prasanthi Printers.

Joshi, Vijay & Little, I. M. D. 1987. Indian macroeconomic policies. *Economic and Political Weekly*, 28 February.

Karat, Prakash 1976. The Peasant Movement in Malabar 1934–40. *Social Scientist* (Tvm), no. 50.

— 1977. Organised Struggles of Malabar Peasantry 1934–40. *Social Scientist* (Tvm), no. 56.

Kogelkar, S. V. & Park, R. L. (eds.) 1956. *Reports on the Indian General Elections, 1951–52*. New Delhi, Government of India.

Kohli, Atul 1987. *The State and Poverty in India*. Cambridge, Cambridge University Press.

Konar, Harekrishna 1977. *Selected Works*. Calcutta, Gour Saha.

Krishnaji, N. 1979. Agrarian relations and the Left movement in Kerala: a note on recent trends. *Economic and Political Weekly*, 3 March.

Krishnan, T. V. 1971. *Kerala's First Communist: Life of 'Sakhavu' Krishna Pillai*. New Delhi, CPI.

Kumar, Sunil 1987. Man of Iron. Bombay, *Illustrated Weekly of India*, 16 August.

Kurian, K. Mathew (ed.) 1972. *India: State and Society*. New Delhi, Orient Longman.

Leiten, Georges Kristoffel 1979. Progressive State Government: an Assessment of the First Communist Ministry in Kerala. *Economic and Political Weekly*, 6 January.

Malaviya, H. D. 1958. *Kerala: A Report to the Nation*. New Delhi, People's Publishing House.

Marx, Karl 1936. *Letters on India*, (eds.) B. P. L. and Freda Bedi. Lahore, Contemporary India Publication.

Mencher, Joan P. 1966. Namboodiri Brahmins: an analysis of a traditional elite in Kerala. *Journal of Asian and African Studies*, vol. 1.

— 1980. The lessons and non-lessons of Kerala: agricultural labourers and poverty. *Economic and Political Weekly*, Special No. October.

Menon, Achutha 1958. *The Kerala Agrarian Relations Bill: An Interpretation*. New Delhi.

—— 1969. *What Happened in Kerala: Review of the 30 Months of Namboodiripad Government*. New Delhi, CPI.

—— 1970. *Link*, 12 July.

Menon, P. K. K. 1972. *History of the Freedom Movement in Kerala*. Tvm, Government of Kerala.

Miller, Peter 1988. Kerala's unpredictable paradise. *National Geographical Magazine*, May.

Miller, Roland E. 1976. *Mappila Muslims in Kerala*. New Delhi, Orient Longman.

Morris-Jones, W. H. 1971. *The Government and Politics of India*, 3rd rev. edn. London. Hutchinson.

—— 1977. Creeping but uneasy authoritarianism. *Government and Opposition*.

Mullick, B. N. 1972. *My Years with Nehru 1948-64*. New Delhi, Allied Publishers.

Myrdal, Gunnar 1968. *Asian Drama: An Inquiry into the Poverty of Nations*. New York, Pantheon/Twentieth Century Fund.

Nair, R. Ramakrishnan 1965. *How Communists Came to Power in Kerala*. Tvm, Kerala Academy of Political Science.

Namboodiripad, E. M. S. 1943. *A Short History of the Peasant Movement in Kerala*. Bombay, People's Publishing House.

—— 1952. *On the Agrarian Question in India*. Bombay, People's Publishing House.

—— 1953a. Questions and answers: nationalities and the Right of Secession. *Crossroads*, 6 September.

—— 1953b. Stalin and Mao on the National Liberation Movement. *New Age*, November.

—— 1953c. Why no socialism now in India. *New Age*, November.

—— 1954. *The Peasant in National Economic Reconstruction*. Delhi, People's Publishing House.

—— 1964. *Note for the Programme of the CPI*. New Delhi, 4 Windsor Place.

—— 1965. *Revisionism and Dogmatism in the CPI*. New Delhi, New Age Press.

—— 1968. *Yesterday, Today and Tomorrow*, 2nd edn. Calcutta, National Book Agency.

—— 1969. *Right Communist Betrayal of Kerala United Front and Government*. Calcutta, CPI(M).

—— 1974a. *Conflicts and Crisis, Political India: 1974*. New Delhi, Sangam Books Orient Longman.

—— 1974b. *Indian Planning in Crisis*. Tvm, Chintha.

—— 1976. Marxism and India. *Sunday Standard*, Madras, 4 April 1976.

—— 1982. *Selected Writings*, vol. 1. Calcutta, National Agency.

—— 1986. *A History of Indian Freedom Struggle*. Tvm, Social Science Press.

—— 1987. *Reminiscences of an Indian Communist*. New Delhi, National Book Centre.

Nossiter, T. J. 1977-8. Coalition governments, Kerala 1969-75 (Parts 1-3). *Focus* (Tvm, Legislative Assembly), vol. 7.

—— 1982. *Communism in Kerala: a Study in Political Adaptation*. London, C. Hurst; University of California Press; New Delhi, Oxford University Press.

Nossiter, T. J. 1985. Communism in Rajiv Gandhi's India. *Third World Quarterly*, vol. 7, no. 4, October.

Oommen, T. K. 1985. *From Mobilization to Institutionalization: the Dynamics of Agrarian Movement in 20th Century Kerala*. London, Sangam Books.

Overstreet, Gene D. & Windmiller, Marshall 1960. *Communism in India*. Berkeley, University of California Press.

Palme-Dutt, R. 1949. *India Today*. Bombay, People's Publishing House (2nd rev. Indian edn).

Potter, David C. 1987. *India's Political Administrators, 1919-1983*. Oxford, Oxford University Press.

Prakash, B. A. 1975. Impact of foreign remittances: a case study of Chavakkad village in Kerala. *Economic and Political Weekly*, 8 July.

Ram, Mohan 1969. *Indian Communism: Split within a Split*. New Delhi, Vikas.

— 1971. *Maoism in India*. New Delhi, Vikas.

Ranadive, B. T. 1978. Eurocommunism and the State. *Social Scientist* (Tvm), no. 75, October.

— 1987. Review of forty years of Indian Independence. *The Marxist*, vol. 5, nos. 2-3, April-September.

Rao, M. B. (ed.) 1976. *Documents of the History of the Communist Party of India*, vol. VII (1948-50). New Delhi, CPI.

Rasul, M. A. 1974. *A History of the All India Kisan Sabha*. Calcutta, National Book Agency.

Retzlaff, Ralph 1965. Revisionism and dogmatism in the Communist Party of India. In R. A. Scalapino (ed.), *The Communist Revolution in Asia*. Berkeley, Calif., Prentice Hall.

Roy, Subodh (ed.) 1972. *Communism in India: Unpublished Documents 1925-1934*. Calcutta, CPI.

— 1976. *Communism in India: Unpublished Documents, 1934-1945*. Calcutta, CPI.

Sarkar, Sumit 1973. *Swadeshi Movement in Bengal 1903-8*. New Delhi, People's Publishing House.

Sathyamurthy, T. V. 1985. *India Since Independence: Vol. 1. Centre State Relations, The Case of Kerala*. New Delhi, Ajanta Publications.

Sen, A. et al. 1982. *Three Studies on the Agrarian Structure in Bengal 1890-1947*. Calcutta, Oxford University Press.

Sen, Mohit (ed.) 1977. *Documents of the History of the CPI*, vol. VIII 1951-56. New Delhi, People's Publishing House.

Sen, Tripur Chandra 1970. *Tripura in Transition 1923-47*. Agartala.

Singh, S. Nihal 1986. *The Yogi and the Bear*. London, Mansell.

Spate, O. H. K. 1954. *India and Pakistan: a General and Regional Geography*. London, Methuen.

Tripura Agricultural Workers' Association. *Reports of the 2nd State Conference*, 16-18 February 1986. Agartala n.d.

Varghese, T. C. 1970. *Agrarian Change and Economic Consequences: Land Tenures in Kerala 1850-1960.* Calcutta, Allied Publishers.
Varkey, Ouseph 1979. The CPI-Congress Alliance in India. *Asian Survey*, vol. 19, no. 9, September.
Westergaard, Kirsten 1986. *People's Participation, Local Government and Rural Development in West Bengal.* Centre for Development Research, Copenhagen, Mimeo.
Woodcock, George 1967. *Kerala: a Portrait of the Malabar Coast.* London, Faber & Faber.
Zagoria, D. S. 1973. The social bases of communism in Kerala and West Bengal: a study in contrast. *Problems of Communism*, vol. 22, no. 1.
Zinkin, Taya 1962. *Reporting India.* London, Chatto & Windus.

Newspapers and Periodicals

(B — Bengali; M — Malayalam; T — Tripuri)
Amrita Patrika Bazaar B
Bangadoot B
Blitz
Business Standard
Chandrika M
Chiniha B
   (ed. Roy, Prabhat & Thakur, Bansi)
Chiniha M
Commerce (Bombay)
Crossroads
Daily Telegraph (London)
Deepika M
Deshabhimani M
Economic and Political Weekly
Economic Review (B)
Frontline
The Guardian
The Hindu
Hindustan Times
Indian Express
Illustrated Weekly of India
India Today
Janayugam M
Kerala Kaumudi M
Link
Mainstream
Malayalam Manorama M

The Marxist
   (New Delhi, CPI(M) theoretical quarterly)
Mathrubhoomi M
New Age
Patriot (New Delhi)
People's Democracy
Seminar
Sunday (Calcutta)
The Sunday Observer
The Statesman (Calcutta)
Social Scientist (Trivandrum)
The Telegraph (Calcutta)
The Times of India
Tripurar Katha B
World Marxist Review

Index

Administration 76–81, 183
agrarian change 115
Agrarian Land Reform Act 140
agrarian movements 47–8
agrarian reform 69–73, 141
Agrarian Relations Bill 70
agrarian unions 192
Agricultural Labourers' Union 52
Agricultural Workers' Act 70, 98
AITUC 80
A. K. Gopalan Centre 193
All India Agricultural Workers' Union 36
All India Congress Committee 48
All India Democratic Women's Association (AIDWA) 37
All India Kisan Sabha 36
All India Services 7
All Indian Coordination Committee of Communist Revolutionaries 24
All Malabar Peasants Union 48
Alleppey 52
Amritsar Massacre 124
Andhra Pradesh 33
Andhra Rice Deal 77
Anti-Terrorist Act 150
Antony, A. K. 97, 101
Aryans 1
Asiatic Society 3
Assam 27, 33
Avadi Resolution 17

bandh 23
Bardhan 10
Basu, Amrita 140
Basu, Jyoti 21, 126, 131, 139, 171, 197
Battle of Plassey 111
Bava, Imbichi 90, 91
Benares 1
Bengal 5
Bengal Provincial Congress (BPC) 124–5
Bihar 33
birth-control campaigns 4

Black Hole of Calcutta 111
Bose, Subhas Chandra 48, 127
Buddhism 1

Calcutta 109, 111, 114, 122, 142
Carmichael, Lord 122
caste and communal segmentation 191
Catholic Church 72, 73
Central Assistance 8
central investment 8
centre-state relations 186–8
Chacko, P. T. 78
Chakraborty, Nripen 151, 160
China 19, 20, 23, 26, 27
Chowdhury, Benoy 140
Christians 1, 38, 49, 51, 72, 73
CITU 36
Civil Disobedience Movement 14
Clive, Robert, Baron of Plassey 111, 112
Cochin 46, 48, 53
Cochin-Ernakulam 40
Comintern 14
communism, history of Indian 14–37
Communist Party of India (CPI), *see* CPI
Congress *see* Indian National Congress
Constitution of India 6
Cooch Behar 138
CPGB 17, 19
CPI 5, 46, 48, 116, 129, 131, 136, 159, 178
   Coordinating Committee 27
   history 14–37
   membership 30–7
   National Council 20, 28, 29, 33
   organization 28–30
CPI(M) 7, 10, 34–7, 116, 149, 151, 159, 165, 167, 168, 174, 176–80, 187, 188, 193, 194
   Central Executive Committee 28, 29
   hegemony of 137–43
   history 21–31, 82–102, 129–36
   membership 32
   see also Left and Democratic Front

CPI(ML) 23, 24, 134, 174
CPSU 15, 16, 17, 18, 19, 26, 27
CSP 15, 46, 48, 53
Curzon, Lord 118

Damodaran, K. 177
Dange, Shripat Amrit 20, 25
Das, C. R. 124, 125, 126
Das Gupta, Promode 143, 160
Datta, Biren 157, 167–9
Deb, Dasarath 151, 157
Deccan 1
Democratic centralism 29
Deshpande, Mrs 25
Devbarma, Aghore 157, 161
Dey, Manik 150
Disraeli, Benjamin 2

East India Company 2, 45, 46, 111, 112
economy 9–13
Emergency, 1975–7 9, 99–102
Engels, F. 173, 174
Ezhavas 50, 191

Finance Commission 7
First World War 5
From the Gutter 42

Gandhi, Mahatma 4, 5, 42, 47, 124, 127
Gandhi, Mrs Indira 6, 11, 12, 25–7, 73, 96, 100, 106, 129, 132, 134, 135, 137, 138
Gandhi, Rajiv 6, 13, 28, 107, 138, 139, 162, 186, 190, 195, 197
Gandhi, Sanjay 11, 12, 25
GDP 5
Ghisingh, Subhas 195
Ghosh, Ajoy 17, 18, 20
Ghosh, Atulya 130
Ghosh, P. C. 133
Giri, V. V. 24
Gladstone, William 5
Golghati Incident 157
Gopalan, A. K. 91, 107
Gorbachëv 27
Gordon, Leonard 116
Government of India Act 1919 123
Government of India Act 1935 5, 6, 48
Green Revolution 9

guerrilla warfare 5
Gupta, Bhabani Sen 174
Guru, Sree Narayana 50

Haq, Fazlul 123
Higher education 185
Hindus 1, 4, 44, 48, 49, 149
Hrangkhwal, Bijoy 160
Hyder Ali 43
Hydro-electric power, 38

Independence 16
India Act 1774 112
Indian Army 2
Indian Mutiny 2
Indian National Army 5
Indian National Congress 5, 11, 12, 14, 15, 16, 17, 18, 19, 24, 25, 47, 48, 53, 64, 65, 66, 67, 68, 69, 70, 76, 84, 86, 87, 95–102, 103, 106, 107, 108, 125, 129, 130, 133, 134, 135, 136, 137, 138, 149, 150, 159, 168
Indo-Gangetic Plain 1
Indus Valley 1
industrialization 9

Jainism 1
jenmi 44
Joint Political Congress (JPC) 51
Joshi, P. C. 15

Kanaran, C. H. 91, 193
kanomdars 44
Karnataka 38
Karunakaran, K. 106
Kerala 4, 7, 8, 15, 18, 22, 23, 25, 33, 35, 37
  area 38
  cities 40
  climate 38
  communism in, 1940–50 53–4
  CPI split 82–4
  education 57–63
  employment 55–6
  history and political traditions 38–54
  language 41
  national consciousness 42
  natural divisions, 39
  natural resources 38–9

political history, 1792–1918 43–6
political history, 1919–1939 46–53
population 38, 40, 55–6
pre-colonial socio-economic structure, 38
settlement pattern 40
social structure 55–63
Kerala Congress Committee 42
Kerala, Yesterday, Today and Tomorrow 43
Khan, Alivardi 111
Khrushchev 17, 18
kisan sabhas 34
Konar, Harekrishna 134
Kozhikode 40
KPCC 42
Krishak Praja Party 125
Krishna Iyer, V. R. 68
Kurukkal, N. P. 52

landscape 1
law and order 74–6
Left Democratic Alternative 27
Left Democratic Front 179
Left and Democratic Front (LDF) 103–8, 194
Left Front 137–42, 162–9
Lenin 14, 175
Liberation Struggle 71, 74–6
life expectancy 4
Linguistic Reorganization Commission 42
literacy 191
  in Kerala 42, 57–9
  in Tripura 144, 153, 154
  in West Bengal 115
Lok Sabha 6, 17

Maharashtra 33
Maintenance of Internal Security Act 137
Majumdar, Sudhir Ranjan 150
Malabar 43, 44, 47–8
Malabar Tenancy Act 1929 47
Malayalam 41–2
Malayalis 41
Marx, Karl 2–3, 18, 173, 174
Menon, A. R. 68
Menon, C. Achutha 69, 93, 105, 171, 179
Menon, Govinda 74
Mitra, Ashok 29, 142, 183
Moplah Outrages 44
Moplah Rebellion 44, 45

Mughals 1, 2, 111–13
Mukherjee, Ajoy 130, 131, 133, 135
Mundasserry, Joseh 72
Munshi, Das 195
Muslims 1, 38, 44, 118–19, 123, 124, 149, 157, 158
Mysorean Wars 44

Nair, M. N. Govindan 76, 90, 179
Nair Service Society 50, 73
Namboodiripad, E. M. S. 19, 21, 23, 43, 67–9, 75–8, 89, 90, 91, 103, 107, 171, 174, 186
Narayanan, Jayprakash 98
National Congress 42
National Democratic Front 24
National Rural Employment Programme 141
nationality question 144, 160–2
Naxalitism 24, 31, 91–2
Nayanar, E. K. 104, 106
Nehru, Pandit 5–6, 128, 146, 197

On Certain Harmful Practices in Internal Party Life 29
Operation Barga 139

Pakistan 11, 126, 135
panchayat 7
panchayati raj 7
Parliament 6
Peasant-Workers Party (KMPP) 64
People's Democracy 16, 20, 21
People's Democratic Front 21, 22
People's United Socialist Front (PUSF) 128–9
PEPSU 185
Pillai, Mannath Padmanabha 73
Pillai, P. Krishna 47
Planning Commission 8, 9
population 1, 4, 5
poverty 4
Presidential Rule 6
Punjab 5, 27, 33
Punnapra-Vayalar Rising 53

Quit India Movement 128

Raghavan, Azhikodan 88, 193
Rajya Sabha 6
Ramakrishnan, T. K. 104, 105

Ramaswamy Aiyar, Sir C. P. 51, 72
Ranadive, B. T. 173
Rao, T. Madhava 45
Ray, Siddhartha Sankar 136
Regulating Act 1773 112
religion 1
Reserve Bank of India 8
Rowlatt Act 124
Roy, M. N. 14, 15, 109, 126, 155
Rural Landless Employment Generation Programme 141

Saha, Hari Charan 157
Sankar, R. 50
Sarkar, Sumit 116
Scavenger's Son 42
Sengupta, Sukhumay 149
Seth, Jagath 112
Shashtri, Lal Bahadur 11
Sikhs 1
Singha, Sacindralal 149
SNDP 50, 51
Soviet Union 5, 15, 17, 20, 26
Stalin 18
Students' Federation of India 36–7
Syrian Christians 49

Tagore, Rabindranath 109
taluk 7
Tamil Nadu 22, 33, 36, 38
taxation 7
terrorism 5, 16
Thomas, T. V. 80
Tibet 19
Tipu Sultan 43, 46
Tiyyas 50
trade unions 34, 35, 36, 192
Travancore 45–53
Travancore-Cochin 52, 54
Travancore Labour Association (TLA) 52
Travancore State Congress (TSC) 51

Tribal Autonomous District Council 184
Tripura 31, 33, 35, 144–69
  economic situation in 157
  food crisis 157
  municipal election results 168
  social roots of radicalism 152–60
  tribal area autonomous district council results 152
Tripura Agricultural Worker's Association 161
Tripura National Volunteers (TNV) 160
Tripura Tribal Areas Autonomous District Council Act 161, 184
Trivandrum 40, 52
Two Measures of Rice 42

Unemployment Enquiry Committee 52
United Front 107
  1965–67 85–6
  1967–69 87–94
United Left Front (ULF) 178, 179
United Socialist Organization of India (USOI) 128–9
University of Calcutta 116, 122, 181
urbanization 4
Uttar Pradesh 4, 8, 33

Venad 45
Vira, Dharma 132
Viswanathan, V. 90
Vivekananda, Swami 49, 124

West Bengal 4, 7, 8, 15, 16, 22–4, 31, 33, 35–7
  1905–42 122–7
  1947–72 127–36, 194–6
  1972–85 137–43
  historical background 111–21
  modern history of 122–36
WPP 14

Zedong, Mao 24